ROADS TO BE TAKEN

The Intellectual Odyssey
of Charles H. Sandage

ROADS TO BE TAKEN

The Intellectual Odyssey of Charles H. Sandage

By Charles H. Sandage

Center for the Study of Free Enterprise and
Entrepreneurship
Graceland College
Lamoni, Iowa

Copyright © 1993
Center for the Study of Free Enterprise
  and Entrepreneurship
Graceland College
Lamoni, Iowa
Printed in the United States of America

ISBN 0-9636457-0-6

96 95 94 93   1 2 3 4

To my wife Elizabeth

Table of Contents

PART III: MIAMI UNIVERSITY, OXFORD, OHIO

National Advertising Review Board
American Association of Advertising
    Agencies Education Foundation
American Marketing Association
Champaign-Urbana Advertising Club
Better Business Bureau

PART V: POST-ACADEMIC YEARS

Foreword

I was delighted when asked to write the foreword to this book because it provided me the opportunity to reflect on a thirty-year relationship with C. H. "Sandy" Sandage. I first met Dr. Sandage in the fall of 1962 at an Alpha Delta Sigma (professional advertising organization) convention in New York City. We were there representing our respective universities—his, the University of Illinois, and mine, the University of Houston. The sales representative of the Richard D. Irwin Company, Sandy's textbook publisher, had arranged a meeting for the two of us to discuss a possible teaching position at Illinois. For me, a doctoral student at the time, this was a heady event—getting to meet first hand THE most recognized and celebrated advertising educator in the country, indeed the world.

I did not want to leave Texas without having my Ph.D. degree in hand, so we deferred an interview until the following October (1963), when I visited the Illinois campus in Urbana. After getting me settled in at the Urbana Lincoln Hotel, we had dinner in the hotel's Lincoln Room, seated before a roaring fireplace. Although our dinner discussion surely must have been about the esoteric issues of academia, I cannot recall the slightest particle of that conversation. What I do remember—vividly as if yesterday—is that we both shared a liking of calf's liver and pipe smoking, especially pipes known as "pot" shaped. After that wonderful meal of liver and crisp bacon pieces, we both lit up our pipes before the fireplace and puffed away (my, how dietary habits and societal norms have changed in thirty years!).

After accepting the position, our family (wife and two small daughters) moved to Urbana in August 1964, thus commencing a long relationship with the University of Illinois and Sandy. Sandy and I had almost daily contact at the university, and by the fall of 1965 I also was involved with his research operation, Farm Research Institute (FRI), an involvement that was continuous until 1983. Since 1983, when I returned to the South for another teaching position, we have remained in contact through monthly telephone exchanges and an occasional visit to Urbana.

What did I learn from Sandy Sandage over these past thirty years, and what are my perceptions of him as a scholar, businessman, and person? Perhaps the one thing that most personifies Sandy, and permeates his being, is the ability to generate ideas—ideas that are definitive, innovative, crisp with logic...ideas that sparkle with the natural excitement they generate. He deals with everything—from subjects with the greatest intellectual challenge to the most mundane—with a fresh viewpoint and infuses the issue at hand with creativity and insight. His success as an entrepreneur comes from this trait. Whether attempting to encourage a merger of the cities of Urbana and Champaign, developing a research protocol to solve a company's marketing problem, establishing a rationale for the discipline of advertising in the university community, or protesting a stop sign location by the Urbana police department, Sandy provides solutions that fascinate the imagination.

When thinking about Sandy, I also marvel at his dedication, diligence, and perseverance. When I first started working with him in 1964, and he was a young-ster of sixty-two, it was typical of him to put in a twelve-hour workday, six days a week, with a cutback to eight hours on Sunday (he probably could have worked a bit more had it not been for his penchant to arise no earlier than 8 a.m.). Of course, by the time he reached age eighty, he had become slothful and worked only nine hours a day. Aside, though, from merely working many hours, it is Sandy's intense dedication to the task that is distinct, bringing a strong desire to solve problems that in some way, however small, make a contribution to matters of consequence.

Sandy's devotion to fairness, in all aspects of his life, is another characteristic I have observed and from which I personally benefited and learned. He never approaches a situation solely from the "me" viewpoint. It always is from the perspective of the "greater good." For example, when we were asked by FRI clients to solve a particular marketing or advertising problem, the first questions he asked always dealt with "What benefits can we provide?" Certainly, as a successful entrepre-neur, he was not embarrassed to make a profit, but the money to be derived was not the driving motivation. On a personal level, I often felt that his willingness to take on a research project at FRI was more to provide me, a young academician with a family trying to supplement teaching income, with a bit of cash.

One cannot think of Sandy Sandage without a thought about his wonderful sense of humor, especially where he personally is the target of the humor. I telephoned to wish him happy birthday in his ninetieth year, commenting, "How does it feel to be 110 years old?" His very quick retort, "125, actually!" Some of the warmest recollections I have are observing Sandy after he has told—or heard—a story of humor; his broad smile breaks out like the sun at dawn, his entire body moves with the flow of the story, and he characteristically slaps his thigh in tune with the tenor of the joke.

The few attributes of Sandy Sandage I have mentioned here, plus many more, should be readily discernible to the reader of this book. You will learn of his earliest years as the son of a farm family in Missouri in the early years of this soon-to-be-gone century. You will be able to note how the formative years of boyhood influenced his character and served him later as a scholar of international repute and a successful businessman and consultant. You also will learn something about a host of interesting subjects: farm life—its business and social aspects—in the early 1900s; one-room school education and a "classical" education in the truest sense of that term at Graceland College; academic life; the United States government; research methodology; architecture; curriculum development; the insurance industry; and entrepreneurship. Plus much more.

And all of these things are related in a delightfully casual and personal way so that, although the story told is not a mystery, you nevertheless will not want to put the book down until you read "just one more chapter." So...find a comfortable chair...adjust the reading lamp to its best height and level of brightness...kick off your shoes...make yourself comfortable...and start reading a thoroughly marvelous story......of a most remarkable and wonderful person.

Arnold M. Barban
Tuscaloosa, Alabama
December 1992

Introduction

Amid the tumult and confusion—one might even say the gathering chaos—of the dying years of the twentieth century, it is heartening, inspiring, and enormously uplifting to find among us one individual whose life spans 90 percent of this century, whose mind is still youthful, active, and prodigiously productive, who still heads and operates his own business, who remains an optimist thriving on a positive outlook, whose sense of humor enlivens all encounters, and who began writing his life story in his eighty-sixth year. There had been a great deal of conversation between us for the preceding fifteen years about such a book, but the trigger that got it started was a request from a colleague at Miami University in Oxford, Ohio, for material to include in a history of that institution's marketing department. Once engaged in that project it seemed a shame to stop there, so he continued.

By the time he began work on his autobiography, macular degeneration had robbed him of the central vision that is essential for reading and for all visual discrimination of fine details. Undaunted, he organized the entire book in his mind and dictated it to me. His files, kept over the many years of his professional life, were in such order that when he needed to check facts, dates, details, it was not difficult for me to find the needed material.

Work on the book was squeezed in between heavy schedules for both of us at his research business (Farm Research Institute) so there would be weeks at a time without much getting done on it. Thus it was completed in January 1992, taking about three and one-half years. While he included some details of his personal and family life,* the principal focus of this book is on his professional life.

Always years ahead of his time, he pioneered, originated, and built, leaving a thriving new academic discipline, the study of advertising as a significant social and economic institution, firmly established not only at the University of Illinois but in universities throughout the country. His contribution was truly unique. Until C. H. Sandage, no one had ever viewed advertising from this perspective or had recognized the vital economic and social function that advertising as an institution performs. His legacy is studded with innovations that sprang from his fertile imagination. His perception that the purpose of business and marketing is to serve the needs and wants of consumers was significant. That advertising is a necessary function of marketing so that consumers can be provided with information about the need and want satisfying qualities of products and services was an innovative way of defining advertising.

A lifelong advocate of the value of research, he introduced a unique course in his first advertising classes which he developed as part of the marketing program at Miami of Ohio. The course initially was called "Advertising Procedures" and later "Advertising Campaigns." It remains an integral part of advertising curricula around the country. He pioneered panel research and the use of consumer diaries to log purchases

---

*Those readers who are not particularly interested in the details of his childhood and life on the farm at that time may wish to skip chapter one and begin with chapter two. It is in this chapter that the first stirrings of his lifelong intellectual odyssey are recorded.

of various products and thus test advertising effectiveness. He introduced the idea of grade labeling of food products in the early days of the consumer movement. The "firsts" that he introduced in marketing and advertising research go on and on. The appellation, "The Father of Advertising Education," bestowed on him by his peers is singularly appropriate and well deserved.

He used the Socratic method in teaching, a technique that posed a stream of provocative questions to the students in his classroom, forcing them to think logically and to acquire problem-recognition and problem-solving expertise. The effect his approach to education had on students has often been expressed in their letters to him. For example, "I've carried your teachings throughout my professional career. I was a James Webb Young scholar.... God bless you, Sandy." Or, "Thank you so very much for making a profound difference in my life."

In a somewhat lighter vein, reacting to Sandy's unique sense of humor, one former student wrote, "Now some twenty-three years out of the master's program, I can assure you that what I learned from you has been invaluable.... I still remember not only the rigor and wisdom of your classes, but also part of your advice to me just before I left to teach at the University of Georgia.... You were ahead of your time, even then, in that you always did address the whole person and take a personal interest in your students. That advice? It was to get a haircut. I did. Now I simply feel fortunate that there's still something left to cut.... You may be pleased to know that even in the harsh glare of business, I carry your legacy forward by teaching, when I can.... For me, Bonnie Blair didn't put Champaign on the map. You did."

A tireless worker, even through his ninetieth year, Sandy has carried with him throughout his life the nineteenth-century work ethic that was instilled in him as a child on the farm in northern Missouri. His philosophy about work is simply to find the work one enjoys doing and devote one's life to it. Such work is pleasure, something to look forward to eagerly each day. Productivity, creativity, and a multiplicity of psychic rewards result. It is his contention that to go into a profession or a job with making money as the primary goal is a recipe for personal misery and probable failure. To do work for the sheer pleasure of it will bring monetary reward without making that a goal. With regard to the accumulation of money, he advocates stewardship as the appropriate mode of thought and action.

Finally, he has always looked optimistically to the future rather than dwelling in the past, even though the world around him has been in a mess with no signs of improvement. While he is not blindly Pollyannaish in his appraisal of events, yet with great good humor he sees always what he can do rather than bemoaning what he can't. This attitude of mind is exemplified in a comment he wrote to a former student who was among the more than 100 who sent him cards and notes on the occasion of his ninetieth birthday. He wrote, "The Nonagenarian Club is an exclusive one. A number of its members are inactive and wondering how they got there. I consider myself as one of the fortunate in that I am still active and wondering where I am going rather than how I got here."

On a personal note, I can tell you from the heart that living with this amazing man has been an endlessly fascinating experience. He was sixty-eight when I became part of his life, an age generally described as in "the twilight years." For him it was still high noon, and his sun has yet to drop very low on the horizon. As with every other life he has touched, he has changed mine substantially, and I firmly believe changed it for the better.

If his autobiography is an inspiration to even one young person, it will be well worth the writing.

Elizabeth Sandage

Acknowledgments

No book is ever written without the help of others. That is especially true when the contents of the book cover a span of ninety years. There is not sufficient room to name all the individuals who could be named who helped to shape and influence my life and work.

Among that list I would include my parents, siblings, classmates, teachers, professors, colleagues, and business associates. Of particular significance are the many students whose minds interacted with mine, who stimulated my thinking, and who added intellectual zest to my life.

There are, however, a few whom I wish to name and acknowledge who made important contributions in the actual writing. My faithful secretary, Patricia Herron, was very helpful in serving as my eyes in searching the files and supplying me with materials used in my writing.

I am indeed grateful to Barbara Higdon who read the manuscript, made valuable suggestions, and as director, accepted it for publication by the Center for the Study of Free Enterprise and Entrepreneurship.

I am indebted to Kim Rotzoll for reading the manuscript, publishing one chapter as a departmental working paper, and urging the publication of the entire manuscript. He suggested the title for this book.

I am especially grateful to Arnold Barban for preparing a foreword for the book. Our close professional and personal association over a period of many years enriched my life and helped to sharpen my mind.

I owe my greatest debt to my wife Elizabeth. She kept the pressure on me over several years to "get with it" and start writing. Every word in the manuscript was dictated to her. She transcribed, edited, and prepared material for transmission to the publisher. My dedication of the book to her is a loving "thank you" for her help.

C. H. Sandage

PART I
MY EARLY YEARS

Chapter 1

Pre-High School Days

Sometime after Thanksgiving 1901, Mode and Matie Sandage conceived what emerged as a squalling twelve-pound boy on August 21, 1902. Whether life began at Thanksgiving 1901, sometime between then and August 1902, or not until the twenty-first day of August is left for the theorists, physicians, biologists, and jurists to decide. It was not, however, until the August date that the youngster was christened Charles Harold.

The "Charles" was for a close neighbor, friend, religious leader, and patriarch in the community, Charles Jones. The "Harold" had no significance other than Mother liked it. Soon after my eighth birthday, my namesake gave me a Bible signed in his own handwriting. I still have that Bible even though many of its pages are dog-eared.

The site of my entry into this world was in a cottage on a small, hilly farm in Harrison County, Missouri. A country doctor residing five miles away apparently attended the birth. In anticipation of the event, my two brothers (Neil, seven, and Orville, two and a half) had been sent to the home of an uncle to spend the night. It apparently was quite the custom of families to maintain strict privacy in the birth of a new human being. That, in retrospect, seems rather strange in view of the fact that the birth of colts, calves, lambs, and pigs were common occurrences and youngsters often participated in assisting or viewing such events.

The events in the first four or five years of my life can be recalled primarily from my memory of comments made by my parents and brothers. It appeared that my parents were somewhat disappointed their third child was not a girl. Even so, I was accorded special attention and apparent affection as the baby brother. This special attention, however, vanished after two and a half years at the birth of my sister, Ruby. She became the darling of the family, which status never changed.

The Utility Player

Our farm was only 100 acres, but even so it was labor intensive. The only power source was either horse or human. The distribution of human labor on the farm generally resulted in male family members doing most or all of the outside work and the female members doing the inside work. My entry on the scene resulted in four male members of the family and only one female (Mother). Obviously, during the first four or five years of my life little labor was expected of me. When I became old enough to contribute to the family labor force, there was much more need for someone to help Mother with inside-the-house work than for an additional farm hand. Mother's "little helper" became my moniker; it stayed with me for a long time, the only change being the elimination of the word "little." I became quite proficient in most kinds of inside work including cooking and housecleaning. Also, I learned some "non-manly" things, such as tatting, crocheting, and embroidering. In some respects I also became a tutor to my sister in "educating" her into the arts of cooking and crocheting. No one, however, could ever consider me as being a "sissy."

There was a time when I was reluctant to comment on my excursion into the realm of needlework. After Rosie Grier demonstrated that needlework was not necessarily associated with femininity, I became rather proud of my childhood accomplishments in that area. I do not have any of my own work that was kept, but I did crochet some squares as part of an afghan. I also tatted some edges for pillow slips. I suspect somewhere in a forgotten part of my personal belongings is an embroidery hoop and just maybe a partly finished design on a stretched cloth.

Some might think it was unfortunate and maybe detrimental that I spent considerable time inside the house helping my mother when I was young and while Ruby was growing up. Actually, I did not feel abused. I apparently considered it as a natural function for the number-three male sibling to have that kind of assignment. In any event it provided an excellent educational experience. I learned to cook and prepare several types of food. I could prepare chicken starting at the hen house, scalding water bucket, butcher table, frying pan, and on to the table. I could do a good job of frying steak and recall that after frying either chicken or steak I would make milk gravy. The bits of chicken or steak with the grease in the skillet would be mixed with flour and enough milk stirred in to make a properly thickened gravy. Obviously, I did not learn these things from a cookbook. My tutor was always my mother, who was patient and thorough in her instructions. If I erred in performing some of those cooking functions, she used that as a way for me to learn rather than to criticize.

My young sister, when she reached a certain age, was also to help in the kitchen and to do some of the things that I had been or was doing. I guess, unfortunately for my sister, Mother often told her she would let Charley do it. In some respects, then, I became a tutor to Ruby.

I wanted to emulate the work of my brothers and succeeded in participating often in some of the outside farm work. I learned at an early age to milk cows and operate the cream separator. I had my own pony. At the age of eight or nine I learned how to harness horses and hitch them up to a wagon or buggy. It was, at times, a struggle to throw the heavy harness onto the horse. One time I dropped a harness and part of it hit my front tooth, breaking off a corner that eventually required special dental work. By the age of eleven I was a regular outside hand during the real busy season. I could hitch a team of horses to a twelve-inch bottom plow and do my share of the spring plowing.

One time when my folks had gone somewhere I was left to do some plowing. On one round I plowed out a snake, which frightened me. I did not want to continue plowing for fear I would run across another snake, so I pulled the linchpin from the double-tree, left the plow in the field, and drove the team back to the barn. I tried to claim that the pin got lost some way or other but did not get too far with the story and had to confess eventually that my lack of bravery drove me to such a stunt.

I guess if one could use baseball terms, I would have been considered a "utility player." I could play a number of positions inside the house and also many positions in general farm work. I was a regular on the milking detail at home until I left to go to a campus-oriented high school and junior college where I did jobs of milking cows, cutting weeds out of corn fields, and serving as breakfast chef in the kitchen. I became a fairly proficient cook at home. If my parents or my mother were away for a day or more to go to town thirteen miles distant or to visit mother's parents in Kansas City, I was always responsible for doing the cooking for those of us left at home.

There were two experiences with chickens that are perhaps worthy of comment. One has to do with my first use of the family's double-barreled 12-gauge shotgun. By age ten I had never shot that gun, although I had seen my father and older brothers do so and felt that I knew how. One day when my father and mother were helping out one of our neighbors and my brothers were out in the field, I thought it would be a good time to experiment with shooting the shotgun. I loaded it and went out to find something to shoot at. I saw a hen down in the barnyard and thought that would be a good target. The gun was a little too heavy for me to hold without a prop, so I rested the barrel on the wheel of a wagon parked not too far distant from the hen. I took a bead on the target and pulled the trigger, but had failed to hold the butt of the gun tightly against my shoulder. The kick of the gun was such that it fell from my shoulder and dropped to the ground. After regaining my composure from that, I looked to see what had happened to the hen and found that I had killed it. The problem then was what to do with it. There was an uncapped, dry well resulting from the failure to find water, so I thought I could drop the hen in that well and nobody would know what had happened. I then picked up the carcass and was walking toward the well when someone in a loud voice called my name and asked what I was doing. My brothers were coming in from the field and one had called out to me. They recognized that the hen was a healthy one and would make good eating. Since I was already caught in the act, we might as well

31

clean it and have it for a meal. I suppose the major thing I learned from that experience was to make sure I kept the butt of the gun tightly against my shoulder anytime I wanted to shoot it.

Another episode with chickens was related to my tendency to walk in my sleep. One night I left my bed and went outside, down to the chicken house, completely oblivious to what I was doing. The disturbance to the chickens resulted in substantial noise that brought me half awake, at least enough to start me back to the house. The noise also awakened my father who suspected chicken thieves. With his gun he came outside to challenge the thieves and saw a figure walking toward him. He yelled out asking who was there. That really awakened me, and I cried, "It's me, Charley!" That could have been a close call.

Use of Tobacco

It is almost embarrassing to comment on my rather extensive experience with tobacco at an early age. My father did not use tobacco himself and was strongly opposed to it. He made it extremely clear that if he ever caught any of his boys using tobacco he would apply the whip. That challenged us to see how far we could go. All three of us boys experimented from time to time with rolling corn silks into a cigar-sized shape and smoking it as though it were tobacco.

My oldest brother, Neil, was not particularly interested in experimenting with smoking. He was almost a man before I was a boy, and he associated with neighbors more than with his two brothers. My brother Orville and I had a very close relationship and if one became interested in something the other one automatically did so, too. We had two cousins about our same ages living less than a mile away. Their father grew some tobacco. One fall, when I was about ten years old, the four of us experimented by taking some of my uncle's half-cured tobacco and rolling it into cigars to smoke it. I became very sick from that experience but it did not cure me from further experimentation with tobacco.

There was a little country store less than a mile from our farm that handled all kinds of items including pipe and chewing tobacco. The proprietor also bought eggs from farm people. It was an easy thing to take a dozen eggs to the store and trade them for a tin of smoking tobacco—Prince Albert, Edgeworth, Briggs, Velvet, or Tuxedo—or a plug of chewing tobacco—Star, Horse-shoe, Masterpiece, or Peachy Plug. Cigarette papers were also available at the store. We learned how to roll cigarettes using the specialized paper. We also learned how to smoke a pipe and made our own from corn cobs. The pipe stem was made from pieces cut from a branch of a box elder tree, its pithy center punched out with a wire.

We obviously did not smoke much, but we thought it a great accomplishment to do it undetected. We were extremely careful to keep our tobacco and matches hidden. Because we were so conscious of the potential fire hazard if matches were left unprotected in our hiding place at the barn, we therefore left our matches in an empty tobacco tin. We were successful in keeping our smoking and the location of our cache secreted from our father, but Neil knew where it was. On one occasion we got into an argument with Neil, who thought he would teach his younger brothers a lesson, suggesting to Dad that he might go down to the barn and look in a particular place and see what he would find. He found the tobacco, and it was obvious that Orville and I had been using it. That brought out a branch off the willow tree. The ultimate result was that we changed our hiding place and made sure that we never again confided in Neil.

If we wanted to use some tobacco when Dad was nearby, we would cut off a sliver from a plug of Masterpiece or Peachy Plug and nestle it under our upper lip. We thought it was very smart to be able to have that in our mouths while working with Dad and he not knowing what was going on.

My use of tobacco as a youngster came to a rather abrupt stop when I was thirteen. The basic cause for my resolve to stop playing with the "filthy weed" was not the admonitions of parents but rather those emanating from religion. My parents were very religious people and active members of the Reorganized Church of Jesus Christ of Latter Day Saints (RLDS Church). Most farm families in the area had been drawn there because of the influence of that church. The area was called Lone Rock, and the Lone Rock Church served as the community center and the focus of most community activities.

That church would not accept baptism of youngsters before they reached the age of eight. The philosophy was that the individual should make his or her decision as to whether he or she wanted to become a church member. Most youngsters in the community chose to be baptized and become members as soon as they reached the age of eight. I chose not to do so. But when I reached thirteen, I offered myself for baptism and church membership. It is quite normal for boys of that age to experience the emotional struggle that accompanies entry into manhood. My penchant for inquiry had led me to analyze various aspects of religion. I felt that I was now capable of understanding, which did not exist when I was eight, and I concluded it was time for me to join the church. The church emphasized the detrimental effects of tobacco. Therefore I eliminated all use of tobacco in any form. I was not to take up its use again until I was in my late twenties or early thirties.

Our Farm Environment

Our farm of 100 acres was not real good crop land, being for the most part hilly with some so-called bottom land. Because the acreage had to provide sustenance for the entire family, this meant our farming was a highly diversified operation. Crops were grown that could be plowed without resulting in excessive erosion. Pasture land was used for livestock. We had five or six dairy cattle, some beef cattle, horses, hogs, chickens, and turkeys. We grew most of the feed for the livestock but did buy a small amount of supplemental feed including tankage and oil meal. Fruit orchards occupied a smaller part of the land as well as an area for a large garden. Buildings occupied the rest of the area.

Crops consisted of corn, wheat, oats, millet, timothy, and clover and were regularly rotated so that corn would not be grown consecutively on the same area for more than a two-year period. Wheat would often be planted on corn land in the early fall with clover and/or timothy seeded along with the wheat. Eventually the so-called cover crop would be plowed under providing some green manure for fertilization followed with corn again.

Farm Chores

By the time I was twelve I was considered to be a regular in field work. My labor was especially involved at harvesttime. I helped in picking up bundles of wheat, oats, or hay that were dropped from the binder and put them into shocks. When threshing time came, I might be on the wagon used to haul bundles from the field to the threshing machine. That job involved using a pitch-fork to distribute the bundles on the wagon in an appropriate manner. In the case of hay, I might also be used to drive the team that would lift the "stacker" loaded with hay and have it dumped on the stack that was being built.

A winter job involved hauling hay from haystacks in the field and scattering it in the pasture for cattle to eat. This was a job for people other than myself, although I was intrigued in noting how the hay would be forked out of the stack. The hay in a stack was always tightly packed together, which made moving it fork by fork very difficult. A hay knife was therefore used to cut out smaller areas to be removed. The hay knife was a slightly curved, deeply serrated blade eighteen to twenty-four inches long. It had two handles to facilitate the application of human muscle in cutting through the packed hay. The severed block of hay could then more easily be forked out of the stack.

An early winter job consisted of driving through parts of the fields where rocks had been brought to the surface. These rocks would be picked up, thrown into a wagon, and hauled to a rock pile. I would be one of the picker-uppers or would drive the team. Dad usually was the leader and whatever boys were available, in-cluding myself, would help.

Spring sometimes brought a job that was both inter-esting and educational to a young person. It involved cutting young branches from willow trees and pushing them into the soft earth in the small stream that ran through part of our farm. These small branches were supposed to take root and grow into trees. Dad was very conscious of the problem of soil erosion. Corn was sometimes grown on some of the hilly parts of our farm bordering the stream. Terracing and contour plowing had not become a part of protection against erosion at that time. Hence, substantial erosion might occur after a heavy rain and valuable soil washed into the creek to be carried off downstream. The purpose of developing trees in that stream was to reduce the amount of soil carried beyond the boundary of our farm. We would also sometimes build small dams in the creek to keep the rush of water from torrential rains from eroding the banks and deepening the channel. We might use brush and rocks in building such dams.

There was another winter job that some might have considered work but at least I thought it was fun. This involved hunting rabbits and squirrels. The objective was not to provide pleasure but food for the table or carcasses for sale.

A firearm was a part of the equipment of every farm male. We had both shotguns and .22-caliber rifles. Shotguns were generally considered belonging to Dad or as "community" (family) property, but each of us boys had a .22-caliber rifle. The rabbit and squirrel populations were substantial, and we were not limited to hunting on our own farm. I became a reasonably good shot with a rifle, probably by the time I was eleven, and with a shotgun shortly thereafter. I also soon learned how to dress a rabbit or squirrel and to cut them up for frying or stewing. Rabbit became a common source of meat during the winter. We would occasionally resort to squirrel meat, but none in the family seemed to care too much for that.

There was a fair market for rabbit as a source of meat. I recall one winter day after a fairly heavy snow, Dad decided to have a real rabbit hunt to obtain rabbits that we could take to the market and get cash. He hitched up a team to a sled to be used to haul our rabbits back to the house after our hunt. Dad had his double-barreled shotgun, Neil a rifle, Orville had a .420-gauge shotgun, and I had a rifle. Neil was a good shot and could often hit a running rabbit with his rifle. I was never that good, but I got several rabbits that I found sitting and added to the collection. We would flush rabbits from their living quarters if they were not found already out in the open. We ended our hunt with a big pile of rabbits on the sled that we took home, gutted, left out to freeze, took to town the next day, and sold.

There were other wild animals in our area, including civet cats, skunks, muskrats, and mink. Many farm boys would trap such animals for their skins, which would bring a price in town. Neither Neil nor Orville were interested in trapping, but I was, although I limited my trapping to civet cats and skunks, probably because we did not have areas close by that served as a habitat for muskrats and mink. I checked a string of traps every morning before going to school. If I caught an animal, I used my rifle to kill it before removing it from the trap, if possible shooting it through the head to avoid damaging its pelt. I would then skin the animal at home, stretch the skin on a board made especially for that purpose, scrape any extra fat from it, and hang it up to dry and cure. After the season was over, I would then take my pelts to town and collect some money for them.

I recall one morning I had a good, almost black skunk in a trap. I took it home and proceeded to skin it before going to school. Unfortunately, in that process I accidentally cut the odorous gland that generally served the skunk well as a defense mechanism. In this case, it permeated my clothing. That did not bother me as I was concerned primarily for the value of the hide. I was also concerned about not being too late in getting to school. It was not long after getting into the warm school building that it was obvious something unusual had happened to me. I was summarily dismissed by the teacher and sent home to bathe and change clothes. The pelt brought a premium price, though.

Our dairy cows required milking twice a day. I became a member of the milking detail at a rather early age, perhaps six or seven years. It was a very uncomfortable way to start the day to be aroused out of bed, often before daylight, carry a lantern to the barn, get cows into the stanchions for milking, and milk them. This was always bad in the winter, but not so bad in the summer.

Our small herd of beef cattle was kept primarily for sale although we always butchered a baby beef for our winter meat supply. I did not have many duties associated with the beef cattle. However, there was one episode associated with beef cows that I distinctly remember. Orville and I went out to bring the cows in from the pasture. There were two or three cows with young calves and I was apparently trying to direct one of the calves toward the barn when the mother of the calf decided to object to my action. She took out after me and butted me with her head. She caught me mid-body so that I was balanced over her head as she raised me off the ground. My brother saw what was happening and ran to stop the animal and succeeded in having me dropped. I was actually not hurt, but exceedingly fortunate that I was caught where I would be lifted rather than trampled. I took the episode in stride, figuring it was all in a day's work.

Dad became very interested in his beef stock. He was caught up in the emphasis on developing quality in animals, which he would read about in the farm magazines, and decided to upgrade his herd. He worked toward the eventual development of a registered herd of white-faced Hereford stock by buying a registered Hereford bull and then an occasional registered Hereford female calf. He became very proud of his accomplishments in this area.

Hogs were perhaps our principal livestock cash crop. Farrowing was usually planned to provide most hogs to be marketed in the fall but a smaller crop for spring marketing. Pork was an important meat staple for our table. I usually did not participate in the butchering but always got pleasure observing, and at times I helped in the processing that took place in the kitchen. The first meal after butchering usually consisted of liver, but the choice meals immediately following included pork tenderloin.

Poultry was kept for both egg production and for meat. Some breeds of chickens were better for egg production and others better for meat. Leghorns would be kept primarily for eggs and Rhode Island Reds and Buff Orpingtons were common breeds for meat as well as eggs. Nests were provided in the hen house for hens to lay their eggs in, but since the chickens were allowed to roam the entire barnyard area, some hens selected their own nests in various parts of the outbuildings. Such nests were almost always located and the eggs gathered from them on a regular basis. Occasionally a nest would not be discovered. In such cases the hen completed her laying cycle after perhaps a dozen or so eggs and then sat on the eggs intermittently for three weeks, turning each egg daily with her beak until the hatching process occurred. This was an uneconomical way of producing chickens. We therefore depended primarily on an incubator kept in the back part of the house. Heat for the incubator was supplied by coal oil lamps. Eggs were turned manually on a daily basis. When chicks were hatched, they were kept in a heated enclosure until they were old enough to turn outside with the adult chickens. Poultry provided a vital part of our food supply.

We occasionally had a flock of turkeys, but they were somewhat of a nuisance to take care of. They would not tolerate being cooped up in pens and houses. They wanted to seek their own roosting and nesting places. They might develop a nest out in the edge of a pasture or in the tall grass or brush area along a creek as a place to lay their eggs and hatch their chicks. If we found a nest early so that we could collect eggs while they were fresh, we would include them as part of our supply of food. Primarily, however, the turkeys supplied meat for our table.

Orchard

A fruit orchard was another part of our diversified agriculture that helped in providing a self-sufficient physical existence. We had cherries, plums, peaches, apricots, pears, and apples. Commercial sprays were nonexistent for us at that early date so we had the job of sorting out the bad or wormy fruit at harvest and either throwing them away or feeding them to the hogs. We had different varieties of peaches and apples se-lected so that the fruit would be ready for harvest at different times of the season. I was especially fond of apples, so much so that I was often called "Apple Charley." Our summer apples were usually made into applesauce and canned for use the year round. Our winter apples (I remember the varieties of Ben Davis, MacIntosh, and Greening) were stored in barrels and kept in the cellar. We became very conscious of the statement that "One bad apple in a barrel can damage all the rest" and kept the apples sorted, removing those that had started to spoil. We were not allowed, however, to throw the partly spoiled apples away but rather to cut out the rotten part and consume the rest. There were times when two of us boys would be assigned to empty a partly filled barrel of apples, separating the good from the bad and keeping the good ones. We never enjoyed that task as it was always done in a dark, damp cellar. When these fruits were ripe, they were canned to provide fruit throughout the year. Some fruits, including apples, peaches, and apricots, were dried in addition to those that were canned.

We also had some small fruit including strawberries, gooseberries, raspberries, blackberries, and grapes. These were usually used to produce jams, jellies, and preserves. I often helped in their production. I should mention, too, that a favorite and delicious use Mother made of the different fruits we grew was in pies, which were wonderful and frequent additions to our meals.

Garden

We always had a large garden which provided us with vegetables throughout the year. During the summer, of course, we had vegetables fresh from the garden and the rest of the year from cans and storage bins in the cellar. The storage bins contained potatoes, carrots, turnips, and parsnips. We also had dried beans, both navy and lima, and black-eyed peas. Squash and pumpkins could be stored for several weeks or months and used for regular dishes or pies.

Different plantings of sweet corn were spaced to provide a two-week interval between harvesting. At harvesttime we had corn on the cob and creamed corn, freshly cut off the cob. Corn not consumed during the short harvest period would be dried or canned.

A large variety of other vegetables grew in our spacious garden, including various kinds of beans, lettuce, radishes, salsify, rhubarb, peas, tomatoes, cabbage, peppers, onions, cucumbers, melons, and beets. We did not have in our garden the more exotic vegetables such as broccoli, cauliflower, and asparagus. Cucumbers and beets were generally pickled. Cabbage could be stored for awhile but it mostly was made into sauerkraut. Onions were hung from the rafters in the small milk house adjacent to the kitchen.

The younger boys (I being the youngest) were regularly assigned to garden work. This included regular hoeing both to keep the weeds down and provide some cultivation for mulch and penetration of rain. There was also the problem of bugs and worms that fed on tender plants. We had no pesticides for spraying or dusting, but there were some "homemade" remedies, the exact nature of which I do not recall, that were used to discourage such pests. I recall that one of our homemade remedies for potato bugs involved a liquid mixture of some kind which we would pour on the plants. That also was a boy's job. Tomato worms, if found, would be picked off and stepped on.

I always enjoyed participating in the potato harvest. Because potatoes provided an important staple food for all-year consumption, we always grew a lot of them. Harvesting consisted of Dad hitching a team of horses to a lister that he would drive down each row, turning the potatoes out of the ground and onto the loose soil. We boys would follow with buckets, picking potatoes out of the mellow soil and carrying them to the house for storage.

Wash Days

Other than Sunday, there were two days of the week that had special concern for me as well as for some other family members. These were Monday and Saturday.

Monday was generally washday. It took place in our large kitchen. As a young observer, I noted the preparation for doing the weekly family washing. It included setting up a stand that would hold washtubs with a hand-operated wringer between them. Mother would use a washboard to rub out stains and dirt before putting the clothes into a copper boiler placed on the kitchen wood-and-coal-burning range where they would be boiled as a part of the laundering process. Mother would take a broomstick handle to lift the clothes from the copper boiler and return them to the tub of wash water. Then the clothes would be run through a ringer to another tub for rinsing purposes. The clothes were rung into a second rinse to which Mother added bluing to whiten and brighten the fabrics. White clothes were always washed first, followed by the colored ones. After rinsing, the clothes would again be run through the ringer and carried outdoors to be hung on long clotheslines. The outdoors lines were used both summer and winter except when it was either raining or snowing, in which case the clothes would be hung in various rooms in the house. The appearance of frozen clothes on lines was always an intriguing sight. The term "freeze drying" became a meaningful one to me.

When I was somewhat older a mechanical washing machine was purchased and this lightened somewhat the Monday drudgery, except for me or my brothers. A mechanical washing machine required human muscle to push a lever back and forth to turn gears that operated the clothing agitators in the tub. That was never fun.

Another aspect of washday was the fact that the laundry soap used was homemade lye soap. Sophisticated detergents were not available, or at least not known by us. Mother and Father made soap usually once a year, as I recall, an out-of-doors process that followed not too long after Dad did the butchering in the fall. I remember the smell of the soap being cut into bars and laid out to dry and solidify. It had a brown color somewhat similar to Fels Naphtha soap with which we got acquainted at a somewhat later date. Homemade lye soap was too harsh to be used as a hand soap.

Saturday was also a washday and involved the use of washtubs. It, however, did not mean washing clothes but rather washing one's whole body. This was a shivering operation except in the hot summer weather, but Mother never permitted the temperature or the weather to interfere with this weekly ritual. In fact, there were times when the ritual was more than a weekly experience.

We had two sources of water for drinking, cooking, and washing. Water for drinking and cooking came from a well located not far from the house. A hand pump was installed in that well. It was usually a job of one or more of the boys to pump water from the well and keep a teakettle and a pail full of water in the kitchen. It is almost embarrassing to report that the dipper was kept in the pail of water from which each member of the family would take a drink.

Water for all other household purposes came from a cistern. Water from the roof of the house was carried into a large, charcoal-filled tile and then into the cistern. The charcoal served as a filter to provide a cleaner soft water. There was no pump to lift water from the cistern, but rather a rope attached to "an old oaken bucket" on one end and a large cylinder on the other. A handle was attached to the cylinder for purposes of turning and wrapping the rope to hoist the bucketful of water from the cistern. (An incidental use of the cistern was to place milk or other perishables in the bucket and lower them into the cistern as a cooler place for temporary storage.)

We had two wells on the farm to provide water for livestock. Eventually Dad was able to buy a windmill to provide power for pumping water from one of these wells. Before that was done, however, large water tanks had to be filled by pumping water from the wells by hand. That was obviously a frequent job for one or more of us boys. It was never a pleasant task.

Shopping and Leisure Time

There were not many occasions during a year all the time I was living on the farm that much time or attention were given to going to town on pure shopping expeditions. Much of the shopping for clothes, household items, tools, small farm equipment, harness for the horses, and even some food items was done from the Sears Roebuck catalog. Such purchases were usually made two or three times a year. The entire family would be excited when notice was received that a large shipment, fully crated, was waiting at the railroad depot thirteen miles away. After the crated items were opened and distributed we felt very elated.

While work was a normal and important part of the activities of all family members, there was still time available for social and recreational activities. Sunday was always a day of relative leisure. The Bible admonition to rest on the Sabbath was rigidly adhered to, with only the necessary work of taking care of the livestock included in the day's activities. After completing the milking and feeding of livestock and eating breakfast, we would all hasten to clean up, put on our "Sunday clothes," hitch a team of horses to a two-seated buggy, and take the entire family to church. There would be a Sunday school with classes for different age groups for youngsters and adults. This would be followed with a sermon usually given by a lay preacher.

It was almost a universal practice of our family to leave the church after the service and either go to a friend's home or have friends come to our home for Sunday dinner. After dinner younger members of the two families would engage in some kind of play. Such play would usually be much more restrained than play that occurred during the week because we were always admonished on Sunday to be careful to not damage our Sunday clothes.

Non-Sunday leisure time varied considerably. We would get together with neighbor youngsters occasionally to play barnyard games, race horses, swim in somebody's pond, go sleigh riding, or ride horseless four-wheeled carts down steep hills. We might also have contests on accuracy in hitting targets with small rocks or pebbles. The glass balls on lightning rods on top of the barn unfortunately and unwisely were selected as targets. The boy who succeeded in hitting a glass ball and shattering it would strut like a hero until he was otherwise chastised by his dad.

Each of us youngsters also became somewhat adept at developing individual or solitary ways of using any leisure time. I enjoyed reading and had a special place in my room for that purpose. My father had purchased an abandoned school desk with its sloping lid. He placed it in one corner of the room used jointly with my two brothers, but it was labeled as my desk. I could raise the lid and store papers and books in the bin and keep them out of sight from others. Although you might think I would secret in the bin some risqué reading material, there was none. My parents would never have permitted such in the house if they knew about it. The closest to any material of that sort that might be found in the house was the Sears Roebuck catalog. I must confess that I turned the pages in that catalog rather frequently—not at the desk in my room but in a little outbuilding down toward the chicken house that had a half-moon in the door. Strange as it may seem, the one book that I did not want anyone seeing me read, which I would quickly slide into the bin and close the lid if someone came into my room, was the Bible. I guess I had developed a reputation of not being interested in religion and didn't want anyone to know I was. Perhaps to cover up I used swear words when the occasion seemed to provide an opportunity.

As a young boy on the farm, I often dreamed of what kind of farm I might have when I became an adult. Such dreaming at times took on the aspects of an architect. On rainy days I would often plan the kind of livestock I might have on my farm and the kind of buildings and fenced in fields appropriate to my vision of future operations. I used corn cobs for preparing "blueprints," to fence off the areas for hogs, cattle, and horses, and to divide the barn into grain storage, wagon storage, cow stanchions, and horse stalls. Those were as good as Lincoln Logs in this creative venture.

Another type of recreation or use of leisure time was the four-wheeled cart, which was really a chassis of an abandoned buggy. Neil had fashioned a seat close enough to the front axle so that when sitting on the seat his legs would be close enough to the axle so that he could use his feet to guide the cart when racing down a hill. There was also room behind the driver's seat for others to sit. The game we would play with that contraption was to load it with passengers (usually three of us) and ride down the rather steep hill, at the bottom of which was a fairly narrow bridge crossing a small stream. The art in the game was to guide the vehicle across that bridge without being wrecked. That was great fun!

When we would get together with neighbor boys we would sometimes play "shinny." I do not know how it came to be named that. The game might be referred to as "barnyard hockey" and consisted of dividing up into two teams. Each player would have a club (homemade hockey stick), and a tin can would be used for the puck. We would then see which team would be most proficient in moving the tin can into the other's territory and outside the playing field.

Halloween provided an excuse for a particular kind of "recreation." One fairly common procedure in the area was placing a buggy, wagon, or other vehicle or implement on the roof of a barn. Adults learned to accept that as a youthful prank and seldom chastised their offspring for such a performance. Parents seldom asked whether any of their boys were a party to such operation.

It was fairly common, particularly in good weather, to play a prank on a newlywed couple. Few if any married couples left the area immediately after the ceremony to get away from their friends and pranksters. In the first place there were not many places where they could go and also little or no money to take them. The married couple would therefore be closeted in a house—their parents' or friends'—but youngsters in the neighborhood would know where they were, sometimes surprising them with an evening of revelry to celebrate the marriage.

Some of the activities associated with the community church might be classified as making use of leisure time, although some would question that designation. I refer to such activities as Children's Day and Ice Cream Socials. Children's Day was designed to give youngsters an activity that would be both stimulating and instructive. Preparation for such a day involved numerous meetings to practice plays and individual presentations. Some youngsters enjoyed this and others participated under duress. Those parents responsible for instructing and coaching youngsters would hardly call the time devoted to such as "leisure time." It did, however, bring people together and reduced somewhat the monotony of daily farm operation.

The Ice Cream Social was an annual affair and sometimes was held more than one time during the summer. Some might refer to it as an experience in gluttonous living. Each participating family would bring to the church grounds a freezer full of homemade ice cream and/or a cake. There would be no limit in the amount one might consume. In fact, some would compete to see who could eat the most ice cream or sample each of the various varieties available. The varieties would include vanilla, lemon, banana, strawberry, cherry, coconut, and chocolate. The ice creams were not made from skim milk or brought from the "Dairy Queen." Farm women usually included extra quantities of real cream with the whole milk, eggs, sugar, and flavorings in their ice cream. The Ice Cream Social was a highlight in summer social gatherings and enjoyed by all members of the participating families.

We certainly did not look upon the community Ice Cream Social as a unique opportunity to enjoy ice cream and cake. These delicacies were common fare in our home. There was an ice house in our area where we could get ice in the summer to make ice cream.

Pets

We had both cats and dogs as part of the standard residents of our farm. I say "residents of the farm" because they did not live in the house. They had their own living quarters outside the house. Cats were usually fairly plentiful and not generally recognized as pets. They were considered to be helpful in keeping the mice and rat population under control.

Dogs were a different matter. They were indeed pets. We often had two or three dogs at the same time, but each had its own master. My favorite dog was a large, bushy collie named Shep. He was my companion and protector. I recall one summer day Orville and I got into a friendly tussle in the house. Shep was on the front porch and became conscious of our tussle. The regular door to the room was open but the screen door was closed. Shep, undoubtedly thinking his master was being injured, tore the screen wire off the door, plunged through, and took my brother off of me.

One of the saddest moments in my young life was when I left the house one morning and Shep was not there to greet me. He was later found some three-quarters of a mile away, dead, having been shot by someone, most obviously the neighbor on whose property Shep was found. There had been some talk of sheep that had been harassed by dogs and one had been killed. We supposed that the neighbor was trying to protect his sheep and thought any dog was suspect. Eventually a replacement was obtained for Shep, but he was never the same.

Improvements

Any family farm must have a variety of buildings, usually referred to as "improvements." Our farm was no exception. When I appeared on the scene the buildings consisted of a small barn, a carriage house, a chicken house, a privy, and a small house or cottage. My parents recognized the need for an additional barn and a larger house. I remember family discussions when I was five or six years old as to which should come first, a large house or a new barn. My father pointed out that the new barn would help increase family income by permitting some expansion in the livestock part of our farming operation. He indicated that a larger house would not increase family income, hence we should have the barn first to help accumulate funds for the house. And that is the program that was adopted. The new barn was built when I was six.

My father, as was true of all good farmers, was a man of many skills: a mechanic, a shoe repairman, a veterinarian, an animal midwife, a blacksmith, a shoe-er of horses, a mason, and a carpenter. In building both the new barn and the house he contributed his own labor and skill on a regular basis although he had a professional carpenter assume the leadership role in constructing these buildings.

Three years after the barn was built work started on a new house, a large, square structure. There was no basement, but there was a cellar located below the milk house and storage area. The cellar could be entered through that building. The downstairs of the main house contained a kitchen, dining room, sitting room, parlor, screened-in porch, and a large pantry. The upstairs consisted of four large rooms. My parents had one room. My sister Ruby had a room of her own. We three boys were all in one room in which we had three beds. The fourth room was used for storage. It was not long after the house was built that Neil left home to work for others and that left only Orville and me to share the one room.

There was, of course, no central heat or electric lighting at that time. Coal oil lamps provided the source of light. A wood and coal burning cookstove provided heat in the kitchen. We also had a coal burning stove in the large dining room and another one in the sitting room. There was no heat (or air conditioning) in the downstairs parlor or any of the upstairs bedrooms. On cold winter nights Mother would heat flatirons, wrap them in paper or towels, and place them under the covers at the bottom of the beds to help keep feet warm. In the wintertime it was always a cold awakening of a morning, but Dad always got up early to stir up the banked fire in the stoves and get the downstairs rooms warm for us to run to get dressed in a warm area.

In retrospect, I marvel at the economic accomplishments of my parents. They inherited fifty acres of land, later bought another fifty acres, raised a family of three boys and a girl, added new buildings on the farm, added another twenty acres to their holding, bought an automobile in the early days of automobiles, always paid their debts, and received no government grants or handouts. In modern terms our family would have been listed among the poor, their income and assets placing them below the poverty line. And yet we were rich in spirit and in accomplishment. We were free and sensed that we were responsible for our own livelihood and future.

Chapter 2

The Country School

Our public school consisted of a one-room building for all eight grades. It was a locally controlled school system with policies set by a local school board. My father was a member of that board for a number of years. The board was responsible for hiring the school teacher and paying the teacher from locally generated taxes. About the only government supervision of local school boards was at the county level. I cannot recall any exercise of such supervision until I was finishing the eighth grade.

I was introduced to our one-room country school at an early age. I felt left out when I saw my two brothers leave with their dinner pails to go to school and I had to stay home. As I remember, I was allowed to accompany my brothers to school in the spring before my fifth birthday. I became a regular attendant in the fall after my fifth birthday in August.

The school building was located about a mile from our house and we always walked to and from. I believe school opened fairly early in the day, probably 8:30, and there was a recess of probably fifteen minutes between the opening and lunchtime. Everyone brought their own lunch. We probably had about an hour set aside for lunch and games played in the yard or in the building if the weather was bad. We had another recess in the middle of the afternoon, and school closed around 4 o'clock.

The recesses and noon period after lunch were devoted to different types of games. We would choose up sides for some kind of ball game. Andy-Over was a very popular game for boys. This consisted of dividing the boys into two teams. One team stationed itself on the east side of the school building and the other team on the west side. A ball would be thrown over the building by one team and members of the other team would try to catch the ball. Whether caught or retrieved, it was then thrown back over the building to the original team. This process would be continued until we got tired or it was time to return to our desks.

During the winter, if there was snow on the ground, we would often have snowball fights. In the spring we would sometimes create new types of activities utilizing the natural resources at hand. One such activity involved the use of clay mud rolled into balls and stuck on pointed, whip-like branches cut from willow trees. We used the whip to see how far we could fling the clay ball. We sometimes used the front of the school building as our target and then counted the number of balls that stuck to the building. Naturally, in my first few years at school I was an observer of such games, but as I got older became a participant.

The size of the school building was such that it could accommodate as many as twenty-four or twenty-six pupils, although I doubt whether there were ever that many attending at any one time. There were times when there were no pupils in one or more of the grades. The desks were anchored to the floor and each accommodated two pupils. The top of the desk was slanted and hinged so that the top, when raised, provided access to storage space where pupils could keep note paper, slates, and pencil boxes. The four or five inches of the desk top to which the sloping top was hinged contained two ink wells, one for each occupant. The writing instruments which were dipped into the ink wells were somewhat superior to the quills of an earlier age, but quite inferior to the later fountain and ballpoint pens.

A rather standard procedure was followed by the teacher in conducting classes. When it was time for school to open or to call pupils in from recess or after lunch, a hand bell would be rung. Pupils were then supposed to come in, take their seats, and be ready for instruction. The teacher's desk was at the front of the room, and in front of her desk was a long bench. The teacher would call a particular class, say first grade, by announcing "The first grade please rise, come forward, be seated." Members of that class would then receive whatever instruction the teacher provided. A standard number of minutes was allowed for each such class. At the end of the allotted time, the teacher would then go through a similar process of having the pupils rise, return to their seats, and sit down.

While a particular class was being instructed or asked to recite, the rest of the pupils in the room were supposed to be reading or working on assignments. It was obvious, however, that many youngsters preferred to listen to what was going on between the teacher and those on the bench rather than to try to concentrate on their own reading or working arithmetic problems. I know that I learned a great deal by listening to the upper grades before I became a member of such upper grades.

Incidentally, all of us in any of the grades where geography was being taught got a directional mind set that was out of kilter with reality when examining a map. The pupils' desks all faced south, but when we opened our geography books we were looking at a map in which the top pointed north, east was to the right, and west to the left of the page. This has always disturbed my sense of direction. As a result, I have ever since needed to mechanically train my mind to realize that left is west and right is east when viewing a map.

The teacher in our school during all of the time I spent there was almost always a woman. There was only one year in which I had a male teacher. I use the term "woman" in referring to my teachers, but I probably should change that to "girl." I doubt whether any of my country school female teachers were more than twenty years old. The most formal education any one of them had was two years of high school. The male teacher was hired primarily because the school board recognized that there was a disciplinary problem and wanted a teacher who could keep the pupils in line. I don't know whether the male teacher was any more successful in maintaining discipline than were the female ones. My memory is very vivid concerning one teacher, a young woman not more than nineteen years old, who never had a disciplinary problem of any kind. She had the superior quality of engendering in her pupils a desire to learn and was thus able to lead them into books and competition at the blackboard and make such activity highly desirable.

Except for that one great teacher, I think there was never another who did not at one time or other use corporal punishment as a method of trying to maintain discipline. It was fairly standard practice to keep four or five switches standing in the corner of the room, available to lay on some obstreperous big boy or smart aleck. I recall that one time some of us "doctored" those switches when the teacher was not there. We took our pocket knives (every boy carried one) and carefully made thin cuts in three or four places around the circumference of each switch. The purpose of these cuts was to make the switches easy to break into pieces if used to whip a youngster. This happened in one instance and created an interesting situation.

It might seem ironic that modern "human rights" legislation and court decisions have made anything in the least resembling corporal punishment a forbidden action and the teacher subject to a fine, dismissal, or, in some cases, imprisonment. At the same time, we have an increase in student dropouts and a diminished stimulation to learn. Many who do not drop out of school remain to create havoc and dare the teachers to try to discipline them.

As much as 80 percent of a youngster's learning depends on oneself and 20 percent on the intellectual contribution of a teacher. Motivation is vital to learning. Maybe teachers who can motivate are more valuable in the classroom than those who have superior technical skills and degrees from colleges of education and no ability to motivate.

The community involvement in the school was enhanced by parents taking an active part in supporting and attending school functions such as special programs put on by pupils at specific times such as Thanksgiving, Christmas, or Easter. One special annual evening function was a box supper. My sister, who was a public school teacher, described this event as follows:

> The teacher usually had at least one pie and box social during the year, which was well attended. Entertainment usually preceded the auction. Women and girls tried to see who could bring the most attractively deco-

rated box. The food inside was either a pie or a whole lunch. The fellows made a big to-do trying to find who had brought which box. Some bidders were very competitive and often paid a big price in order to eat with the girl of their choice. The money taken in was usually used to purchase something for the school. Eating the goodies and visiting with each other was the climax of an enjoyable evening.*

There were only one or two situations during my grade school days in which my activity might be considered somewhat unique. About the time I was finishing the eighth grade, a legal regulation was passed requiring an examination given and supervised by the county superintendent of schools. Anyone passing that examination would be awarded a certificate indicating successful completion of eight grades of school. My memory is somewhat dull, but to the best of my knowledge I was the first person in our school district to take that examination. I do recall that it was a very nervous experience but a happy one after I learned I had passed and that a certificate was on its way. I was so proud of that certificate that I had it framed to hang on my wall. It remained there until replaced by my high school certificate.

I enjoyed school a great deal and wanted to move on to high school after finishing the eighth grade. The closest high school was at Hatfield, located about five miles distant from our farm. I believe it offered only two or maybe three years of high school work. It was too far away for me to live at home and travel to and from school every day. While my parents were not enthusiastic about me seeking "higher learning," they agreed

---

* Ruby Sandage Herring, *Whoa!! Back Up!* (Urbana, Illinois: Farm Research Institute, 1986), 84.

that if we could find some place in Hatfield for me to live and do some work for my room and board, I could enter the Hatfield high school. They were successful in finding such a place. It was the home of a widower who wanted someone to do chores around the house, some cooking, and provide some companionship. After a little more than a week of such working and living it became intolerable to me because the householder was an alcoholic and was usually half drunk. My parents, therefore, thought it best for me to leave that situation.

A somewhat unsatisfactory compromise was worked out that permitted me to return to the one-room country school from which I had just graduated. The new teacher had two or three years of high school work and agreed to let me attend her school where she could let me study algebra plus a reading program involving history, geography, and literature.

My desire for continuing formal education was not satisfied with this temporary post-eighth-grade work at our country school. There was a potential solution for satisfying that desire fairly close at hand. Located thirteen miles away in Lamoni, Iowa, was Graceland Academy and Junior College, sponsored by the RLDS Church. That facility provided dormitories for campus living. My parents agreed that we would seek a meeting with the officials of that institution to see what arrangements might be made that would permit me to attend the school. My parents could in no way afford to pay the tuition, board, and room required of all students, so it was necessary to ascertain whether one could work to pay for some or all of those expenses.

We did get an appointment to talk with school officials. The result of our conference made me ecstatic. The school would not require payment of tuition until after graduating from the academy, and I could work four hours a day, seven days a week, with an extra two hours on Saturday, to pay for my board and room. We agreed that would be done. I therefore became a student in the Graceland Academy starting in September 1917.

Chapter 3

My Graceland Years

In late August or early September 1917 my parents drove me to Lamoni, Iowa, so I could be settled at Graceland and registered for classes to start immediately after Labor Day. My clothing and personal belongings took up very little space and could be packed in a large suitcase. I was duly registered at the academy and assigned to a room in what was called the College Farmhouse. I had a roommate by the name of Grant Snethen. He had already moved in, and like me, was scheduled to work for his board and room.

Working for Room and Board

My first regularly assigned job was working with the herd of dairy cattle maintained by the academy, which meant milking twice a day. The first milking took place before breakfast. It involved getting up at about 4:30 a.m., bringing the cows in from the pasture, putting them in their stanchions, and feeding and milking them. The milk was then cooled and used for drinking at meals. We usually had more milk than needed for drinking and cooking. The surplus was run through a separator with the cream sold and the skim milk fed to calves or other animals.

I was assigned additional work on my first Saturday on the campus because classes had not yet started and will never forget that experience. There were two or three of us involved that made up a crew to take hoes and walk through a corn field and cut out noxious weeds with special attention given to cockleburs. It was a hot, dry day and we worked from fairly early in the morning until dinnertime at night with an hour off for a noontime meal. I had only one pair of shoes and they were already too small to be worn with any comfort. After walking most of the day up and down corn rows, my feet hurt me so much that the pain was almost unbearable. I had no money, but my distress was so complete that it motivated me to hobble to town and buy a larger pair of shoes. The owner of the store knew my folks. He recognized my predicament and said that he would take the risk of collecting from them.

Adjustment to my new environment was an experience in itself. I knew no one in the student group. My roommate was a stranger with living habits quite different from mine. My Farmhouse environment was not particularly different from my past, but the school buildings and dormitories were quite different. There was no running water at the Farmhouse, but I was quite familiar with that type of situation. There were, however, running water and "modern" facilities in the campus buildings. I am somewhat reluctant to say that it took me some time to feel comfortable with such amenities as flush toilets and shower baths.

After about two weeks on the campus, a most fortunate change in my work status occurred. Mrs. Guss, who presided over the kitchen and dining facilities at the commissary that served all students, needed some male help and asked that I be assigned to her. Her request was granted. I was then moved from the Farmhouse to Marietta Hall, the primary boys' dormitory on the campus. I also gained a different roommate—Allen

Trachsel, an upperclassman. He served as a fair tutor in educating me to this new form of living.

Graceland made no distinction between academy freshmen and students in the junior college with respect to housing and social activities, thus my good fortune in getting an older person as my roommate. My roommate was actually eight years older than I. He had stayed out of school a number of years before becoming a student at Graceland Academy. He, like a number of students at the school, was of an age that made him a prime candidate for the military draft in World War I.

The United States had entered the war in April 1917. Of course, this occurred before I enrolled at Graceland, but I was very conscious of its impact on individuals and families. My older brother, Neil, enlisted in the Army Air Corps soon after we had declared war, and my other brother, Orville, was registered and within a year of being inducted into the military. I was much too young to even have a draft card, but having a brother already in the war, another brother eligible for induction before long, and now a roommate who was of military age, brought the war very close to me. My roommate enlisted in the Navy before the end of my freshman year, and I knew he would not be my roommate for the ensuing year. He was sent to the Great Lakes Naval Training Station for his basic training. It was a sad day when news came that Allen had died of influenza in camp in September 1918.

My assignment to Mrs. Guss did not permit me to sleep any later in the morning, but it did give me work and an environment that I enjoyed more than I had at the Farmhouse. My job was varied. I got up early and peeled potatoes before breakfast. A peck of potatoes looked awfully big. I also pumped water into buckets from the centrally located well on the campus and carried them to the kitchen for both drinking and cooking. I recall one morning when loaded with two such buckets, I met Miss Royce, my English teacher, and greeted her with "Howdy." She very gently but firmly replied that it would be more proper to say, "Good morning." It is no doubt a truism that an off-hand comment made by a teacher often has a much greater impact on the listener than the teacher would ever suspect.

My water-carrying job also involved filling jugs of water on the second and third floors of the girls' dormitories. I always called out in a loud voice when mounting the steps, "Man on second" or "Man on third." I doubt whether such an announcement would ever be used today.

My kitchen and commissary job did not change during my freshman year. At the close of school I stayed on the campus during the summer and worked full time in physical labor. This was to continue each summer with one exception. My summer jobs were varied and included painting, house cleaning, some field work, and general maintenance work. One summer, however, a new building (eventually named Briggs Hall) was being constructed. Students made up a significant part of the unskilled labor force in the construction of that building. I can still remember pushing many wheelbarrow loads of cement to be used in the foundation, walls, and floor of that building.

When school started for the beginning of my second year, I was still assigned to the kitchen and commissary area as a helper to Mrs. Guss. I had, however, been promoted to a more enjoyable job than peeling potatoes and preparing vegetables. I became the breakfast chef.

That was not only more pleasant work than that of the previous year, but it also had certain social values. I would often help in serving the food to students as they came in to breakfast and thus increased the frequency of meeting and conversing with most of the students on the campus. I also helped in the serving of the noon and evening meals but had no chef responsibilities for these.

The one summer not spent working on the school campus was the one following my junior year in the academy (1920). There were two wonderful girls in my class whose home was in Goodland, Kansas. Their parents operated a large farm or ranch and the girls suggested that it might be a pleasant experience if I would come out to Goodland to help in the wheat harvest. This sounded like a good idea to me and to Harve Elefson and Walter Walden. The three of us agreed that we would try to leave Lamoni immediately after the close of school and seek work in the Goodland, Kansas, area and remain until time to return for fall classes. My only problem was obtaining permission from my parents and having them give me enough money to pay train fare for the trip. My parents were solidly against the idea. They thought I was too young and physically unprepared to perform the hard labor associated with harvesting wheat. Harve and Walter apparently had no problem in getting permission and I used that as leverage in pressuring my parents for permission. Eventually I won out, but my father said that he would pay for only a one-way ticket for the 500-mile trip to Goodland and that it would therefore be necessary for me to earn enough to return in the fall. That was good enough for me.

The three of us arrived at Goodland in early June, about two weeks before the wheat was ripe enough to combine. Therefore, we'd have to wait at least two weeks to get a harvest field job. We did get temporary jobs but at different places and this separated us until the weekend when we got back together at a rooming house. My job was out on a farm doing odd jobs. These included hoeing the garden but primarily painting some of the farm buildings.

When we got together Saturday night back at the rooming house, we mourned the fact that we had to be separated during the week. I had become very home-sick, and had my father not been wise enough to limit my railroad ticket to one-way, I probably would have caved in and gone home. Therefore, the idea of finding work where the three of us could be together was paramount in my thinking. Because I had been paint-ing, I suggested that the three of us offer our services as painters and follow that until wheat harvest started. My idea was accepted and we proceeded to seek paint-ing jobs in town. We were fortunate in getting all of the painting we could do. Instead of working by the hour, we contracted for an entire job.

I recall one very interesting but disturbing experi-ence. We had finished putting a coat of paint on one house just before leaving for dinner at our rooming house. During dinner the wind started to blow rather heavily and the sun was blocked out by what I thought were clouds. The local people, however, said this was a sand/dust storm. It lasted for maybe ten minutes and then stopped. After dinner we went around to examine our house with its wet paint. It looked more like a stuccoed than a smoothly painted house. The owner was a marvelous individual who said the paint was used primarily to preserve the wood and that we might as well apply the second and last coat of paint over the sand spotted surface.

Our "occupation" as painters lasted for another ten days when the three of us got harvest field jobs. After working in getting the wheat cut and either bound in bundles or stacked, we signed on as members of a threshing crew. The crew was mobile in that it moved from one job to another. It maintained its own mobile living quarters as well as its own chuck wagon. We remained with that crew until time to return for fall classes.

The summer in the Goodland, Kansas, area was devoted primarily to work. It did, however, have its social and recreational aspects. Our Graceland girl-friends, whose suggestion brought us to Goodland, found us spending some time with them on various weekends. The problem of transportation in getting to their home was generally solved by borrowing some-one's car for an evening. There were no emotional ties to our Graceland girlfriends. Our interest in spending the summer in the Goodland area was primarily of adventure rather than drawn by an emotional attach-ment.

There were two purely recreational adventures that I have never forgotten. One involved taking a trip into the sagebrush area of Colorado to hunt sage chickens. We were successful in our hunting and enjoyed roasted sage chicken over a campfire on the prairie. I remember that the natural sage seasoning was especially pro-nounced. The other bit of recreation also involved hunt-ing. This time it was Canadian geese as they were winging south in the early fall. Our threshing was interrupted for a full week because of rain. We were located not too far from several ponds that migrating geese used as stopover points on their southward journey. We built blinds on these ponds and tolerated the mosquitoes until we got our quota of fowl. We had sumptuous meals during that week. The chuck wagon was presided over by an excellent Norwegian cook who knew exactly what to do with the geese that we brought to her. I recall that I gained five pounds in those seven days.

The year 1920 was an economically prosperous one. Perhaps some of the prosperity was like fool's gold in that monetary inflation had resulted in significantly higher prices for both wages and commodities without recognizing that there might be a reversal at a later date. The high wages we were earning encouraged us to spend rather lavishly on clothes that we could take back to Graceland and show off to our fellow students. One would think that I would have been encouraged to save substantial sums from my high wages to reduce the number of hours I needed to work for my board and room at the school. At that age, however, I suppose that for one who had been living in relative poverty, the adage "Easy come, easy go" not too surprisingly applied.

It did not take long to get back into the routine of classes plus four hours a day of work. Actually, the work was enjoyable. It kept me in constant relationship with fellow students. My summer flirting with riches would never be forgotten, but primarily because of the broadening of my horizons rather than the temporary economic gain it brought.

After graduating from the academy and entering the junior college, I "lost" my kitchen and commissary job and was appointed as manager of the school bookstore. This was a great opportunity. The store occupied a small room on the first floor of the Administration

Building. The term "cubbyhole" would probably be more accurate than the term "room." It was not large enough to permit potential customers to enter and examine any of the books available for purchase. There was an open window where a customer could ask the store attendant for whatever book he wanted to purchase. Flanking the open window were mailboxes, one for each resident student. The mail carrier delivered all student mail to the store manager and he was responsible for sorting and placing the mail in the appropriate boxes.

When I was appointed to assume the responsibility for running the bookstore, J. A. Gunsolley, the college business manager, informed me that the bookstore was operated primarily as a service to the students, that it had never made a profit, and that it would probably continue to be operated at a loss.

As soon as I took on that job, I took an inventory of the books and supplies. I found that 100 or more books in inventory were no longer being used as texts and that there appeared to be no prospect for selling them. Previous managers had felt that the price of a book was a fixed figure that could not be changed. I thought there was no purpose in keeping books on the bookstore shelves year after year that were unsalable at the fixed price. It might be better to give them away than to continue to let them occupy space that could be used for something else. I got permission from the business manager to reduce the price of these books dramatically and offer them to students. As there was no room in the store for students to come in and browse, I placed all such books on a table in the hall and prepared a sign stating that any book on the table could be purchased for twenty-five cents. After a few days probably 70 percent of the books had been taken. I then altered the sign and dropped the price to a dime. Eventually practically every book had been purchased.

There was now some space in the room that could be used for other purposes. There was a section close to the mailboxes that could be used for displaying certain items. I thought it might be appropriate if the bookstore could get felt pennants and pillow covers with the Graceland name and seal and others with the name of the three literary societies that served as substitutes for sororities and fraternities. A manufacturer agreed to produce such and let us have them on consignment. These proved to be very much in demand and profitable.

I also got in touch with a candy distributor and included popular candy bars and various chocolate confections as items that students could buy through the bookstore. I recall that chocolate covered cherries were extremely popular with the students. Some other items were also added to merchandise available for purchase, but because of the size of the store (or cubbyhole) there was a definite limit to the extent of expansion.

These changes in the operation of the school-backed bookstore resulted in eliminating financial loss and provided a reasonable profit to the school. The president and business manager seemed to be somewhat surprised, but I do not recall that they bestowed any particular praise on the manager. I did not need praise because I thoroughly enjoyed what I was doing. In retrospect, I appreciated the opportunity at a young age to experiment with different approaches to business management. I did not recognize until years later that this was really an exercise in entrepreneurship.

Academic Life

I do not recall all of the subjects I studied in my four years at the academy and two years at the junior college. I know, however, that they included Latin, English, English literature, Bible, history, general science, algebra, geometry, philosophy, psychology, education, biology, geography, economics, accounting, typing, typesetting, and printing processes. In addition to class instruction, thirty minutes each morning was set aside for an assemblage labeled "chapel" attended by all students and faculty. Chapel was usually opened with reading a short item from the Bible, statements from eminent scholars, or material from secular writers and philosophers. Following that the president or a member of the faculty would present to the students a discussion on some item of educational value. It might be a reading from some noted philosopher or writer, a challenge to students to excel in their intellectual pursuits, or the importance of certain basic values in one's life. I recall one such reading that is still fairly vivid in my memory. It was "The Message to Garcia." The basic theme of the story was one of completing the job to be done regardless of obstacles that might be encountered.

I was a fairly good student and enjoyed the stimulation of learning. I was usually in the classroom and chapel four or five hours a day, and I worked an average of four hours a day. The rest of the time was spent in eating, studying, and sleeping. My normal weekday involved getting up at 4:30 a.m. and going to bed generally by 11 p.m., with most of my studying done in the evening.

The courses I took in education would permit me to obtain a teaching certificate after graduating from the college. One such course involved practice teaching

73

under supervision. Most students did their practice teaching in the public schools of Lamoni and surrounding areas. I did mine on the campus teaching a course in general science in the academy. I probably learned more teaching that course than any one of my students learned.

Extracurricular Activities

Debate

There were extracurricular activities of educational value although they carried no class credit. One such activity that I pursued in both the academy and college was debate. The debating team during my last year in the academy consisted of Addie Belle Chappell, Mary Tennery, and myself. We competed in statewide high school debating contests, traveling to various towns in south central and southwest Iowa for debates during that year. We finished second place in the state.

Music

Another extracurricular activity involved music. I sang baritone in a music group called "The Harmony Eight" and was also a member of the community glee club. At least half of its members were Graceland students and the director was the Graceland director of music. We rehearsed and presented two major programs a year—at Christmas and Easter. These productions were classical oratorios such as "Messiah," "Elijah," and "The Seven Last Words."

The Acacia

The school year 1921-1922 was a difficult one financially. In the spring college officials wondered if they could finance a yearbook for the Class of 1923. There was a prospect, therefore, of passing that year without an Acacia. Adding to the difficulty was a report by the staff of the 1922 Acacia that in their opinion there was insufficient talent in the Class of 1923 to put out an effective yearbook. As a result of the financial situation and that report, college officials decided to have no yearbook for 1923. There was a weekly publication called the Graceland Record which would be continued, but that would be the only student publication.

A few of us in the Class of 1923 were somewhat outraged at the suggestion that there was a paucity of talent in our class and decided to do something about it. I led a group with the idea that we edit the *Graceland Record* in a manner that would permit us to put the different weekly issues together at the end of the year in a way that would produce an effective yearbook. I took the idea to college officials, and they accepted it on the condition that I would serve as business manager for that project. This I agreed to do. An editor-in-chief was then appointed to work with me in getting plans organized for combining the *Record* and *Acacia*. Frank Smith, a student from Illinois, was appointed editor-in-chief. We had several meetings before school closed in June, after which he returned to Illinois to spend the summer with his parents.

Unfortunately, Frank became ill during the summer and never recovered from that illness. His death placed upon me the entire burden of getting plans for the combined *Record/Acacia* worked out during the summer and having them in place when the school opened in September. This was no small task. It meant getting the thirty-four issues planned and laid out in a manner that would permit assembling them to provide a logical and effective yearbook at the end of the school year. It was my plan then to have a blueprint of all thirty-four issues laid out by the time school opened. The first issue would be one that could eventually be placed in a business section of the *Acacia* and contain advertising from the local merchants. However, I planned two additional issues to be placed in the business section, the second to appear in December, before Christmas, and the third one in March, before Easter. Each of those three issues appearing at various times during the year would appear together in the business section at the end of the year in the *Acacia.* The second issue would provide a message of welcome to new students and would, therefore, eventually appear in the early part of the *Acacia.* The last issue would be the first item in the final bound volume. It would contain frontispiece material such as the listing of the staff and faculty.

An editor-in-chief was appointed during the first week of school: Dorothy Briggs, who lived in Lamoni and, incidentally, was the daughter of the school president. She served as editor-in-chief for the first semester and asked to be relieved because of the pressure of work. Duane Anderson was appointed editor-in-chief for the second half of the year.

During the summer I also developed a direct mail advertising campaign to solicit orders for the bound *Record/Acacia* yearbook that would appear at the end of the school year. It was necessary, I thought, to have a specific print order at the beginning of the school year. It was the plan to have the printer produce enough copies of each issue of the *Record* to be used in the eventual bound volume. This meant we would need a print order number as early as September. The copies to be printed for eventual binding would be stored at the print shop until the last issue was printed and then they would be assembled in the order laid out in my blueprint for the eventual yearbook.

The result of this combination of the *Record* and *Acacia* was highly successful. The yearbook was considered to be one of the more successful ones that had been produced. All of us who served on the staff were glad to be able to demonstrate that there was talent in the Class of '23 who could do effective work. All we needed was the opportunity and encouragement to demonstrate that ability.

Literary Societies

Graceland had no social fraternities or sororities. Instead there were three literary societies organized as substitutes for Greek letter social groups, but with emphasis on educational values. Each society had regular meetings and at least once a month would present some kind of dramatic production. The scheduling of such major productions was made so there would be no conflict of offerings by the separate societies. This provided some competition with each society trying to outdo the others.

As a member of the Niketes Society I was involved in the planning of a major dramatic production during my last year at Graceland (1922-23) that brought statewide attention to me and the school. Plans for the production were developed by a fellow student and myself. We thought a mock jury trial would make an interesting dramatic production. We wanted to create a dramatic situation which would result in the development of a villain, a victim, and a full-blown trial with a judge, jury, prosecutor, and defense lawyer. I was to be the villain and my fellow student, the victim. I was manager of the college bookstore and handed out mail to students as they were on their way to morning chapel. My colleague was to come in a little late and ask for his mail as I was closing the door to go to chapel. I was to refuse him and in a loud voice tell him that if he wanted his mail, he had to get there on time. He was to get mad, call me a no-good bum, and hit me. This he did, with a little more realism than either of us had planned, while two or three other late students observed the altercation. I responded to his blow by telling him that I would kill him for this. He went on to chapel, but I stayed away. My college roommate came in quite late, saw me in the hall with my shirt collar awry and a flushed face, and asked me what happened. I told him that Propst got mad at me and smashed my jaw, and that I would kill him for that. My roommate went upstairs to chapel, but I still stayed away.

As the chapel program was nearing an end, I entered the room, stalked down the aisle, spotted Propst, yelled out "You will bash me, will you? Take this," pulled out a gun, and "shot" him. This, of course, was prearranged, and Propst, who had secreted an ink dropper with red ink under his shirt, pressed it and thus displayed simulated blood to make the situation appear real. Actually, it was so real that one member of the faculty sitting on the stage fainted. Two burly students grabbed me, almost wrenching my arms out of their sockets, and persuaded school authorities to lock me in one of the dormitory rooms and post a guard over me.

President G. N. Briggs and J. A. Gunsolley, the business manager, had been advised of the episode we were to develop, and the gun I used had actually been provided by Mr. Gunsolley. After my shot rang out in the chapel, the president tried to calm the audience by saying, "Apparently this is some type of hoax that is being performed," but that was obviously not believed. The dean of men, Lonzo Jones, wanted to check for himself and came to my "prison" to talk with me. When he came in the only thing I would say was, "What will they do to me? What will they do to me?" He tried to console me but got nothing more from me. When he went back to the president's office, he said he knew it was real because he had been over and talked with me, so in essence he accused the president of trying to cover up the "crime."

The victim got nothing but sympathy. Two students carried him out of the chapel and rushed him downtown to a doctor's office. Inside, Propst confided that this was a fake operation but asked him to go along with it and got the doctor to issue a statement that "If the bullet had gone an inch closer to his heart, it would have killed him." Propst was then taken back to the dormitory and put to bed.

An enterprising news reporter sent information to the *Des Moines Register*, and a report of the shooting appeared in the next issue of the paper. Also, one of the faculty members called my parents to indicate that something had happened and to alert them that their son might be in trouble.

The chapel episode took place at about 10 a.m., but it was not until 4 p.m. that a safe and healthy Propst was "discovered" and I was released from my "prison."

I was overjoyed to think that we really had the basis for a mock trial, but my joy was shattered when we were not permitted to go ahead with our program. This was probably appropriate because the suspense had already been taken out of the project.

There was an organization on the campus called "The College Players." Membership consisted of students who were interested in the dramatic arts and participated in the college plays. I had never been interested in that aspect of education, but after the shooting episode I was invited and urged to become a member. I still have my College Players pin somewhere.

Graceland placed major emphasis on learning. Extracurricular activities were viewed as important as a part of the learning process, but scholarly achievement in the completion of formal courses was measured by grades. A Greek letter society, Lambda Delta Sigma, was organized to honor outstanding scholarship achievement as Graceland's equivalent to Phi Beta Kappa. I was fortunate enough to be a member of that society.

Social Life

During my six years at Graceland, I never felt that there were class distinctions. There were, of course, differences in ages but there were no recognized "upper" and "lower" social groups. There were no sororities or fraternities. I was not even conscious of significant social differences between college and academy students. We had a number of academy students who were actually older than students in the junior college. One of my very close friends was Walter Daykin. He was married and in his late twenties when he came to school as a freshman in the academy. He had been a coal miner in Illinois and decided he wanted an education. He learned of the existence of Graceland Academy through his church and was told that he would not be out of place there because of his older age.

I was a timid individual when I arrived on the campus. I was not the only farm boy, but the fact that I had no previous association with young people from towns and cities, or even with groups larger than the fifteen or so youngsters in our farm area, church, and school, created a difficult period of social adjustment for me as a newcomer in a group of 200 or 300 people. Nature, however, tends to take care of situations of that sort, but nature was helped along in my case by the efforts of older students.

One of the most popular individuals on the campus was David Hopkins, a student in the junior college. He recognized my timidity and thought I ought to begin dating some young lady. He arranged a date for me with Blanch Derry, a girl from Colorado. It was actually a somewhat uncomfortable, but I suppose necessary, experience in one's young life. I can't recall my dating experiences except that they were infrequent and varied until late in my senior year in the academy. It was then that a young lady became a very important part of my Graceland life. She was Geneva Rogers from Jonesport, Maine, a freshman in the junior college. She was thus a sophomore when I enrolled as a freshman in the college in 1921. We were largely inseparable during that year. She returned to Maine after her graduation and I was primarily a stranded, lonesome person, at least during the first half of my sophomore college year. My lonesomeness was allayed when another young lady rekindled my spirits. That young lady was Dorothy Briggs, also a sophomore in the college. She had been appointed as editor of the *Acacia* at the beginning of the academic year to fill the vacancy left by the death of

Frank Smith. The close relationship brought about by our work on the *Acacia* demonstrated that we had a lot in common. Our relationship continued to flower and culminated in marriage a year or so after we graduated from Graceland.

Social life, in general, was centered around skill activities. Dancing was a prohibited item, but there usually were weekend activities that brought students together. These might be musical or dramatic events. During the fall there was intercollegiate football played in the town park. There would be individual group parties following home games. We had baseball games in the spring. I was neither a football nor baseball player, but I attended all games and was a member and, at one time, head of the Pep Committee who served as cheerleaders at games.

There were two or three facilities downtown that were frequented by students. These included a moving picture theater and an ice cream parlor. I seldom went to a movie because that cost money. I did, however, find a way of participating in activities in the popular ice cream parlor by taking a part-time job behind the soda fountain. This not only provided a little income but also had social value for me. I became rather expert in preparing root beer floats, cherry fizzes, and banana splits. The latter was a work of art. I can still see two halves of a banana on the bottom of a dish made especially for that delicacy, scoops of three different flavors of ice cream placed on top with chocolate, caramel and strawberry topping, sprinkled with chopped nuts. The final touch was a red maraschino cherry.

There was a pool hall in town but it was off limits to Graceland students.

Health and Physical Well-Being

It was a relatively short time after the beginning of my second year in the academy that the flu epidemic invaded the campus. Many students succumbed to the virus as well as a number of the faculty. It did not catch up with me until near the end of the epidemic. This enabled me and a few others to help in taking care of the sick. My contribution was largely in the form of labor such as carrying food trays, delivering medicines, and functioning as nurse's aide. The virus eventually caught up with me and put me completely out of commission. I was incapacitated for quite some time, ran a very high fever, became delirious, and lost most of my hair. Obviously, I survived. My hair eventually returned, but with the semblance of a wave rather than completely straight.

The flu disrupted normal operations, and the school actually functioned more like a hospital than an educational institution for two or three months. I do not recall specific figures, but at the peak of the epidemic well over half of the campus population was afflicted.

I had another but less serious illness during the summer following my sophomore year in the academy. I remained on the campus as a laborer devoting much of my time to building maintenance work. Included in that work was painting floors in the dormitories. I began suffering with pain in my joints and found it difficult to wield the paint brush. This went on for several days with increased intensity. The pains appeared in most of my joints, and I also became feverish. Eventually, my supervisor recognized the difficulty I was having and had me taken to a doctor. I was suffering from rheumatic fever.

In general, I maintained good health during my six years on the campus. There were only two other occasions in which I experienced any illness of significance. One resulted in an appendectomy and the other a tonsillectomy. In retrospect, I have sometimes wondered whether either of these operations was necessary. The tonsillectomy resulted in severe hemorrhaging, which was probably more damaging than the infected tonsils.

Getting Ready to Leave Graceland

The spring of 1923 marked the beginning of my last weeks at Graceland. It was with mixed feelings that I recognized that I would soon be leaving the school and be forced to move out "into the world" and a completely different environment. I would not be able to continue my education by transferring to a four-year university because it was necessary that I get a job to pay for the six years of tuition which Graceland had agreed would not need to be paid until after I had graduated.

It appeared that the best prospect of a job was in the field of teaching. An A.A. (junior college) degree with a few courses in education were sufficient to receive a teaching certificate. I started seeking a teaching job quite some time before the day of graduation. I developed a direct mail approach to placing my application before school boards in various parts of the country. I mailed a personalized letter together with a resume of my presumed qualifications to schools where names and addresses had been made available to the college. I do not recall how many applications I mailed out, but do remember that I eventually had received offers from four different schools.

I accepted one of the early offers. It was to teach history, algebra, and geometry in the Township High School in Dunlap, Illinois, which was 300 miles from home, at a salary of $1,200 for the nine-month school year. The position carried the highest salary of any offer, and that was my primary motivation for taking it. A few days after I accepted the Dunlap offer, I received a letter from a high school in Devil's Lake, North Dakota, offering me a salary of $1,400. The extra $200 for the year would have been readily accepted had the offer been received before I had accepted the Illinois job. I had already given my word to Dunlap, and I could not go back on my word. I have often wondered how my life would have been different had I gone to Devil's Lake instead of Dunlap. The fact that I had a job in hand at the time of graduation gave me confidence.

The happy but sad graduation day at Graceland eventually arrived. It meant separation from friends and entering the job market. A number of my class-mates left Graceland and enrolled in a four-year college or university to work for the prized bachelor's degree. Even though I was now finished with my academic education at Graceland, I stayed on the campus for the summer and worked as a day laborer. This helped to reduce some of my Graceland debt.

PART II
ON TO HIGHER
EDUCATION

Chapter 4

Life Between Graceland and the University of Iowa

Dunlap, Illinois, High School Teacher

I was supposed to arrive in Dunlap in time for the start of school, but I thought it appropriate to get there a little early to find a place to live before the opening of school. I found a room to rent and got well settled a few days before classes started.

I recall that the school board president greeted me and wanted to help me get acquainted with the community. He invited me to some kind of an evening meeting that was to be held out in the country on somebody's farm. I, of course, accepted the invitation but was somewhat confused concerning the nature of the gathering. It turned out to be a meeting in which the presumed merits of the Ku Klux Klan were presented. That was something with which I was at the time unfamiliar. People were not clothed in the traditional KKK robes, and I do not remember much of the content of the speeches that were made. There was nothing, however, during my two-year stay in Dunlap that would suggest any abnormal social or political intolerance by people in the community.

It was both interesting and exciting to get started as a full-fledged teacher. My classes kept me busy, but I still found time to supplement my teaching with part-time work that would increase my compensation. I signed up as an insurance agent and also did some painting jobs after school and on Saturday. I was a bachelor in a small town with very little social life other than that associated with school. Social life, however, meant very little to me because I was engaged to Dorothy Briggs and my moral values would not permit me to date other girls. As a substitute, I enrolled in a correspondence course from the State University of Iowa and that became my mistress. This provided academic credit that would apply toward my bachelor's degree when I found the time and finances that would permit me to enter the university on a full-time basis.

The first correspondence course I took was in education, and it dovetailed beautifully with my teaching. One of the course assignments dealt with the problem of classroom discipline. I used an example from my own experience in completing the assignment and felt honored when the professor wrote to say he was not returning my report but rather kept it to use in his classes as an illustration of how one teacher handled a problem of discipline.

A young, inexperienced teacher probably gives more thought to the problem of discipline than would an experienced teacher. In the case on which I reported, I had two students in the back of the classroom who did a lot of whispering while I was trying to present various materials. I would try to break up the whispering by calling on one or the other boy to answer questions, but once that was done the whispering was renewed. After a week or so of that kind of operation, I called one of the boys into my room after class and told him I would like to have his help in my teaching. I praised him as one of the leaders in school, said that other students looked up to him for guidance, and that I would like to have him help me keep appropriate discipline in class. He could do that by eliminating his own whispering and refusing to listen to his seat mate who might want to whisper. The approach worked. The boy felt honored and my discipline problem was eliminated.

Near the end of the term the school superintendent informed me that he would like to have me serve as the athletics coach for the next year. That would involve coaching basketball, baseball, and tennis. I demurred because I knew little or nothing about any of these sports, not having played them in either high school or college. However, I was told that they could not hire a full-time person to coach, that the part-time coach we then had could not be rehired for the next year because of moral indiscretions, and because I was the only male member of the faculty other than himself, I was it.

Summer School at U of Iowa

I had planned to enroll at the University of Iowa for summer courses. That plan was only slightly altered by my adding a class in basketball coaching to my summer curriculum. One of my academic classes was "Intermediate Accounting" taught by Professor Ross Walker, who later became a professor of accounting at the Harvard Graduate School of Business Administration. I was later to become a colleague of his when I served as a visiting professor of business research at Harvard. I mention that accounting course and Professor Walker for a particular reason. I had taken a beginning course in accounting at Graceland but that course was more one of appreciation of accounting than to teach how to do it. Hence, the summer course in intermediate accounting required a lot of time and effort to do the work. I was somewhat astounded at the end of the course by having Professor Walker call me into his office and tell me that I was the only student in the class who got an "A," and he wondered what I was going to take in the fall. I told him I could not afford to stay in school but would have to go back to my job. However, I hoped someday to get back to Iowa and finish work for my bachelor's degree. He urged me not to postpone my return any longer than necessary and to let him know if there was ever anything he could do to help when I was ready to come back.

Wedding Plans

I did not tell Professor Walker that another reason for my continuing my teaching at Dunlap was that I was planning to be married within a couple of weeks and take my bride with me as a teacher of music in the Dunlap school. My fiancée was Dorothy Briggs, who had graduated from Graceland the same time I did. She had been teaching at a high school in Woodbine, Iowa, but had accepted an appointment to start teaching at Dunlap where we would be on the same faculty during the first year of our marriage.

The marriage ceremony was performed in her parents' home in Lamoni, Iowa, on August 4, 1924. My wedding day was not like the storied events written up in the society sections of newspapers. Instead, it was a quiet home ceremony attended only by close friends and relatives. My mother had died two years before my marriage and only my father and sister were able to be at the wedding. My best man was a fellow Graceland graduate, Cecil Bernett. My bride's large family (she was the eldest of eight siblings) together with her grandmother and aunt were also there. Dorothy's maid-of-honor was Ramona Judson, a close Graceland friend.

Some might wonder why the president of Graceland College did not give his daughter a large, public, heavily attended church wedding. It was not because of any antipathy to religion. Actually, Dorothy's father was also an ordained minister and performed the ceremony. The reason was primarily the lack of money to finance a large wedding. The groom did not even pay the preacher.

A reference must be made to the weather associated with our wedding. A half-hour before the ceremony was scheduled to take place a torrential rain hit the area. This was a good omen for the farming community but created some travel difficulties for us. My father and sister lived two miles in the country and that is where my best man and I were getting prepared for the wedding. It was a dirt road from the farmhouse to town. We were to drive there by car but we did not get started until after the downpour occurred. We put chains on the car and decided to drive through the mud to town. We got almost to our destination when we got thoroughly stuck in the mud. Fortunately, my father had decided to depend on a team of horses and a buggy and came along to deliver his son to the home of the bride, even though a little late. Dorothy's grandmother was to arrive by train for the wedding and bring the wedding cake to be served after the ceremony. She, too, was late but did arrive before the vows were exchanged. If one were superstitious, one might conclude that the weather cast a somber omen on the future of that marriage. Instead, it actually could better be viewed as a rich christening that provided sustenance to bring forth the flowers of wedded bliss.

The storybooks tell of a wonderful honeymoon that occurs immediately after marriage. We had a honeymoon quite different from that of the storybooks. We had planned to take off in my new Ford roadster to Lake Okoboji in the northwest corner of Iowa, but the heavy rainstorm kept us from leaving immediately after the ceremony. Instead we stayed at the home of my father and left the next morning for the lake even though the roads were still muddy.

It might seem strange that after only one year of full-time employment I would have made peace with my creditors and have enough money to buy a car, but in fact I had been able to do just that. I often remarked that as soon as I was able to buy a car and a marriage license I got married. The new car was purchased for cash and cost approximately $400. I do not recall whether my father provided some financial help, but if he did it was slight.

On our trip to Lake Okoboji we traveled like most poor people did at that time. We borrowed a lean-to tent and folding cots so that we could camp out, not only going to and from the lake but also at the lake itself. Today, such folk would be classified as deprived, poverty stricken people who should be wards of the government. In our case, we did not know that we were deprived, and the phrase "below the poverty line" had not yet been invented. We had faith in ourselves, we had jobs waiting for us, and we had visions of continued self-improvement.

Settling into Married Life

Soon after returning from Lake Okoboji we packed our car and drove to Dunlap for the start of the new school year. I had already arranged for an apartment in the home of Mr. and Mrs. Simmons where I had a room during my first year in Dunlap. Because I had lived in Dunlap in the Simmons' home for a year before my marriage, my new bride was accepted, not as a stranger, but more as a member of the community family.

Mrs. Simmons operated a tea room in one part of the home, and Dorothy often helped on weekends in the tea room as a daughter would help her mother. Both the Simmonses and the community seemed to be happy that I had become a married man and welcomed my bride as one of them.

Our apartment consisted of two rooms. One served as a kitchen and dining area and the other as a living and bedroom. Dunlap was a small town and our apartment was located only three blocks from the school building.

Dorothy taught music and served the entire school system including both high school and grade school. I continued to teach history, algebra, and geometry but added coaching. The latter was primarily a "free will offering." I served as disciplinarian and chaperon with some attempts at putting into action some of the things I had learned in my one coaching course the previous summer. Fortunately, the young athletes were very cooperative and we had an interesting and somewhat successful year.

As the Christmas vacation period approached, we debated whether we should risk driving the 300 miles to Lamoni to spend Christmas with our families. It was not much of a debate because Dorothy pointed out that it would be a great disappointment and also unseemly if we did not go back home for Christmas. The term "home" meant "parents." We enjoyed our apartment in Dunlap but it was not yet our home.

The school Christmas vacation did not start until after classes ended on December 23. We decided to leave Dunlap immediately after classes and drive to Burlington, Iowa, stay all night there and drive on to Lamoni on Christmas Eve day. The weather was not very cooperative. We got out of classes about 3:30 in the afternoon and a snow storm had already started. The temperature had plummeted to a very cold level. We had a manifold heater in the Ford roadster and isinglass curtains to provide some protection against the weather. Mrs. Simmons had two soapstones that she had heated in the oven and wrapped in cloth to be placed on the floor of the roadster to keep our feet warm.

We made it to Burlington without difficulty and took a room in the hotel. When we awakened the next morning the storm was over, the sun was shining, and we looked forward to a pleasant trip. Our soapstones had not been reheated, hence the only warmth we had in the car was from the manifold heater. We got started early but after about twenty-five miles we were getting quite cold so we stopped in the next town to get some gasoline and warm up a bit. The gas station attendant pointed to the thermometer at the station which read 20 below zero. Some twenty miles later, I noticed we were getting some steam coming through the manifold into the car from an overheated radiator. It was obvious that we had a small leak somewhere but I thought we could tough it out until we got to Lamoni, even though I recognized we would need to stop and refill the radiator at least every twenty or thirty miles. It finally became apparent that it would not be possible to complete our journey without doing something about the leaking radiator. It was early evening when we drove into a garage in a town fifty miles short of our destination to get the necessary repairs done. The garage people said they had no one who could work on the car, that it was Christmas Eve, and that there wasn't anything they could do. We did, however, locate the nature of the leak. An engine gasket had blown at a point which permitted a leak in the circulating water that cooled the engine. I persuaded the garage people to lend me the necessary tools to make the repair, to provide me with a new gasket, and I would do the work. This was done and eventually, repair accomplished, we resumed our journey. We arrived in Lamoni shortly after midnight. After a brief talk with our family we went to bed to get some rest. It was only two or three hours later that I awoke with severe pain in my toes. They had become frozen because of the lack of heat in the car, but the damage was not permanent.

We enjoyed the stay with our parents even though we were somewhat nervous anticipating what troubles might be ahead on our way back to Dunlap. Fortunately, the weather improved greatly and the return trip was a pleasant one. It was also pleasant to get back into the classroom because I had learned to thoroughly enjoy teaching.

Future Plans

In addition to my teaching, I continued to take correspondence courses from the University of Iowa. I had developed a blueprint which would permit me to obtain my bachelor's degree from Iowa if I attended two summer school sessions, took a few correspondence courses, and spent two academic semesters in residence. I had already spent one summer and had taken some correspondence courses. I planned to spend the next summer and the following two semesters in residence and graduate in June 1926.

To follow that blueprint, it meant I would resign from Dunlap at the end of the 1924-25 school year and we would move to Iowa City. I needed to have some kind of paid job in Iowa City. We also wanted to start a family and thus should not expect Dorothy to obtain a full-time job. I remembered the request Professor Walker made of me that if I needed any financial help in returning to the university to let him know and he would see what he could do. I then wrote him in January 1925 saying that I did need help. To my great delight, Professor Walker wrote back saying that I could have a job in the College of Commerce grading accounting papers for the accounting professors. This would not only provide a cash income but would also provide some free tuition. I readily accepted his offer. We were now psychologically set to leave Dunlap at the end of the school year, move to Iowa City, and start a new chapter in our life.

Chapter 5

Our Life in Iowa City

Move from Dunlap to Iowa City

We moved directly from Dunlap to Iowa City and looked for a place to live. We were able to find a house that someone wanted to sublease for the summer, and we readily took it. Also, one of Dorothy's sisters came to live with us during the summer and took some classes at the university. Dorothy obtained a clerical job and I enrolled for summer school classes.

Our lease of the house lasted only until September, at which time we moved into an apartment. Our apartment consisted of two rooms somewhat similar to the ones we had in Dunlap. They were upstairs in an older residence with the landlady living in the downstairs part of the house. The place was located about three-quarters of a mile from the campus. This provided me with ample exercise walking to and from school morning, noon, and night. We had sold the Ford roadster earlier, recognizing that we could get along without it and that we needed the money for education.

I was registered in the College of Commerce working for a bachelor's degree in business. I had no clear-cut vocational or professional objective but planned to let the market determine what I would do after graduation. That, however, was modified in December when the dean of the College of Commerce called me to his office and proposed that I continue in graduate school after my undergraduate work. He said he had two graduate assistantships available and that I could have one of these if I stayed to work for a master's degree. He did not require me to make a decision then but suggested that I think it over and let him know sometime after Christmas.

The thought of graduate work was intriguing and I decided to give it a try. I would, of course, do my work in commerce. In analyzing the graduate program, I noted that a number of courses I was planning to take during my last semester for the bachelor's degree were also courses that carried graduate credit. I thought, why not postpone taking these until the next year and elect courses during my last undergraduate semester that I could not take for credit as a graduate student? I already had enough courses in economics to meet the requirement as an economics major in the College of Liberal Arts and Sciences. Why not, therefore, transfer from commerce to liberal arts for my bachelor's degree and devote my last semester to courses in history and psychology, thus saving additional business courses for my master's program?

I went to the dean's office to make an appointment to talk with him about my thoughts and seek his approval. Fortunately or unfortunately, he had left for an extended trip recruiting new faculty members. He would not be back on campus until after it was necessary that a decision be made. My decision was to transfer from commerce to liberal arts and follow the plan I had devised.

When Dean Phillips returned to campus, I told him what I had done, thinking that he would be delighted at my incisiveness. To my chagrin he expressed great disappointment. He somewhat subtly suggested that he was not sure that the graduate assistantship would now be available to me. I had failed to realize the importance deans and department heads placed on keeping good students on their turf. Fortunately for me, he did not deny me the graduate assistantship when he realized that I would be returning to his school to work for a master's degree. An unexpected by-product that resulted from my transfer to liberal arts was my election to Phi Beta Kappa. Had I stayed in the College of Commerce I would have been eligible for its honorary society but not Phi Beta Kappa.

I thus graduated in June 1926 with an A.B. degree in economics rather than a B.S. degree in business. There was another very cherished degree conferred on me a few days after receiving the A.B. in economics. That was the "PA" degree in parenthood; Allan was born in Iowa City on June 18, 1926.

Graduate Work

My graduate assistantship did not start until September 1926, but I enrolled in the graduate program at the beginning of summer school. I was given a job, however, working in the commerce library and also grading papers in business law for Professor Hill.

There were specific responsibilities associated with my graduate assistantship. I was assigned to teach one section of the introductory course in accounting and, in addition, to do some research in the Bureau of Business Research. I was not particularly interested in accounting and did not select it as a major, but since I was to teach the course, I thought it appropriate to enroll in some advanced accounting courses. I therefore took a course in cost accounting and also one in auditing before completing work for the master's degree. Teaching the introductory course required a lot of work. The course I had with Professor Walker a year earlier was helpful, but I had to spend an inordinate amount of time the first several weeks of the semester on mastering the material to be covered in the classroom.

My work in the bureau was very interesting. I was assigned the job of researching the importance of the automobile in Iowa and the relative costs of constructing and maintaining different types of roads and highways. I spent much time in the library and in government offices in Des Moines pursuing my research. I computed from various data the relative costs of dirt versus gravel versus paved roads. Included in my cost analyses were wear and tear on vehicles, cost of motor fuel, and cost of highway maintenance and disruption because of weather to the flow of commodities from farm to market. The result of my research appeared in printed form as a bulletin with the title, "The Motor Vehicle in Iowa," published by the bureau. It was my first academic publication.

One of the requirements for the master's degree was a thesis composed of a piece of original research. I was not allowed to use my "Motor Vehicle in Iowa" research for my thesis. Instead, I elected to study what labor unions were doing in the area of workers' education. This research gave me an opportunity to study and evaluate labor unions and provided an insight into the working relationship developed between corporate management and labor.

I was moving toward graduating with a master's degree in June 1927. Again, Dean Phillips called me into his office and said he thought I should plan to continue in graduate school and work for a doctorate degree. I indicated it would be necessary for me to get a job after my master's, that I was in debt and now had a family to support. He indicated I could do much of my work during summer school, that he could probably provide some kind of help on tuition, and that my research for the doctorate could probably be done off campus. He thought that could be done easily in connection with a job if I would enter the teaching profession. This all sounded good to me, and I agreed to follow this advice. I would seek a college teaching job for the upcoming year, start my Ph.D. work in the upcoming summer school, and reserve the following summer for continuation of work on campus. Shortly before receiving the master's degree I accepted an offer from Simpson College in Indianola, Iowa, as an assistant professor of economics to start in September 1927. I was to teach a number of different classes including economics, finance, and transportation.

Before that, however, I was offered an instructorship at Graceland College, my alma mater. Graceland was an RLDS Church-supported school. The church would be classified as fundamentalist in its orientation at that time. It included in its philosophy those elements in the New Testament that referred to a gathering into Zion of the faithful in anticipation of the second coming of Christ. The gathering would place responsibility on church leadership to utilize the talents of its intelligentsia and also to provide for the health and comfort of the poor and indigent among the membership. Some attention was given to how to financially support the welfare aspects of such a program. It was recognized that talented members would have to be "taxed," "assessed," or "persuaded" to contribute financially to the establishment of a "storehouse" of goods that could be drawn on by those in need. There were differences of opinion as to how to arrange for such support. The kind of organizational and financial structure that might be developed was discussed under the general title, "The Economics of Zion." No course under that title had ever been offered at Graceland, but the president thought such a course would be an appropriate addition to the Graceland curriculum. I was asked to consider joining the faculty and to teach such a course.

I was honored and flattered to be asked to go back to my alma mater as a member of the faculty. I could not consider such a move or accept the responsibility of offering a course that had never been offered by anyone before unless I could develop a plan that I thought would be effective and meet the basic tenets of an economic system in a free society. After much study, I came up with a proposal. It contained several elements: (1) all employees of the church would be paid market wages; (2) the church would encourage talented members to organize and operate basic business firms; (3) church members and others would be encouraged to contribute to the capital necessary to operate business firms (this would be done by buying stock and thus have an ownership stake in the property); and (4) the two kinds of firms suggested as ones to be first developed were banks and insurance companies.

It seemed to me that such an approach to the "Economics of Zion" would encourage saving, provide a self-propelled development of an annuity or pension after retirement, and demonstrate the significance of stewardship in managing one's life and talents.

This proposal was submitted to the college officials who in turn submitted it to the financial leaders of the church. It was not dismissed out of hand, but I felt it was not embraced with any enthusiasm. I felt that my youth was a handicap in getting such a proposal accepted. I chose, therefore, to accept the offer from Simpson College. That became my first full-time college teaching position.

Nonacademic Activities

Our social life in Iowa City was a restricted but happy one. I was not a typical undergraduate student. Most of my classmates had been on campus for all of their college work. I did not join them until the senior year. I was also married and in that day this was a most unusual thing. In addition, Dorothy was pregnant.

It was our good fortune to have two families from our Graceland years who were students at Iowa City. They were Cecil and Ramona Bernett, who had been my best man and Dorothy's maid-of-honor at our wedding, and Walter and Sarah Daykin. Walter Daykin was an especially close friend, older than I and a real scholar. He had been a coal miner in Illinois with only an eighth grade education, but quit his coal mining job and brought his wife with him to Graceland Academy so that he could "get an education." He finished his high school work in two years, stayed on for his A.A. degree, transferred to the University of Illinois where he stayed for one year, then transferred to the University of Iowa where he received his bachelor's degree and eventually his Ph.D. We three families got together often.

We had several residences in Iowa City. Our first apartment was not to be our abode for the rest of our stay at Iowa City. When our landlady learned that Dorothy was pregnant and that I was planning to stay for another year at the university, she told us that we could not have the apartment. She did not want a baby in the house. This information was passed on to us in

May. My graduation was coming up, the birth of our child was also scheduled about the same time, and now I had to look for another place to live. I found something that seemed ideal. It was an apartment in a building with pleasant surroundings, and we could move in on June first. That we did. After we went to bed the first night we did not go to sleep. We had company—something neither of us knew much about. We had had no previous experience with them. They were bed bugs. The next morning I told the landlord that I wanted my deposit back and that we were moving. So I spent the day finding some other place to live. I eventually was successful. We again had an upstairs apartment which was more spacious than the one we had left. Also, I could pay much of the rent by taking care of the yard and furnace. We got moved in and lived in that apartment until we left for Simpson College more than a year later.

Our stay in Iowa City covered three summers and two full academic years. I was enrolled for courses during all of that time. I also had appointments for work at the university as a graduate assistant, paper grader, researcher, and assistant in the library. Dorothy had various types of jobs, mostly on a part-time basis, some of which could be done at home, such as typing student reports and theses. I also did some typing of other students' reports.

My full-time academic schedule, extra time devoted to my research in the Bureau of Business Research, my teaching, and nonacademic work such as tending the apartment furnace, taking tickets at athletic events, side jobs of typing, and devoting cherished time to our new baby assessed a toll on my physical well-being that was noticed by my academic mentor. He called me into

his office and expressed concern for what he had noticed as a loss of weight. My weight had dropped from
136 to 116 pounds. I was not personally disturbed by
that. I was not sick, although I usually felt tired, but
considered that as a very normal thing. This situation
was to change after leaving Iowa City for a full-time,
well-paid job.

Chapter 6

Work as an Itinerant Professor

Leaving Iowa City for Simpson College

It was with mixed feelings that I left Iowa City. The academic environment with its extensive library and stimulating professors brought additional excitement and pleasure to my life. Professor Phillips, who was dean of the College of Commerce, was also a professor in finance and taught a course, "Money and Banking," which I had taken. Professor Walker's help and personal interest in me would never be forgotten. I had several classes with Professor Frank Knight, who was a giant in the field of economics. Professor Sydney Miller was my Ph.D. dissertation chairman. Professor Root, in history, had earlier refused to let me register for three courses in history my last semester as an undergraduate because he did not think anyone could handle as much reading as these courses would take along with two or three other courses, but finally he let me register for them after I convinced him that I would assume personal responsibility for handling them. (I got A's in all three.) Professor Seashore in psychology opened another window in my mind. These and other professors would be difficult to leave, but I would meet others now as colleagues at Simpson College. The transition from student and neophyte teacher as a graduate assistant, to a *full-time PROFESSOR** meant that I now had a quite different responsibility. It was now my role to foster the joy of learning in others and to help smooth the path in the learning process.

Simpson College was an excellent, small liberal arts college located in Indianola, Iowa, about fifteen miles south of Des Moines. We were able to find a furnished house as our new home in Indianola. We could thus abandon cramped apartment living and have a complete house to ourselves. It was located only a block or so from the college campus.

Written information had been received from the president of the college in late summer announcing a meeting of the faculty the day before the registration of students for the new school year. At that meeting three new faculty members were announced and introduced. The president gave none of us new members specific registration responsibility, but suggested that we appear on campus and be available to help if and when help might be needed. It was also suggested that we might volunteer to help when we felt there was an area that needed assistance. Of course, as new members, we were each interested in volunteering to do anything we might be asked to do. I became very active in some of the registration work and kept quite busy. During a lull in the work, an older member of the faculty called me aside and asked if I was an upper classman who had been asked to help in registration. I was somewhat crushed to think that I did not look like a professor even if an assistant professor, but I nevertheless told my questioner that the president had hired me as one of his colleagues. We were both embarrassed.

---

* Even though only an assistant professor.

I had a very heavy, but at the time standard, teaching load. It consisted of five different three-hour courses each semester. The preparation for each class took a lot of time, but it was not drudgery. In many respects, it was a continuation of the learning process. It may be a truism that a teacher learns more than the student the first time he teaches a new course. Classes at Simpson started at 7:30 in the morning. I had a 7:30 class three times a week. No classes were held from 9:30 to 10:00 a.m. That period was set aside for a student/faculty assembly. Simpson was a church school supported by the Methodists. Chapel, therefore, always carried a religious message of some sort. The responsibility for conducting chapel service was passed around to various faculty members. It was always a struggle for me to come up with an appropriate program when I was tapped to be in charge of the assembly.

Our nonacademic life in Indianola was much less harried than our experience in Iowa City. I did not have the financial pressure and Dorothy was experiencing the joy of being a young mother. A former Graceland student, Tommy McGeorge, and his wife were living in Indianola, with Tommy being a full-time student completing work for his bachelor's degree. We thus had a social relationship that was comfortable.

I did some nonacademic work, however. Because I now had a full-time paying job, we thought we should have an automobile. I persuaded the local Dodge dealer to let me be a part-time weekend salesman, selling used and new Dodge cars. The first sale I made was to myself.

I did not spend all of every weekend trying to sell cars, particularly during the hunting season. I had persuaded myself that I wanted a shotgun and hence found enough money somewhere to buy a gun. I used it frequently on weekends when Tommy McGeorge and I would go hunting. We were able to bring home some ducks for good eating during the time that ducks were migrating.

Now that we were again a possessor of an automobile, we were no longer substantially confined to town and campus. We were only eighteen miles from Des Moines and eighty miles from Lamoni, where Dorothy's parents and my father, stepmother, and sister lived. My two brothers and their families also lived within the general area. We therefore spent an occasional weekend visiting with relatives.

I was not unhappy at Simpson but thought a larger school might provide greater opportunities. I therefore let it be known that I would be willing to change jobs if a better one presented itself. I received a tempting offer from Drake University in Des Moines that would pay me more than I was then receiving and offered a lighter teaching load. It would thus give me more time to do the research I had already started for my Ph.D. dissertation. The only aspect of the offer about which I had any question was that most of my teaching would be concentrated in the field of accounting. I did not particularly object to that, but I had not found the same degree of satisfaction in that field as I had in economics and various business courses. Nevertheless, I wrote my acceptance and had it ready to mail but failed to put the letter out for the mail carrier to pick up before I went to my classes at the college. When I came home for lunch there was a letter from the University of Kansas at Lawrence offering me a job there. The teaching load would be even lighter than at Drake. It also included teaching two courses in accounting but another course in economics. I would have an additional course in economics in Kansas City, Missouri, one evening a week. The salary offered was somewhat more than I was getting at Simpson but less than Drake was offering. I held out my letter of acceptance to Drake to give me time to compare the two offers and accept one or the other. I finally chose to take the University of Kansas job even though the salary was smaller. It was a major university and would give me, I felt, more opportunity to do research and hasten the completion of my work for the Ph.D. at Iowa.

Moving to Lawrence, Kansas, and KU

My work at Simpson was finished in early June 1928, and I was to be moved to Lawrence by early September. My educational blueprint called for me to go to graduate school for the summer. I could go back to Iowa City or I could choose another university and have the credits I would earn there transferred to apply to my Ph.D. requirements. I therefore chose to obtain some experience from another university and spent that summer as a student at the University of Illinois in Urbana. Dorothy and Allan stayed with her parents during the summer, and I concentrated all my time in taking three courses at Illinois.

In contemplating my move to Kansas I wondered whether my colleagues there would look upon me as a callow youth as was the case at Simpson. That thought caused me, while I was on my own at the University of Illinois during the summer, to grow a mustache. I thought that would make me look older and maybe somewhat professorial. I did not comment in my letters to Dorothy about what I was doing, but planned to wait and surprise her when I returned to Lamoni after summer school. And surprise her I did. She was obviously disappointed and broke down and cried. She was so distraught that I promised that I would shave it off at Christmastime but I wanted to keep it until then. I did keep the mustache until Christmas at which time I kept my promise and shaved it off. I did not announce my intention to keep my promise, so again I surprised Dorothy and again she broke down and cried. She had gotten used to my mustache and now with it off she thought I looked too young and weak. So a few months later, I grew the mustache again and kept it as a part of my anatomy for seventeen more years, shaving it only just before I moved to the University of Illinois.

The move to Lawrence was not uneventful. We had accumulated a number of physical possessions which could not all be packed into our automobile. I thought it would be more economical if I could have a small trailer hitched to the car for hauling our possessions. There were no U-Hauls in those days and trailers that did exist were generally homemade affairs. I went to a junk yard and found parts for a two-wheel chassis on which I could build a box large enough to carry our possessions. I had a blacksmith make the hitch to be used to connect the trailer to the car. I felt very proud of my accomplishment. I was now ready to get things packed and loaded for the trip to Lawrence. We really did not have a good deal to pack, most of which could go into a trunk and some additional small boxes. All other things would be packed in the car itself. I thought it appropriate that I test out the trailer, so after getting it loaded I went out on the road to see how it worked. Everything seemed to be going along well the first four or five miles. Then the trailer seemed to start weaving and I began to have difficulty with the balance of materials. It was fairly clear to me that we would never get to Lawrence pulling that thing. I therefore changed my mind immediately and took the trunk and boxes to the Express office and shipped them by public transportation. I left the trailer at the automobile dealership where I had sold a few cars, hoping that they might find someone who would pay a little money for it. The trailer experience was fairly costly but very educational.

Our living quarters in Lawrence consisted of a furnished duplex located in a nice residential area. As at the University of Iowa and Simpson College, we had former Graceland people to greet us and provide social companionship. It was especially gratifying that the Graceland connection was my good and great friend, Walter Daykin. He had accepted a position a year earlier as a member of the sociology faculty. His Kansas position constituted a short break in his connection with the University of Iowa. He would soon return to Iowa to become professor of labor economics where he remained for the rest of his professional career. In addition to his teaching, he became a nationally known labor arbitrator.

My work at Kansas was, as always, interesting. I did not involve myself in much nonacademic work as had been the case in previous years. I did occasionally help Professor Tupy, who was head of the Department of Accounting, in some of his commercial auditing jobs. I also served as what was called an "expert judge" at high school debates throughout eastern Kansas. These debates were always evening affairs and involved my visiting various Kansas communities.

Kansas City Evening Course

My Kansas City evening course in economics was part of the university's adult education program. My students were older people employed during the day. Some of them were working for a college degree and would use the credited course to count toward their degree. I had one very traumatic experience in that class. It was only two or three sessions before the end of the course and the subject for class discussion was what today would probably be called welfare economics. I do not recall all of the details, but I made some kind of reference to various institutions that might make a contribution to the physical welfare of members of society. I named a few possible institutions including the government, labor unions, business firms, schools, and churches. To stimulate thought, I audibly wondered if Jesus were to return today would he be preaching a type of welfare economics that might label him a radical. I thought I was getting along very well in agitating the minds of students to open up new windows of vision when I was sharply interrupted by a female student sitting in the back of the class who rose to her feet and excoriated me greatly, stating she thought it was terrible that people paid their good taxes to have people like me come out and present such stuff as I was presenting. When she finished, her seatmate arose and continued the tirade. I listened in astonishment and dismay. Then, noting that time was nearly up for the class period, used an appropriate quotation from the Bible which came to mind (which I have now forgotten, probably something like "Peace be unto you" or something like that) and closed the session, saying that I would see them next week.

When I went to my office the next day, I confided my chagrin and remorse to Professor John Ise with whom I shared an office. Professor Ise was an exceedingly popular professor, although a gruff curmudgeon. He might be appropriately labeled a modern Socrates. After I finished telling him my experience and sought his advice on how to correct my teaching, he rose from his chair and came over and shook my hand. He said a person who can get individuals to react, to think, should be proud of that accomplishment and he wanted to congratulate me. It made me feel a lot better.

I returned to the class the following week with trepidation. When I went into the room, I found a gift-wrapped box of chocolates together with a written statement thanking me for the kind of class I had been giving, apologizing for what happened the week before, and signed by every member of the class except the two women.

Teaching Econ vs. Accounting and on to Oxford, Ohio

I enjoyed teaching courses in economics. I did not dislike the courses in accounting that I was teaching, but they did not give me the same degree of satisfaction as did the other courses. Accounting was pretty much a cut-and-dried affair. You set down figures in a particular manner and they always mean the same thing. I occasionally tried to inject a new approach to counting things but such attempts were not encouraged. For example, I might suggest that the standard account in business called "Purchase Discount" could be used to record any money saved if one received a discount for paying cash for merchandise. The total of that account would be listed as an income for the business. I might say, "Would it not be better to change that to an account called 'Purchase Discount *not* Taken?'" The balance of that account would thus show as an expense. It would alert management that their cash flow was either inadequate to take advantage of a cash discount offer, or that management was negligent and wasteful to the extent of the business of that account. Such an operation, particularly in an introductory course in accounting, would generally be frowned upon by colleagues.

I liked teaching, especially the interplay with young minds and to challenge one's thinking. I got much of that from my teaching in economics but not from accounting. Therefore, when an unexpected offer of a new job at another university that included work in new and exciting areas of business was received, I became quite excited. That offer came in mid-summer 1929 from Miami University in Ohio. Miami had established its School of Business two or three years earlier. I was being asked to accept a job at Miami to develop work in the relatively new phase of economics called marketing. That would not take up all of my time, but the additional time would be to teach courses such as transportation and public utilities.

I was intrigued with the opportunities such a position would provide, but I had already accepted the continuation of my position at Kansas for another year. I would not try to break that contract. I chose to discuss this with my dean, express my interest, and ask if there was some way I could honorably be released from my Kansas contract. The dean was very understanding and cooperated fully in permitting me to accept the Miami position. The salary at Miami would be substantially greater than that at Kansas, but it was the subject matter with which I would be concerned that was the major motivating force.

We also had the problem of arranging to take care of the lease we had on our duplex which ran for another year. Our landlord was able to find other renters so he could release us as of the first of September. We were living in Lawrence during the summer although I was registered for dissertation research at the University of Iowa and technically in residence at Iowa. We had one other problem to solve. My sister, Ruby, and Dorothy's sister, Beth, had applied for admission to the University of Kansas to work for their bachelor's degrees. Each had two years of college work at Graceland and would thus be juniors at Kansas. Living arrangements for them at Kansas had not yet been fully established. They could, therefore, keep their plans to enter the university there or they could see if they could be admitted to Miami and move to Oxford, Ohio, with us. This they chose to do. They were each living in Lamoni, Iowa, 170 miles from Lawrence. It would be awkward for them to come to Lawrence to travel with us in our car to Oxford, but they could meet us in Independence, Missouri, and go from there. That took place early in September, and the five of us arrived together in Oxford to start our new life.

PART III
MIAMI UNIVERSITY,
OXFORD, OHIO

Chapter 7

The Miami Years

My first approach to orient myself with my new challenge at Miami was to learn something of the background of the School of Business of which I was now a member. Perhaps the history of marketing at Miami University should start with Harrison C. Dale. He was the first dean of the School of Business Administration established in 1927. Dean Dale believed education in business at the undergraduate level should be built on a strong liberal arts base and that courses in business should provide students with an understanding of each of the various aspects of business operation and management. Marketing was one of the aspects the dean thought was sufficiently important to be included along with production, finance, money and banking, accounting, economics, and statistics.

I do not know whether courses in marketing were offered before the fall of 1929, the date when I became a member of the business faculty. My primary responsibility was to develop a program in marketing, but there could not be enough marketing courses to be offered in 1929 to provide me with the normal fifteen-hour teaching load, so sections in transportation and public utilities were assigned to me to fill up my time.

I developed two courses—"Principles of Marketing" and "Marketing Policy and Management." Completion of the principles course was a prerequisite for taking the policy and management course. The text used in the early offering of the course in principles of marketing was by Maynard, Wydler, and Beckman, all three of whom were members of the faculty at Ohio State University. The text in the second course was *The Harvard Case Studies in Marketing.* I believe the author was Professor Learned.

We soon introduced two courses in advertising and one in retailing. I believe the course titles for advertising were "Principles of Advertising" and "Advertising Procedures." The principles course was a prerequisite for taking the procedures course. I do not recall when the retailing course was offered, but it was sometime after the specific courses in marketing and advertising were introduced. New additions to the business school faculty were required sometime in the early 1930s because of the increased enrollment. One of the additions was Harold Baker who taught the course in retailing.

Because I was charged with the responsibility of building a program in marketing, some comments concerning my philosophy of business and marketing are in order. My academic background as of September 1929 consisted of a bachelor's degree with a major in economics and minor in history, a master's degree in commerce, and completion of most course requirements for a Ph.D. in economics and business. I had taught accounting at the University of Iowa as a graduate assistant; economics, finance, transportation, and money and banking at Simpson College; and economics and accounting at the University of Kansas. I had had one course in marketing and one course in advertising taught by an advertising agency practitioner who commuted from Chicago to Iowa City for a twelve-week weekend course. Such background would seem to be quite inadequate as preparation to build an effective education program in marketing. In retrospect, it might be argued that such background was ideal in that it brought to the project one unencumbered by tradition or undue temptation to duplicate what others were doing. My approach was therefore one in which I persistently continued to ask and to seek answers to the questions: (1) What is the function of business to society? and (2) How could that function be best performed?

There was a substantial amount of literature dealing with business in general and marketing in particular. My reading and studying the many aspects of economics provided me with what I thought was a substantial understanding of various economic systems, with capitalism and the free market winning out as the system having most merit. My philosophy could probably thus be summarized by stating that the function of business was to provide goods and services to meet the needs and wants of consumers. It was the function of marketing to serve essentially as the purchasing agent for consumers. This would involve helping consumers find the products and services they needed or wanted and to transport, store, and distribute such goods and services.

It seemed that an additional function of marketing would be to provide consumers with information concerning the want/need satisfying qualities of products and to persuade consumers to try new items that were available. Advertising, as one of the elements of marketing, seemed to be the appropriate agency to perform the function of providing information and persuasion. The program in marketing at Miami, therefore, was built around the concept of helping consumers meet their needs and wants for physical goods and services thus helping them maximize their satisfactions.

There is no need to go into detail here concerning the particular content of the courses in marketing. Suffice it to say that emphasis was placed on combining business or marketing theory with actual practice. We usually had students carry out certain practical projects to test theory.

It was my belief that while business was designed to serve consumers, that did not relieve consumers of assuming some responsibility for their own welfare. I helped to organize a consumer council in Oxford to facilitate the education of consumers to help them become better buyers. Members became active in researching various products, analyzing their quality, and sharing information with each other. These were the early years of the consumer movement. It was my belief that because the function of business was to serve consumers, that business, and especially marketing and advertising, could logically assume a major leadership role in furthering that movement.

One debated issue around that time was the question of placing a quality grade label on canned food. I thought it would be good to test the hypothesis that grade labeling would benefit the business firms serving consumers best and injure those serving consumers poorly. To test the hypothesis, I purchased one can of every brand available in Oxford of eight different commodities such as tomatoes, peas, corn, peaches, etc. The labels were removed from each can and an identification number, coded against the brand, placed on each can. The coded cans were delivered to the Department of Home Economics at Miami. The department tested and graded each can against U.S. Department of Agriculture standards. After grades were received, a report was prepared matching grade, price, and brand.

The report was published in the local newspaper with identification numbers instead of brand names. A coupon was attached to the article stating that the brand names would be substituted for the identification numbers and made available if the signatory would pledge to use the information personally and not distribute it to others. (This pledge was required for legal protection.) A substantial number wrote and requested identified results.

The highest-priced brand of several commodities consistently graded "C" quality. The next-to-lowest-priced brand of one commodity graded "A." Three days after the identified results had been distributed to those making requests uptown merchants reported they had completely sold out all of the lower-priced grade-A brand. This kind of information served the consumer well, benefited the company providing the "best buy," and stimulated competition that would encourage a closer correlation between price and quality.

Other examples of supplementary classroom work included measurement of consumer purchasing habits, the likes and dislikes of consumers toward specific commodities, readership and listenership measurements of various media, and the application of statistical analysis of local and regional market data. The results of some of these were published in the *Miami Business Review*. One such study was done in 1934 in which focus was placed on the student market for clothing. Thus the December 1934 issue of the *Review* introduced the statistical findings with the following statements:

> In the preceding issue of the *Miami Business Review*, a general analysis was made of the spending habits of the student body of Miami University. Expenditures

were broken down into some two dozen items, some of a strictly school nature and thus confined to a nine months period, and others of a general character covering a full year. The total spent for these items by the "average student" was approximately $792.

The breakdown of this $792 into the items of common use was given (1) as an aid to students and parents in budgeting students' expenses, and (2) as valuable data for the merchant in budgeting his potential sales to a student group. As a further help to both these groups, this issue of the *Review* presents a detailed analysis of student expenditures for clothing.

The material presented in the tables applies to upperclassmen and women. The reason for this limitation is that the data reported by freshmen applied to four and one-half months only. Where freshmen data are significantly different from the average figures appearing in the tables, such difference will be noted.

Hands-on experience was provided students interested in retailing by getting a Cincinnati department store to permit selected marketing students to open the Clothing Wardrobe Corner in uptown Oxford. The students chosen to operate the Corner would be responsible for selecting the various samples of clothing to be included in the wardrobe trunk. These items would be displayed at specified hours during the week and the student attendants would take orders and the merchandise would be delivered later to the purchasers. This operation became so successful that a Cincinnati firm rented an entire store in Oxford and stocked it with merchandise for immediate delivery. The students were in complete charge of the operation with faculty serving only in an advisory capacity.

While some of the work in marketing might be viewed as innovative, the approach to the teaching of advertising might be viewed as pioneering in nature. Courses in advertising were being offered in various colleges and universities. The leading textbook was Otto Klepner's *Advertising Procedure*. Klepner was an advertising agency practitioner, and his book was almost wholly a how-to-do-it treatise. It might more properly have been labeled as a book on the construction and placement of advertise*ments*.

It seemed to me that advertis*ing* is a much broader and more fundamental subject than the construction and placement of advertisements. Advertising has a social function to perform, and practitioners should understand such function and strive to implement that function in their practice. I tended to believe that the function of advertising is to interpret the want/need satisfying qualities of products and services in terms of consumer needs and wants. The function of the practitioner then is to serve as a middleman between the producers of industry and the needs of consumers. To perform that function properly the practitioner needs to know the language of both.

Obviously, if an understanding of function was to precede practice, then the Klepner textbook would not be adequate for a first course. I found no other book that met what I thought was necessary, hence in the "Principles of Advertising" course no textbook was used. Instead, I developed my own outline, placed many books on reserve in the library, and involved students with long reading assignments. I am not sure whether an advertising course was given in the fall of 1929, but I would guess we did not introduce such a course until a year or two later. I started preparing material in mimeographed form covering certain sections of the principles course, thus making it easier for students to read and be more easily guided in their library work.

The mimeographed material eventually resulted in the publication in 1936 of my textbook, *Advertising Theory and Practice.*

Once I started fleshing out the outline I had prepared to organize the advertising principles course, I took the work quite seriously. The government New Deal had established the National Youth Administration along with many other Depression-motivated agencies. That agency provided money to colleges and universities to subsidize students who could not otherwise continue college work. Those students were supposed to devote a maximum number of hours under the supervision of individual faculty members. I requested the time of two students, and my request was granted. I used those students to do some research but primarily to type and mimeograph my longhand written material which could then be distributed to students to cover segments of the course. I spent evenings and weekends in my college office writing and thus kept my student assistants busy.

In the summer of 1934 I left my family in Oxford and went to the University of Michigan where I could isolate myself and concentrate completely on preparing chapters in my outline for later mimeographing. By the middle of the 1934 school year, I had completed approximately three-quarters of the chapters of my outline. I do not know how it happened, but Professor Harold Maynard of Ohio State University had seen a copy of the mimeographed material I had thus far completed. We were both in attendance at the Christmas holiday convention of the Association of Teachers of Marketing and Advertising. Professor Maynard told me he thought my material was worthy of publication and arranged a meeting at the convention with Richard D.

Irwin, who had started his own publishing company with concentration on textbooks in the field of business. He asked for a copy of what had thus far been prepared, which I later sent him. To my surprise he offered me a contract to publish a book if I would complete the outline I was following in the principles course. There was an additional stimulus to concentrate my efforts in getting the manuscript completed. Unfortunately, the manuscript was not finished when I moved to Philadelphia to start work with the Bureau of the Census. However, I took my notes and other necessary material with me and continued to work on the book evenings and weekends in my bachelor quarters in Philadelphia. My family was not to join me in Philadelphia until the end of the first semester of the school year in Oxford. I have a vivid recollection of mailing the last bit of manuscript to the publisher the day before Thanksgiving 1935. The book was published in 1936.

The second course in advertising was called "Advertising Procedures" and the Klepner book was used as a text. The first course, however, was a prerequisite to taking the procedures course. The principles course devoted very little time to the areas of copy and production. Instead, emphasis was placed on how advertising served society and business and what information an advertising practitioner should have to perform his job effectively.

I placed considerable emphasis on the importance of research. It seemed to me that because the function of advertising is to interpret the want satisfying qualities of goods and services in terms of consumers needs and wants, it is highly important for the advertiser to know a lot about consumer needs and wants as well as the qualities of products to be advertised. I therefore introduced in the principles course a new project at the beginning of each semester in which we took a product not yet on the market and researched consumers to ascertain whether the product met some of the needs and wants of the consumers. Some of the products used in the course included a chemical preparation to treat athlete's foot; a product called "Quick Kindlers" to facilitate starting a fireplace fire; a specially designed inkwell to improve the method for filling fountain pens; and special food products.

One of the later products* selected during my tenure at Miami University was a peanut butter manufactured by Swift and Company. Swift was introducing a homogenized peanut butter, which was a changed form of peanut butter from that which was normally offered to the public. Our research consisted of surveying consumers to ascertain the extent to which they used peanut butter, what they liked about it, what they disliked about it, and the relative intensity of specific likes and dislikes. We analyzed our consumer data separately for people in different age groups. This was done because the product Swift was offering carried the name "Oz" and the Swift personnel at the time thought that peanut butter was primarily consumed by youngsters.

The result of our consumer survey indicated that peanut butter consumption was not highly concentrated among the youth but was used to a substantial degree by all age groups. The characteristics disliked most about peanut butter were: (1) hard to spread, (2) it stuck to the roof of the mouth, and (3) the oil separated from the solids. In analyzing the qualities of

---

* Academic year 1941-42, fall semester.

the homogenized Oz peanut butter, it was obvious that homogenization solved the three basic dislikes in general peanut butter consumption. Our research report completed our work in the "Principles of Advertising" course.

Because the principles course was prerequisite to the course in advertising procedure, all students in the latter course had the peanut butter research as factual material to guide them in preparing advertisements and choosing the media for distribution. Students in the procedures course divided into groups of five students each, and each group was to carry through during the semester the development of an advertising campaign for the promotion of the new Swift homogenized peanut butter.

It was relatively easy for the students to select the basic appeal to be used in the campaign. The information from the research was also helpful in selecting media. Most student groups recommended that the name "Oz" be abandoned and that a more general name, "Swift," be used as the brand name.

Swift and Company had agreed to let our students "play" with this project largely because one of our students' father was a company official. We sent a comprehensive report of our research and campaign to Swift. They sent us a nice "thanks," but it was obvious that their advertising agency did not think student work was worthy of reproduction. But six months later their campaign had a lot of resemblance to our campaign. The details given here for the peanut butter project were the same in the two advertising courses each year but using different products each time. While the peanut butter project was carried on in the school year 1941-42, the first year the method was used was probably

1932-33. To the best of my knowledge, this was the first time a course later labeled "Advertising Campaigns" was ever given.

A different type of item was used for an earlier advertising project. It was an invention of a local entrepreneur who thought the product might have a great deal of merit. It was a toothbrush with the end bent to a 90-degree angle. A groove was cut into the end of the bent part of the handle and another groove close to the brush part. Those grooves were to be used to fasten dental floss with sufficient slack to permit a person's finger to pull the thread taut for flossing one's teeth. We did our normal consumer research and in addition placed samples of the product in a number of homes, later checking to ascertain the user's evaluation. After analyzing all aspects of our research we concluded that the product was not worthy of advertising promotion and so recommended to the inventor. Rather than to create the impression that advertising could or should be used to promote products without want satisfying qualities, we did not use that product and the research on it in the procedures course. Instead, we created a hypothetical product and let that be the thread unifying various aspects of the procedures course. The details of the methods and procedures used in the above two examples are typical of those used with all products selected for this assignment.

Supplemental Teaching

Some of the School of Business faculty members taught courses in business in evening schools in nearby cities such as Cincinnati and Dayton. Sometime in the early 1930s I taught a course in salesmanship at the

YMCA Evening School in Dayton, which I did for two semesters. Later I was asked to teach courses in marketing and market research at the University of Cincinnati Evening School of Business. Two or three other Miami professors also taught classes there. This supplemental income was especially helpful during the Depression, although in many respects persons on fixed incomes who kept their jobs and who had no cut in salary found the Depression years prosperous ones. Deflation increased the value of the dollar in contrast to inflation which decreases the value of the dollar. Hence, one's fixed salary check could buy more as prices of things to be purchased declined.

This held at Miami until 1932 when state appropriations were reduced and all Miami professors suffered an across-the-board specific percentage salary cut. That was the only time I think I ever complained about the size of my salary. Our president had placed substantial emphasis on rewarding merit, and faculty members were never given a straight across-the-board increase. Some were increased, some received nothing, and the amount of increase varied for each individual.

I was young, perhaps brash, and wrote to the president emphasizing his position in rewarding merit. I pointed out that merit could be recognized on a downward scale as well as on an upward scale. Why not, therefore, vary the cuts in salary in proportion to the evaluation of one's merit. I was particularly sensitive at that moment in time because I had just recently received my Ph.D. degree from the University of Iowa. I reminded the president that my doctoral degree was the one that permitted the School of Business to qualify as a member of the Collegiate Schools of Business and that

I was "honored" by Miami cutting my salary. The president answered me through my dean, but I still got the same cut as anybody else.

Wolf Chasers

I had the good fortune of having the University of Cincinnati class on the same evening as one taught by Dean Dale. We drove forth and back together, talking about business, the Depression, deflation, the stock market, and other things. Obviously, the stock market had hit bottom although at the time you hit bottom you do not know whether it's bottom or not. We allowed as how it might not be a bad idea to buy stock because of the tremendous deflation that had taken place. We made various comments on what might be the time to act, but eventually mutually agreed that if we organized a small group to invest in stocks that we could hardly lose anything. I was charged with the responsibility of drawing up a charter for such a group. The charter was what today would be called a limited partnership but I believe was organized then under a Massachusetts Trust type document. The charter provided for a limited number of investors, that no one would be permitted to invest more than $75, that we could not buy any stocks that were priced over $5 per share, that we have an investment committee of our members to recommend stocks to buy, that investors be limited to the Miami School of Business faculty, and that there be an executive secretary to handle the details of the organization.

I believe we had only seven or eight investors, and I was stuck being the executive secretary. I devised a name for our organization: the "Wolf Chasers." Had I known more about stock market operations I probably would have chosen "Bear Chasers," but Wolf Chasers was selected with the idea that we would chase the hungry wolf from our doors. I went to Cincinnati to open an account with the brokerage firm Westheimer & Company. Never having had any experience in this area, I talked to the first person on the desk who turned out to be a young man we would call the "customer man." I told him I would like to open an account for Wolf Chasers. He said, "I think you'd better see the manager." So I was ushered in to talk with the top guy. He was intrigued and took our account.

The chairman of our investment committee was the professor of finance. He was very capable and all of his selections turned out to be winners. Obviously, we did not have much to invest but we got some good experience. We continued as a group until the winter of 1935, which found me with the Census Bureau in Philadelphia. No one else wanted to serve as executive secretary, and I did not want to handle that from Philadelphia. We therefore liquidated and distributed to each member a profit of 73 percent.

Involvement with U.S. Bureau of the Census

I was in Philadelphia because in the early summer of 1935 I received a letter from the United States Bureau of the Census offering me a job as assistant chief of the Division of Transportation and Communication in the 1935 Census of Business. The Miami School of Business thought that an appointment of that type for one of its faculty would provide an element of prestige and was willing to give me a two-year leave of absence to accept the government appointment. I recall that I reported for duty in Washington, D.C., on September 13, 1935. The great economic depression starting in the early 1930s had created widespread unemployment. The Works Progress Administration, which funded the 1935 Census of Business, was one of many newly developed government agencies designed to help reduce the ranks of the unemployed. The Census Bureau was charged to recruit most of its clerical personnel from the white collar unemployed ranks. We were housed in Philadelphia because of overcrowding in Washington as a result of the great increase in government activity associated with the Depression.

The Division of Transportation and Communication was responsible for developing questionnaires, collecting data, tabulating questionnaire returns, analyzing results, and writing reports. Businesses included in our division were rail transportation, motor trucking for hire, bus transportation, advertising agencies, public warehousing, and radio broadcasting. Apparently, I was invited to join the staff as assistant chief because I had published a bulletin entitled "The Motor Vehicle in Iowa," and my doctoral dissertation, *Motor Vehicle Taxation for Highway Purposes,* had also been published. The specialty of the division chief was rail transportation, and I was to provide a balance for the division. The chief was transferred to Washington in another government agency in December 1935 and I was then named chief of the division.

The 1935 Census of Radio Broadcasting was the first that had ever been made. Because of its close relationship to advertising, I will comment in some detail on that census. The National Broadcasting Association (the industry trade association) had been making measurements of radio advertising based on a sample of radio stations for several years, but there had never been a complete census taken. A professor at the University of Pennsylvania had been making the sample studies for the association. Because the professor was located in Philadelphia and he was as interested in our work as we were in his background information, we placed him on the government payroll as a dollar-a-year man. It was necessary to put him on the payroll to maintain the Census Bureau pledge of confidentiality. This meant that only government employees would have access to individual schedules.

There were only 557 radio stations in operation in 1935. We had questionnaires from 554. Only three stations refused to answer, but eventually we had information from those as well. One was secured by my conference personally with the radio owner, and the other two by repeated solicitations including telephone calls. Today, we would be quite content with data from a properly drawn sample, but in 1935 the Census Bureau took the word "census" literally, meaning "a complete count."

Advertising revenue was one of the basic measures we were after. We classified stations by wattage power and broke advertising revenue into three categories: national and regional network; national and regional spot (non-network); and local advertising. The custom of the Census Bureau had been to issue preliminary reports before the publication of complete data. We issued such a report showing how total advertising revenue was distributed among the three categories—network, spot, and local. These findings were reported in an issue of Broadcasting Magazine. Two weeks later an article appeared in Broadcasting headlined "Census Data are Erroneous." It was authored by our dollar-a-year man but without his by-line.* The census figures showed relatively more local than regional or national advertising whereas the industry figures pre-census years showed relatively less local advertising.

If census data were erroneous those of us in the bureau wanted to know. If there was error, was it because, as the professor surmised, that radio station owners and management would not give accurate figures to the government? I devised an operation which would, I thought, determine whether radio station management would report differently to the government than to their trade association. The Census Bureau could not disclose the identity of individual stations, but I wrote an article in which I offered to pull out the questionnaires from all of the stations that the industry analyst had used as his sample if we were supplied with the names of those stations, and then we would compare how they answered the industry and the Census Bureau. In my article I suggested that it might be that the industry sample was unduly weighted by large national and regional stations where local advertising would be minimal. I took my article to Broadcasting Magazine, and the editor promised to run it in his next issue even though the association's director might pressure him not to run it. I was going to supply the association director with my copy so that they would be pre-informed. The article did appear but the association refused to give us the names of the stations in their

---

* It was embarrassing in many respects both to the professor and to me because I had been a colleague as a part-time teacher of marketing at the University of Pennsylvania. The Census Bureau chief had approved my teaching stint in response to a request from that university.

sample. This could well be interpreted to mean that they conceded their error.

An interesting sidelight to this episode is that the secretary of commerce had been pressured by the Broadcasting Trade Association director to have me fired. That brought about an invitation from the secretary for me to see him. He congratulated me on what had been done but cautioned me to be more politic in the future.

I did not completely abandon teaching while with the Census Bureau in Philadelphia. The University of Pennsylvania had an unexpected increase in its student enrollment in marketing courses. The dean came to the Census Bureau and asked if he could requisition some of the professors on leave from their universities to help out. I was invited to teach a section of marketing, which I did for a year.

My work at the Census Bureau was completed in June 1937. I had been invited to remain as a permanent civil service employee of the bureau but preferred to stay in teaching and would therefore report to Miami in September for the start of the 1937-38 school year. As a result, I could take a two-months vacation between the time of leaving government service and returning to Miami University. I planned to use that time as a vacation for my family but with me preparing a technical supplement to my advertising textbook.

A fellow educator from Northwestern University had been a retail specialist in the Census Bureau and would also be free for a vacation at the same time. We jointly rented a farmhouse in New Hampshire in the Franconia Notch area for two months. This was fortunate in that my young son and wife had others with whom to explore the area and try out fishing during the day while I was writing, and we could function as a complete unit in the evening.

Why was I writing a technical supplement to the text? The original edition of my text was devoid of detailed material on the preparation of copy and all of the things that went into getting copy prepared for use by the various media. The text focused on the institutional aspects of advertising and its economic and social functions. It was my belief that these aspects of advertising should be presented to students before they were asked to prepare copy. The publisher found that such point of view was accepted by Harvard, Stanford, the University of California, and a few others, but many schools said they could not adopt it as a basic text unless it had some detailed material on creation of ads. The publisher therefore insisted that such details be made a part of the text. This was done by publishing a technical supplement which was distributed to those schools that were using the book as a text. The publisher also used it to influence other schools to adopt the book. The technical supplement was later incorporated in the second edition. The expanded material helped eventually to make the text the leading one in the field.

Grades and Non-Grading

After completing the Census Bureau work and the vacation in the White Mountains, I returned to Oxford in time to start classes in September 1937. It was good to get back into the classroom and enjoy the stimulation of students and research in the areas of marketing and advertising. There was nothing particularly new in respect to classes or methods of instruction. There was, however, one area of experimentation that might be worthy of note. It had occurred to me that students and professors placed undue emphasis on grades. It seemed that many students crammed for exams with their minds geared to a grade rather than to mastery of the subject material, so I experimented with a new and somewhat radical approach.

I had never been enamored with so-called objective tests such as true-false and multiple choice questions. Instead, I used essay questions and did my own grading. I developed a modification of true-false/essay by phrasing a question or making a statement and asking the student to indicate whether he thought the statement was true or false and then tell why he made that choice. I told the students I placed no emphasis on the true or false, but wanted them to decide in their minds how they would answer the question before they started spilling ink. I left maybe three or four inches of space after each statement where they could write their reason, thus forcing them to limit the amount of verbiage used in their support.

I would usually grade the papers in time to pass them back at the next class meeting. The unique part of my experiment was that I placed no grade on the paper. The only mark on the paper was a number showing the order in which the papers were graded. At the next class meeting when I returned the papers, a number of hands would show asking what the number was and where is the grade. My response was always, "Why are you taking this course? Are you taking it for a grade or do you want to master the subject?" That generally confused the students, but most would reply, "I want to master the subject." I told them we would spend the rest of the hour going over the papers and I would give what I would consider to be an appropriate answer. I then would say, "You can follow my discussion and grade your own papers." I would indicate that if I had put grades on the papers and marked the points off each question I would not have the students' complete attention given to my discussion. In other words, if a student had nothing taken off Question 1, he would not listen to my discussion on Question 1. He would be focusing on Question 2 where he had five points taken off and devote his attention to developing an argument on why he was cheated. I also indicated that if grades had been placed on the papers, one would be interested in seeing how his grade compared with that of his seatmate and it might cause psychological trauma to one or the other. I would therefore indicate that I would post the grades after an interval of two weeks, but the student would be identified by the number that appeared on his exam paper.

In the 1930s most students were fairly familiar with the Bible. I sometimes used biblical examples to try to persuade students to the wisdom of this approach to examinations. I compared a "grade against mastery" with the Golden Calf and God. In the latter case, it did not take long for people to worship the golden calf and forget that there was a God. Likewise, unfortunately, many students "worshiped" the grade and forgot there was such a thing as mastering the subject.

After a semester or two of following this method of handling exams and grades, the School of Business faculty voted to adopt the method in all courses except accounting and specific skills courses.

Guest Speakers

Before my two-year leave of absence from Miami, I had followed the practice of inviting well-known marketing or advertising practitioners to talk to my classes.

Generally such speakers were recruited from Dayton, Middletown, Hamilton, or Cincinnati. My evening school teaching in both Dayton and Cincinnati helped me to get acquainted with some of the leading local practitioners and recruit them as guest speakers. One such was James Webb Young, a nationally known figure in the field of advertising and an executive of the J. Walter Thompson Advertising Agency. I got to know him because his sister was a teacher in Miami's McGuffey School and he occasionally came to Oxford to visit her.

The use of occasional guest speakers was renewed upon my return in 1937. I mention this because of the relationship developed with Herbert C. Evans, vice president of Consumer Distribution Corporation, located in New York City. Evans was a specialist in the area of consumer cooperatives. His organization provided counsel and management services for cooperatives that were becoming an important development in the field of marketing. There was not much attention in the standard marketing textbooks given to the philosophy or methods of organization and operation of cooperatives, but I included some material on the subject in my marketing classes. I also learned of Evans and his occasional visits to Indianapolis to confer with people in a farm cooperative and to Cincinnati to work with a consumer cooperative group there. He accepted my invitation to have him come to Miami to talk with my marketing students. A significant educational and personal experience grew out of this. It dealt with a situation in a Cincinnati suburb.

Model Communities—Greenhills

One of the many developments of President Roosevelt's New Deal was the establishment of "model" communities in the suburbs of three major cities. One such development was Greenhills on the outskirts of Cincinnati. These model communities, of which Greenhills was typical, were really thoroughly communal in nature, especially in regard to business operation. All business in the community was to be owned by the residents and operated as a consumer cooperative. Herbert Evans's company had supplemented the government grant with additional capital and assumed a management supervisory role. It was probably in 1939 or 1940 that I received a telephone call from him asking if I would go to Greenhills, review the business situation, and report back to him on my findings. He indicated that business there had thus far always operated at a loss. He wanted to know what caused these losses and what might be done to correct the situation. I agreed to give it a try.

I spent considerable time on some evenings and several weekends in Greenhills. I met with the manager, various employees, and the board of directors. I developed a questionnaire to be submitted to each resident in an attempt to measure the extent to which residents patronized the business, what they liked and disliked about it, and obtain comments concerning the operation. I submitted my report to Evans together with recommendations for change. He replied and asked me to assume the responsibility of getting changes implemented and ride herd on the operation. Implementing change was not an easy matter, but a number of changes were accomplished. It was a very pleasant experience to report at the end of the fifth month that operations were in the black. That favorable picture continued for several months, at the end of which it was appropriate that I close my relationship with Greenhills.

Mr. Evans apparently spoke kindly of me to officials of the Indiana Farm Bureau Cooperative Association in Indianapolis. That organization had done little in the way of marketing or seeking to know the real needs and wants of its consumers. I was invited to Indianapolis to talk to the cooperative's management on marketing and how the cooperative could use marketing to its advantage. That grew into a long-term relationship which will be reviewed later.

Summer School at Berkeley

In the spring of 1941, I received a letter from the dean of the business school at the University of California at Berkeley inviting me to teach in the upcoming summer school. I happily accepted and planned to make that also a vacation for my wife and son. We were fortunate to rent a professor's furnished home for the summer. The place was situated about three-fourths of the way to the top of Grizzly Peak which provided a direct view of San Francisco Bay and the Golden Gate Bridge.

I had never been to California, so I anticipated the trip there perhaps as much as the opportunity to teach at the university. Our son, Allan, had developed a keen interest in astronomy even though he would be only fifteen years old that summer. He wanted us to travel to Berkeley by way of Los Angeles-Pasadena. His reason was two-fold: (1) to visit the observatory on top of Mount Wilson and (2) to see the final touches being given the 200-inch mirror that would be housed in the observatory to be built at Palomar. That mirror was located on the campus of California Institute of Technology.*

---

* Years later Allan became a graduate student and a member of the first class in astrophysics at Cal Tech and eventually received his Ph.D. degree there.

I remember the physical environment at Berkeley as much as I do my teaching. There was nothing about the university or its students that I found superior to Miami. I did, however, think that the physical environment was inferior. During the entire period we were there not a drop of rain fell. Every evening a dense fog started rolling in over the Golden Gate and a relatively short time later covered the campus and all of Grizzly Peak. The temperature was generally neither hot nor cold. Its fluctuation between the two required furnace heat almost every evening. I must confess that it was a happy day when summer school was over, our car was packed, and we had started our return to the Midwest. The final exam in my marketing class was given in the morning and I was finished with my class as soon as the students had finished the exam. I did not wait to grade the papers and turn in my grades to the university, but put the papers in my briefcase. I had been so anxious to leave that I did not grade them until we arrived in Reno that evening. I spent most of the evening grading the papers and then mailed the grades back to the university.

Price Officer for OPA

After returning to Miami from Berkeley that summer, it was only a few months before the "day of infamy" created by the Japanese. That recalled our summer experience of seeing a Japanese ship moving in under the Golden Gate Bridge. Our declaration of war brought changes to Miami that affected various faculty members. It was not long afterward that the government placed controls on prices of goods and services. I was invited to serve as the price officer for the State of Ohio. I started my work there on a part-time basis before the spring semester closed and then moved to Columbus on a full-time basis thereafter. I had the responsibility for organizing the Columbus office, staffing it, and getting operations underway. Professor Harold Baker joined the OPA in its regional office in Cleveland.

I recall traveling to many parts of the state talking to groups of retailers explaining the OPA program and urging them to comply with its provisions. I created the term "compliance minutemen" and urged local retailers to assume their role in monitoring themselves and their competitors' adherence to the program. This concept was adopted on a national basis.

I had no intention of not returning to Miami for the fall semester, although on the request of the regional OPA office, Miami permitted me to be two weeks late in reporting for fall classes. I continued to serve as a consultant until the end of the calendar year.

The war brought about many changes in patterns of living. Not only were price controls initiated, there was rationing of many items including fuel oil. Many homes in Oxford had oil-burning furnaces. Thermostats were supposed to be set to provide room temperatures of no more than 65 degrees. Many people increased the use of fireplaces and many whose homes had no fireplaces added such.

Firewood

On the military front, the federal government initiated the development of small airports in various parts of the country, a number of them associated with educational institutions. Oxford/Miami was selected to have one of these airports. A forty-acre piece of land west of Oxford was purchased and a contractor was employed to prepare the facility. There were several acres of mature trees of various varieties on the site and the contractor proceeded to cut all of them down. They were to be bulldozed into piles and burned.

In view of 65-degree temperatures in homes with oil-fueled furnaces and no restrictions on the use of wood-burning fireplaces, I was appalled at the wanton destruction of beautiful, potential fireplace fuel. I considered it a marketing challenge to figure out some way in which the felled trees could be saved from the "funeral pyre" and focused into fuel-hungry homes. I submitted a plan to the appropriate university administration personnel for approval. This was the plan: advertise the availability of fireplace wood to university people for free if individuals would cut and haul away their own wood. Individuals could go to the site, stake out a small square footage area, post their name, and claim wood property rights in that area. Each would saw his wood into fireplace lengths and be responsible for hauling them away.

The plan was adopted and many faculty and staff members took advantage of this opportunity. It was an interesting sight to go out on weekends and see many people with crosscut saws and improvised sawbucks sawing wood and hauling it away.

Group Health and Accident Insurance

Some members of the Miami faculty were disturbed that there was no health and accident insurance provided by the university. This led to the appointment of a faculty committee to investigate the availability of such insurance and how it might be obtained. I was appointed chairman of that committee.

I do not recall the date the committee was appointed. Whatever the date, it was a period when group H&A

insurance was not a common part of the compensation of employees either in industry or academic circles. Investigation disclosed that there were few, if any, basic policies offered by insurance companies. Most programs tended to be tailor-made to fit the needs or interests of particular groups.

My committee sought information from a number of insurance companies. We finally narrowed our consideration to three. One was a well-recognized national company that had a special appeal because the president of the Miami University Board of Trustees was an agency representative of that company. Of the other two, one was also a well-known national company and the other smaller and at the time regional in its operation.

My committee examined the programs of each of the companies and concluded that the attributes of the smaller one warranted giving it detailed consideration. I was empowered to negotiate with the representative in developing a plan that would fit the needs of our faculty.

The name of the company was the Washington Insurance Company with headquarters in Evanston, Illinois. I arranged a meeting with company officials to discuss various plans. I emphasized that our people were concerned with insurance to cover sickness and accidents, but with a special emphasis on coverage to take care of extended incapacity. Our members could absorb the expense of short periods but needed protection against catastrophe. The company worked out a policy with a short-time or monetary deductible but with a multi-month coverage for long-term periods of incapacity.

The university was not willing or able to absorb the cost of a group insurance policy. The university would, however, administer the program and collect the premiums from each member who joined the group. It was agreed that at least 80 percent of the faculty would have to agree to the program before it would be offered. My memory suggests that the university agreed to continue the salary of a faculty member for thirty days in the event of sickness or accident but not beyond that period. Thus, the group insurance paid for by individual contributions would take effect after thirty days' absence.

The rate offered by the company would be the same for each member of the group regardless of age and no physical examination would be needed. I negotiated a special arrangement on rates which the company indicated was unique and the first of its kind, at least in their operation. I indicated that we did want the company to profit from providing such insurance but not at an exorbitant level. I suggested that if the payout in benefits during a year amounted to less than 60 percent of premiums collected, that half the amount below 60 percent be refunded to the group. I pointed out that this would, in essence, encourage members to keep their expenses to a minimum because that would react to their own financial benefit. The company accepted that arrangement.

As committee chairman it became my obligation to present our recommendation to the faculty and get an approval or rejection of the plan. My presentation was made separately to each department. I recall that more than 80 percent of all departments approved and signed up for membership, except the Department of English.

One bit of irony developed a few months after the program was inaugurated. One prominent faculty member, who had opposed the program but did join, became ill. His illness became terminal and he collected on his insurance for a number of months. He told me from his sick bed that he was most grateful for the insurance program and thanked me profusely for having pushed it through.

Senior Ball

Back in the 1940s it was common practice for the college senior class to have a senior ball as a means of celebrating their completion of college work and to raise money to provide a gift to their alma mater. I was part of a small faculty group that believed Miami should have a Student Union building to provide a center for unifying the nonacademic activities of students and faculty. We were making considerable progress on promoting the idea when the United States entry into World War II seemed to shelve the project. I had a different idea and proceeded to try to implement it.

The idea was to organize the senior ball for the class of 1943 around a war motif. Members of the class would be assessed a normal fee to finance a ball and raise money for a gift but keep expenses to a minimum. Instead of hiring a nationally known band, they would use the local Campus Owls musical group. They would make their monetary gift to their alma mater to be held in escrow for eventual use in building a part of a Student Union building as a post-war project. The escrow money would be invested in Government War Bonds to relate the gift to the war effort.

It seemed to me that this unique approach of tying the senior ball to the war effort and in anticipating the need for post-war civilian jobs, national attention could be gained for Miami University. *Life* magazine had as a regular part of its publication a section labeled "*Life*

Goes to a Party." Why not, therefore, invite or persuade *Life* to come to the Miami campus to record in picture and story the war-related senior ball/war bonds/future Student Union? I talked at great length with the president of the senior class and he seemed to be enthusiastic about the idea. We wrote to *Life* and received assurance that they would send a crew to the Miami campus for their purpose. The only caveat was that they would have crews in two or three places for potential parties and would select only one to run. I was confident, and I thought the president of the senior class was also, that because of the unique nature of the Miami program it would be a winner. Even if *Life* did not select Miami, the crew would still have been there and the campus would have enjoyed a rather unique marketing experience more satisfying than a traditional senior ball. Unfortunately, I left the campus in February and the president of the senior class was pressured to "play it safe," reject the unique, and stick to the traditional.

Harvard Graduate School of Business Administration

In that fall of 1942 I received a letter from the Graduate School of Business Administration at Harvard University inviting me to come to Cambridge for a conference with some of the business school faculty. That was during our holiday recess so it was easy for me to get away for the trip. I was there two days in which meetings with various faculty members involved discussions of research, teaching, advertising, and marketing. Toward the end of our discussions I realized I was being interviewed for a possible position as a visiting professor of business research with the primary responsibility being to direct a study of radio as an advertising medium for retailers. My last conference was with the dean of the school, who offered me a job starting February 1. I told him I could not accept because I was under contract to Miami, that I had not discussed this at all with anyone at Miami, and in fact no one there knew I was away from the campus. The dean immediately called his secretary and asked her to get President Upham of Miami University on the telephone. When the connection was made, Dean David told President Upham he had one of his professors in his office. He would like to have him join their faculty for a year and a half and would he give him a leave of absence. I could hardly imagine what might be going through President Upham's mind, but he obviously said "yes" and I accepted the Harvard offer.

The decision to take my leave of absence from Miami and move to Harvard for a year and a half created some logistical problems. It was necessary to find a place to live in Cambridge, perhaps rent our Oxford home, and transfer Allan to the Cambridge school system. The first two elements could probably be handled without too much difficulty, but the third presented a real problem. Allan did not want to move. He was a junior in high school and did not relish the idea of leaving his classmates and being thrown in with complete strangers for the rest of his high school work. He was a good student. The armed forces were seeking ways to increase their ranks with top quality personnel. Schools were asked to help in this endeavor. An accelerated program was made available to high school students at the end of their junior year if they met certain requirements. Students who were in the upper ranks of their class and were approved by their principal could skip their senior year in high school and move immediately into college. Allan wanted to enter that accelerated program. We therefore agreed that I would go to Cambridge, rent an apartment, and live by myself for a semester. Dorothy and Allan would stay in Oxford while Allan finished his junior year in high school. He would then enter Miami University as a freshman, live in the dormitory, and his mother would join me in Cambridge. Our home in Oxford was then rented to a naval officer who was a part of the Miami Naval Reserve Officer Training Corp (NROTC).

My leave of absence from Miami was in some respects beneficial to the university because of the great reduction in enrollments in the normal university educational programs. Nugent Wedding was a member of the marketing faculty and could handle most of the demands from the greatly reduced enrollment in that area.

I arrived in Cambridge in either late January or early February 1943. I had rented an apartment in a large apartment building facing the Charles River, and it was a relatively short walk from there to cross the river to the business school campus located on the Boston side of the river. Because gasoline was rationed, little use could be made of our automobile. It was therefore put in dead storage for the duration but could occasionally be brought out for use.

I was given a spacious and beautiful office with a fireplace and a pleasant view from the windows. Also, I was assigned an excellent secretary who had been on the business school staff for several years and hence knew the detailed aspects of school operations.

I was briefed on my visiting professorship and my research responsibilities. The briefing consisted primarily of reporting that the Columbia Broadcasting System had made a substantial grant to the school to fund research in the area of retail advertising. I was to develop a research plan and submit it to an advisory committee of the faculty appointed specifically for this project. The chairman of the committee was Professor Neil H. Borden and the other members were Professor Harry R. Tosdel, Professor Malcolm P. McNair, and Professor Stanley F. Teele. The Harvard Business School was famous for its development of case studies of business firms and using these for class instruction. I therefore included in my research approach the development of case histories of the use of radio advertising by various types of retailers and local service organizations. The detailed information that would be sought from each business firm and the conclusions drawn from collected information was left to me entirely. My appointment was to run through the summer of 1944, and I was expected to complete all research and issue my final report by that time.

The first six months of my time were devoted almost wholly to visiting, interviewing, and recording data from the carefully drawn sample of retailers in various parts of the United States. I interviewed the general manager and personnel involved with radio advertising in department stores, hardware stores, furniture stores, funeral parlors, drug stores, and various specialty stores. I collected data from each source visited in a form that would permit some quantification. A research assistant provided help in editing, coding, and tabulating the quantitative data that I was able to collect. There were also information and impressions gained from interviews that could not be quantified, but which would be helpful in evaluating the nature and impact of radio advertising as used by local business firms.

After the field work was all done and the data reduced to usable forms, the tedious but enjoyable task of analyzing and evaluating the material and preparing a final report began. My final report was submitted to Professor William T. Copeland, director of research, in May 1944, some three months before the end of my appointment. I was told that this was the first research project that had ever been completed by the deadline, let alone three months early.

The report was not limited to presenting case histories. That aspect of the research was basically limited to the first half of the report and the other half provided suggestions aimed at helping retailers improve their radio advertising activities. My manuscript was given to the advisory committee for its evaluation. I learned later that my research assistant, who had been thoroughly schooled in the case history approach, reported to the committee that she thought the report should be greatly modified to eliminate most of the material designed to give advice to retailers. I also learned that the committee approved the entire report as submitted and that Professor McNair voiced special approval. Because Professor McNair was the leading academic authority on retailing and had published case history textbooks, it was especially gratifying to learn of his position.

My report was thought to be of sufficient value that it should be presented in book form. The original donor added funds to employ a graphic artist to provide charts and graphs to highlight much of the quantitative data. The book was completed and issued in 1945 by the Harvard University Press. It went though three printings, the last printing being in 1948.

There was an occasional Miami connection while I was at Harvard, although not a part of my research. The Navy had chosen Harvard as a school to train recruits to serve in its supply corps. Occasionally some Miami students would be in one of the Supply Corps classes. I recall that one such student was Vernon Fryburger. We would invite such Miami students to our apartment for a weekend dinner at various times. We would almost always have chicken since that was not subject to strict rationing.

There was another nonresearch and war-related experience which I have never forgotten. I often ate lunch at the Harvard faculty club and had my first experience in eating horse meat. It was a common item on the menu.

Institute of Transit Advertising

In the spring of 1944, I would catch an occasional hint that at the end of my visiting professorship I might be invited to remain on the faculty on a permanent basis. However, sometime in April or May of that year I received an offer from the Institute of Transit Advertising headquartered in Chicago to join the Institute as a vice president and director of research. The salary offered was more than double the twelve months' salary I was getting at Harvard and three times the nine months' salary I would be getting at Miami should I return there. My ego was stimulated by the reasons the Institute people gave for offering me the job. They wanted someone who was active in the American Marketing Association and I was a national director. They also wanted someone who had published, was recognized in the area of research, and had a doctorate degree. Apparently I qualified on all these counts. Because the war was still on and Miami was not needing my services for the upcoming school year, I was told my leave of absence would be extended if I asked for it. I therefore accepted the Chicago job and agreed to start work there on July 5. I had not discussed the Chicago offer with the Harvard people thinking that to do so might be construed as a feeler to see whether the hints that I had picked up about the possible permanent appointment were real. When I later informed Harvard that I was leaving early because my work was done and there was no point in staying around collecting a salary doing nothing and therefore I had accepted the Chicago job, there was indeed a note of what I construed to be disappointment on their part.

We moved back to Oxford after I finished my work at Harvard and then, on July 5, I arrived in Chicago to start my work with the Institute. Dorothy wanted to remain in Oxford until I found living quarters in Chicago. That task was not an easy one. Housing was extremely scarce due to the war and the national nominating convention of one of the major political parties was to be held in Chicago during the summer. I did, however, find a small apartment that was sublet to me until September and then a good, furnished house which we could occupy in September.

The Institute had offices in the Wrigley Building. Public transportation was excellent from our residence, and with wartime rationing still in effect our automobile was used only occasionally.

The Institute was supported financially by a majority of individual transit advertising operators as a trade association under the name National Transit Ads Inc. The various local transit advertising companies resulted from the breakup of Baron Collier's transit advertising empire. He had largely a monopoly of the entire operation but had gone bankrupt. A large Chicago-based accounting and legal firm headed by George Frazer was appointed by the court to develop reorganization plans for the protection of Collier's creditors.

George Frazer was a very capable individual who had been comptroller at the University of Illinois when Edmond James was president. President James had instituted a rigid rule against nepotism and when Frazer married President James' daughter, he had to sever his connection with the university. He moved to Chicago, organized his own company, and was thus prepared to effectively handle his court-appointed work. In the reorganization Frazer kept for his own operation a transit advertising company serving Chicago and other Midwestern areas. He was the leading force in getting the industry to establish a research organization.

President James had a son, Herman, who became an educator much like his father. Dr. Herman James served as a professor and dean in various schools and was later appointed as president of Ohio University in Athens, Ohio. He was a strong president. That may have been part of the reason that a conflict developed between him and his board of trustees, and he became unemployed shortly after I started work at the Institute. I held the title of vice president and director of research and was also what would be termed today the chief executive officer. The Institute had no president. Herman James was the brother of George Frazer's wife. There was no nepotism rule in the Institute, so Herman James was named president. We became very good friends. Herman James was a true scholar and an excellent historical researcher who preferred to continue his research in that area and spent many hours in Chicago libraries. He also wanted to learn the field of market research, not to participate in the research work of the Institute, but to understand the area.

I was given a free hand to develop a research program. Actually, no research had been done to measure or to test whether advertising in streetcars and buses was effective. I developed a proposal which I thought might answer such questions at least to some degree. I conceived the idea of establishing consumer panels in cities where public transportation was highly important. We would then ask housewife members of the panels to keep weekly charts of their purchases of selected grocery items. Such diaries would be kept on a continuing basis and returned to our office for tabulation and analysis. We could thus establish the purchase patterns of housewives in terms of commodities purchased, brands selected, and frequency. We would then have the panel keep a diary for two weeks of their use of public transportation. The panel would be divided into two groups—riders and nonriders. The purchase patterns of each group could be analyzed separately. We would then, it was hoped, get advertisers who had not used transit advertising to enter the cars and buses with a full showing but change nothing else in their advertising and marketing operation. Our hypothesis would be that since riders would be the only ones exposed to the new advertising there should be a measurable difference in the purchase of advertised items by riders and nonriders.

When I submitted this proposal to my board of trustees there was a negative response from a number of them. They asked, "What if we found out that transit advertising was not effective? Would that not be detri-

162

mental to the industry?" My answer was, "Yes, but if a medium was not effective should not the operators be the first to know?" Also, this was a private organization; it was not obligatory to publicize results. If we found that the medium was not effective, then our research should be directed toward trying to learn why. The trustees eventually were persuaded and gave me the go-ahead sign.

We established panels in Buffalo and Cincinnati. I supplied them with diary forms and followed the procedure I had submitted to the board. I staffed the Institute with individuals who would edit, code, and tabulate them weekly as they were returned to us. Information obtained from these diaries provided insights into shopping behavior independent from any application that might be used to test effectiveness. It seemed to me that such general information would be helpful to operating members of the trade association. I therefore established a monthly publication called "Local Market Facts." We could provide quantitative data showing such things as share of market of different brands of crackers, coffee, ready-to-eat cereals, and pork-and-beans. Comparisons could be made between Buffalo and Cincinnati. Differences in these two cities would emphasize the local nature of markets. We also would report differences in purchases of specific commodities by day of week.

The distribution of our local "Market Facts" stimulated interest in our Institute and also called attention to the medium. It helped us obtain "guinea pigs" for our basic objective to test effectiveness.

We were able to get a substantial number of advertisers willing to cooperate in our research. These included distributors of products such as coffee, macaroni, pork and beans, and ready-to-eat cereal. In the case of ready-to-eat cereal, General Foods used their Wheaties brand in our test. We had already established the purchase pattern for Wheaties by riders and nonriders. Wheaties had never been advertised in the public transportation medium. This made it an excellent subject. A full showing was purchased in the cars and buses in Cincinnati. General Foods wanted to measure readership of their cards and employed another company to do that. Results showed that readership was very high. The company had used their regular cartoon "Breakfast of Champions" theme in their advertising.

When our tabulations were completed for the four weeks involved in this test, my heart sank. There was no significant difference in the purchase pattern for Wheaties by riders and nonriders. On the basis of that one test we might conclude that the medium was not effective, at least for ready-to-eat cereal. These results, of course, were reported to the Wheaties people. It was obvious that riders had seen and could recall the advertising. I raised the question whether the message might be the problem. Would they take another full showing with a changed message? They agreed to do so and used my suggested message, a straight appetite appeal. The card carried a picture of a bowl of Wheaties with rich, yellow cream showing around the edges, a strawberry on top, and a headline, "It Tastes Good! Try it." When the results during the four weeks that message ran came through, there was a significant difference between riders and nonriders in favor of the riders. This one experiment influenced General Foods to stop their cartoon advertising approach and move toward using an appetite appeal.

Return to Academe

My research at the Institute was very interesting and invigorating. Perhaps an old adage that was always whispered about teachers and professors had some influence on my original interest in accepting a full-time job in business. That adage was, "Those who can, do. Those who can't, teach." My work with the Census Bureau was nonteaching but still not business. The Institute was business with its board of directors and its requirement to prove the value of your work and its contribution to profit. The substantial success that was evident in the work we were doing at the Institute satisfied me that "I could do." I did not receive the same personal satisfaction from that kind of work and environment as I did from teaching and the academic environment. I therefore concluded in the spring of 1945 that I would resign my position with the Institute and return to Miami. This would be a substantial reduction in material income, but it would add substantially to my psychic income. When I informed my board of my plan they could not believe I was in earnest. They offered to increase my salary. When they eventually recognized that I was in earnest, they said, "Well, okay, take the Institute work with you back to Miami." This I agreed to do.

While I was still in Chicago it appeared that the war was winding down and would soon be over. This would mean a great return of students to the universities. Administrators were thus looking to not only have professors who were on leave of absence to return but also to add new people to their faculties. I was courted by the University of Chicago, the University of Wisconsin, and the University of Illinois. I indicated in all cases that I owed Miami University at least one year and would return there. In my own mind I thought there was perhaps a probability that I would accept an appointment in some university other than Miami after a year there. Moving the Institute to Miami and the prospect of my leaving for another school at the end of the 1945-46 school year stimulated me to look for an outstanding marketing educator to join me at Miami in the fall of 1945. A former student of mine at Miami had gone to Northwestern where he received his Ph.D. degree studying with some of the top educators in the field and was then teaching at Emory University. I discussed with Miami officials the possibility of offering that individual an appointment with half-time as an employee of the Institute and half-time as a professor of marketing. I felt that if I should leave Miami that individual would be an excellent one to serve the Marketing Department well. That was Dr. Joseph Seibert. The joint appointment was offered and accepted by Joe. I did eventually accept an appointment at the University of Illinois starting in the fall of 1946. The Institute remained at Miami with Dr. Seibert.

After returning to Miami to start the fall semester, the day-to-day operation of the Institute was in the hands of Dr. Seibert. I devoted full time to teaching and university research.

Radio Diary Theory

When in Chicago, I had frequent meetings with other market research people. In these discussions we exchanged points of view and debated various methods of drawing samples, collecting data, and interpreting results.

In measuring listening to radio stations and programs, the audimeter employed by A. C. Nielsen Company was the paramount measurement instrument. That instrument was attached to a radio receiving set and recorded every time the set was turned on or off. This produced a tape from which data could be compiled showing by minute-to-minute or quarter-hour-to-quarter-hour periods when the set was being operated.

In discussions on the pros and cons of that method of measurement, I raised questions such as the composition of those who were listening when the radio was turned on; whether in multi-set homes audimeters were placed on all sets; whether the number of listeners to a particular set varied from time to time; and whether there were times that the set was on and no one was listening. Because I was using consumer panels for measuring purchasing behavior, I suggested the use of panels to measure radio listening. Individuals could be asked to keep diaries of their radio listening on an individual rather than a household basis. I suggested that the diary might be viewed as an audimeter attached to the person instead of the instrument. My ideas were accepted as good conversation but never accepted as a valid or workable approach.

When I returned to Miami, I decided to test my radio diary theory. I therefore introduced a research project that would test this approach as a part of the market research segment of a marketing class.

> The method employed in this local survey consisted of getting each member of representative families in the County to keep a diary of individual listening for seven consecutive days. Persons who cooperated in the survey were located in Hamilton, Middletown, small villages, and on farms. Each of these areas was represented in the sample in proportion to the importance of each area in the total county population.

In soliciting the cooperation of families, personal interviewers called to explain the purpose of the study and to secure pertinent economic and social data. Each family provided the following information for the family or individual members of the family: age, sex, education, family income, telephone service, occupation of those employed, number of radios in home, and specific magazines and newspapers purchased. After such data were secured, an easy-to-keep diary was left for each member of the family. These diaries divided the listening day into 72 fifteen-minute periods from 6 A.M. to midnight. Each potential listener was given a booklet containing seven diaries—one for each day of the week. Stamped, addressed envelopes were supplied for returning completed diaries at the end of the seven-day period.*

The results of that study were printed in the *Miami Business Review*. It provided overall listening patterns not unlike those obtained by the Nielsen audimeter but in much greater detail. It is interesting to note in retrospect that the listener diary method was adopted much later by Nielsen and other rating services. Let me just say that Miami University was the institution at which the personal radio listening diary that I developed was first used and its validity tested.

Acceptance of U of I Appointment

By the end of the holiday season in 1945, I had accepted an appointment by the University of Illinois as a professor of advertising/marketing. It had not been an easy decision to make. I had come to Miami only a

---

* "Radio Listening," Charles H. Sandage, professor of marketing and head of the department, *Miami Business Review* XVII, no. 3 (March 1946), published by the School of Business Administration, Miami University, Oxford, Ohio.

short time after the School of Business had been established and had been a part of its growth to a premier position among business schools. Our work in marketing and advertising had received national recognition and many of our graduates had gone on to achieve success in various areas. We had a strong faculty with members of the marketing faculty called on to serve on various university committees in addition to their teaching and noncurricular duties within the School of Business itself. I had thought that marketing and advertising education had developed to a point where people generally recognized both their business and social value. The popular press and occasional books, however, at times presented a negative view of advertising. One such book that appeared in 1945 was Wakeman's *The Hucksters*. I was shocked one Monday after arriving on the campus to have one of my students tell me about what he heard in his church the day before. His minister had read *The Hucksters* and commented on it from the pulpit, and among other things stated that he could not see how a Christian could go into advertising. I knew the preacher and had considered him a real scholar. I could not, however, as a professor teaching students who might go into advertising as a profession remain silent. I therefore wrote the pastor, who actually held a doctorate degree, the following letter. He never replied.

My dear Dr._____:

Your profession and mine are not vastly different. In fact, there is a considerable degree of harmony between promoting the soul-satisfying doctrine of Christianity and preaching about the want-satisfying qualities of merchandise and business services. Even techniques are often similar. Radio has its Lutheran Hour, Old Fashioned Revival Hour, and Voice of Prophecy as well as its "Love that Soap" program. The printed word is also used extensively in both fields.

You may object to this comparison and claim that even though techniques may be similar, practitioners are different—that in one is to be found Christians and in the other group followers of the fallen Son of the Morning.

Victor Norman threw a stone at advertising, but he was a confessed "sinner." The stone *you* reputedly threw at advertising in a recent sermon was much more telling, because it must have been thrown only after considering the comment of Jesus as recorded by St. John of old.

Of course there is sin in business and its handmaiden, advertising. Such sin could and should be reduced. The professional preachers against sin can help in bringing more purity to advertising. They can dedicate some of their missionary zeal to the task of converting advertising practitioners to the true merits of Christian principles. This can be done not be passing by on the other side of the gutter into which some advertising has fallen, but rather by binding up the sores of advertising with Christian oil and wine.

It is my plea that you dedicate some of your time and talent to this task. We need scholars and persons with integrity to join in such a crusade. We need people motivated by the positive philosophy of Jesus rather than the negative philosophy of Moses—thou shalt rather than thou shalt not. Progress toward improving advertising will be slowed if leaders of thought such as yourself discourage young men and women of integrity and ability from entering the field.

Cordially yours,
C. H. Sandage

The preacher's comments about advertising not only motivated me to write to him, but perhaps more importantly caused me to re-examine my own philosophy. I considered myself a Christian, at least philosophically. I had been teaching students who were interested in developing careers in business in general and marketing in particular. I was transferring to the University of Illinois where my concentration would be even more narrow, namely advertising itself.

I had an academic degree in liberal arts. Emphasis there was on a broad rather than a narrow perspective. Was I violating Christian principles by helping students prepare for a life in business, particularly in marketing and advertising? My conclusion was that instead of violating, I had been following the basic principles enumerated by the "Great Teacher." It was my position that the function of business was to serve the needs and wants of consumers. The function of advertising as an arm of business was to inform and interpret the need and want satisfying qualities of goods and services in terms of consumer needs and wants. Stewardship was an inherent quality of business practitioners who tried to serve consumers effectively. Profit was not a dirty word. Christian principles recognized that the servant was worthy of his hire; further, that the one who served best would profit most. Risk takers and innovators were important elements in business practice. Such elements contributed to the multiplication of inherent talents of persons entering the field of business. Those elements I felt had undergirded my work as an educator in the field of business.

Chapter 8

Family and Personal Life during the Miami Years

As a family, we were young, healthy, energetic and maturing. Allan was three when we arrived in Oxford and was mustered out of the Navy the summer we left.

There are many aspects of academic life that have had particular appeal for me. Teaching, research, and working with young people have been very enjoyable. In addition, time schedules in academia permit a freedom of activity beneficial to family and personal life. It is not an 8 to 5, five days a week, month in and month out, with only two weeks vacation per year schedule. It normally provides a ten-to-sixteen-day vacation at Christmas, a one-week spring break, and two or more months of freedom in the summer. Of course, during the nonvacation periods the academic work week is more like sixty-seventy hours than the normal forty for industrial workers.

I have often said there are three things that make up the good life. One is to love your wife, the second is to love your family, and the third is to like your work. I have had all three.

My Family and My Extended Family in Oxford

I brought quite a family with me to Oxford. There were not only Dorothy and Allan but also my sister, Ruby, and Dorothy's sister, Beth. Ruby and Beth had each graduated from Graceland, a two-year college, and registered as juniors at Miami. Also, Dorothy had not yet received her bachelor's degree and enrolled at Miami on a part-time basis. Allan thus had four people who were ministering to his welfare. At three years of age he enjoyed the extra attention.

We arrived without having a place to live. The dean had written me that there would be no problem in finding housing. So we decided to arrange our timing to arrive in Oxford at the beginning of the day and then, we hoped, find a furnished house or apartment by the end of the day. We found that there were very few choices and none that were furnished. We settled on a rather spacious apartment, but it was unfurnished except for a stove and refrigerator. We were able to get some cots for use until we could buy or rent furniture for the place. We did not experience a very enjoyable first night in Oxford.

The next day, Dorothy and I left Allan with Ruby and Beth and drove to Hamilton, fourteen miles away, to look for furniture. We borrowed enough money to buy the essentials to be delivered that day and then ordered from Sears Roebuck unfinished tables and chairs for dining room and kitchen use. After three days we found our living conditions fairly comfortable and reasonably well organized.

It was months later when I learned that the arrival of our "family" created some interesting whispers. My vita had indicated membership in the Reorganized Church of Jesus Christ of Latter Day Saints. While the RLDS Church was related historically to the Mormon church headquartered in Utah, it was in no sense a part of that church. Polygamy had always been associated with the

Utah Mormons, but the Reorganized Latter Day Saints Church had always been adamantly opposed to that philosophy. Nevertheless, the whispering questioned whether there was more than one wife among the three women I had brought with me.

When school started, Ruby and Beth were full-time students, Dorothy was a part-time student, Allan was in pre-school, and I was also in the classroom—quite an educationally oriented family. Family activity, therefore, for the school year was built almost wholly around education. The adults in the family followed an organized program. Allan got part of his daily education from pre-school, but most of it from the adults in the family during the times they were not studying or in the classroom.

It was not until the summer vacation that we went back to Iowa to visit our parents and friends. We had an experience on the way back from Iowa which could have been disastrous. The road we were traveling took us through Pekin, Illinois. A section of the bridge over the Illinois River could be raised when necessary to accommodate river traffic. Rather than being a cantilever arrangement, the entire movable part of the bridge remained horizontal and was raised vertically. Just as we had driven onto the movable section, I heard the clanking of a bell and the bridge started to rise. Rather than staying on the rising part, I started to back off. The back wheels of the car dropped off the bridge platform onto the pavement, but the bridge had risen with the front wheels of the car still on the bridge and at an angle where the rear bumper of the car was resting on the pavement and hence the car's backward movement was stopped. A number of people were shouting to the bridge tender who then saw what was happening and stopped the upward movement of the bridge. Had the rising of the bridge not been stopped, it would have dumped our car and passengers into the Illinois River. Fortunately, the bridge was stopped and we were able to get out without injury. The bridge was then lowered with only minor damage to the car.

Something had happened to the controls, or negligence on the part of the bridge tender, which kept the gate to close traffic before getting on the bridge from being dropped in place. Naturally, without the gate and without warning, traffic was not stopped. The car behind us happened to be immediately under the steel gate that was dropped when the bridge tender noted the difficulty. The occupant was not injured, but his car was severely damaged.

It was later reported that the bridge tender had been drinking and that he was fired from his job. We were, however, thankful that he stopped the bridge in time to prevent a catastrophe.

One interesting, somewhat amusing, and maybe somewhat morbid aspect of this experience might be worth telling. A gentleman came up to me and introduced himself, saying that he observed the near-catastrophe and had thought he might have to rush to get a rescue squad with grappling hooks to fish us out of the river. He said that if I needed any witnesses to the accident, he would be available and handed me his business card with his name, address, the nature of his business, and telephone number. I later looked at his card carefully and noted that he was a salesman for a tombstone company. Luckily for me and my family he would have to wait a long time to include us as prospects.

After one year in the apartment we were fortunate enough to find a house to rent. The owner was a widow lady whose own home was next door from the place we rented from her. Part of the understanding that went along with the lease was that I would assume responsibility for the physical care of the house we were renting. That meant giving it an occasional coat of new paint.

The house was much more spacious than the apartment in which we had been living. There were two bedrooms downstairs in addition to the normal living room, dining room, and kitchen. There were three rooms upstairs. There was a full basement with a coal-fired furnace for heat. Obviously, there was no air conditioning. I used the small upstairs room as a study, and the other two upstairs rooms were used by Ruby and Beth. Allan had the downstairs room next to our master bedroom. We added enough furniture to our apartment furnishings to make us feel that we were at long last really living. We were a fairly well-organized family with each carrying certain responsibilities including Allan, even at his tender age.

I have never been able to forget one embarrassing episode associated with that house. I was engaged in applying a new coat of paint to the outside one day when a neighbor lady came in to see Dorothy. I was on a step ladder painting the front porch and was partially blocking the front door. When I attempted to get off the ladder, I upset my bucket of paint. It fell all over the floor and quite a bit of it spattered on me. The neighbor lady burst out laughing. The nature of my explosion should not be repeated.

Ruby graduated at the end of the year and took a job as music teacher in a public school in central Ohio. Beth also graduated, but stayed on another year to work in the Miami library. She later left Oxford to pursue graduate work in library science.

Ruby was courted by a young teacher in the same school in which she was teaching which eventually led to marriage. Neither Ruby nor her fiance had parents living close by to plan and put on a large wedding. Also, there were financial considerations. The wedding, therefore, took place in our home. She and her new husband continued to teach for two years in this same school system. Then they each accepted better jobs at a school near Cincinnati. It was there that their first child was born. Dorothy took some time out to be with Ruby for a week after the arrival of the youngster.

Vacation Times

We developed a habit of using vacation periods to do some traveling. This practice provided diversion from one's organized pattern of living and also helped to stretch minds from experience derived from such travel.

We were fortunate one summer in having a cottage on the Canadian side of Lake Erie. This was made possible by the thoughtfulness and generosity of Dorothy's aunt and uncle. Her uncle was a doctor with a medical practice in Erie, Pennsylvania, but he owned a cottage across the lake at Port Stanley.

On another occasion we traveled through Kentucky and southern Indiana following the area in which Abraham Lincoln spent his early years. In that and other travels, we read and talked about the areas to be visited before and during our journeys. I was never sure how much this kind of diversion from routine living stimulated Allan's imagination or contributed to his liberal education, but I am sure it had some effect. It also provided activities as a family unit.

Allan was just nine years old when we moved him from his school in Oxford to Philadelphia. He attended school there for one and one-half years. That in itself was a broadening experience for him. In addition, either Dorothy or I would often take him into Philadelphia on Saturdays to visit historical places and spend time in the Franklin Institute and the Hayden Planetarium. It was during that period that Allan's lifetime interest in astronomy was born.

As noted earlier, our entire summer of 1937 was spent in a vacation house in the White Mountains of New Hampshire. This was in the Franconia Notch area and provided opportunities to explore the wonders of New England.

Allan was eleven years old when we returned to Oxford. The sexual revolution was not to arrive for some decades. Parents at that time, at least this one, were reluctant to discuss various aspects of sexuality with their children. My approach was awkward, but I thought essential, as the age of puberty was at hand. So Allan and I took a trip just by ourselves. The primary purpose of that trip was to have a father and son talk about growing up, the meaning of puberty, and the "proper" way of dealing with the sex drive to assure maximum future happiness. Awkward, late, but maybe effective. We drove to Gatlinburg, Tennessee, rented a cabin, and explored the Smoky Mountains. We talked about various things, weaving in comments on the subject matter which was the foundation of my basic motive for a father and son vacation.

Building Our Home

While still in Philadelphia with the Bureau of the Census, I purchased a lot in Oxford with the idea of building our own house when we returned to the university. On our return, we engaged a local architect to develop plans. Many hours were devoted to thinking through the kind of house we wanted and getting the architect to reduce everything to blueprints for the contractor.

Final plans resulted in a two-story structure plus a full basement. There was an attached garage with a spacious room above to serve as my office at home. There were three upstairs bedrooms: our master bedroom, Allan's room, and a guest room. This was a colonial-type house with a living room, dining room, screened-in porch off the dining room, and a spacious Pullman-type kitchen with all of the built-in conveniences. There was both a downstairs and upstairs bathroom. The basement included a furnace room, recreation room with Ping Pong table, laundry room, and small shop area. There was a fireplace in the living room.

A few years later, when the war brought on fuel oil rationing and turned-down thermostats, the fireplace became a very important part of the house.

It was also during that time that I had a fireplace built into my study. That was fairly easy to do since the study was over the garage and a chimney could be constructed with its base in the garage and carried up through the study and side of the main part of the house.

A builder was engaged and work was started in the fall of 1937. The excavation work and footings for the foundation were completed just as winter arrived, which halted work until the spring. We moved into the new house in June 1938. It was only a short time until we converted from a house to a home.

The section I had staked out in the airport woodlot as a source of supply for fireplace wood became very important. An episode associated with that woodlot was never erased from either my or Allan's memory. It was a Thanksgiving day and we were to have a traditional bountiful dinner. I suggested to Allan that we go out and get a little exercise while waiting for our dinner. The day was cloudy, misty, and rather chilly. I thought it would be both fun and productive if we went out to the airport woodlot to saw up a car-trunk load of fireplace wood. Allan demurred but I thought it was an act and that he actually would enjoy the experience. In any event, we did spend a couple of hours together sawing wood. Apparently my assumption that Allan would enjoy the experience was very erroneous because he has seen to it that I never forget that "I made him help saw wood" on Thanksgiving.

Our home was on a very deep lot. We had room for a good vegetable and flower garden which gave both Dorothy and me much pleasure. I also started a small orchard on the extreme back portion of the lot.

A number of the houses in our area had picket fences enclosing their front yards. I thought we should also have one. I therefore spent spare time during the summer building and painting a new fence. That was before the days of paint spray guns, so my painting was all done with a brush. I had plenty of sun exposure that summer.

Allan's Budding Interest in Science

Allan got himself a paper route and got plenty of use out of his bicycle. He spent more time, however, on following up on his interest in astronomy. He came back from Philadelphia with a small hand-held telescope and now wanted to get a larger one which would require some kind of mounting. He saved up paper route money to help buy a small but fairly good-sized telescope. The question then arose on how to establish an outside mounting. Should he buy or make his own mounting? I thought Allan's interest and aptitude were in science and that it would be good to get him to explore other sciences along with his astronomy. Getting a proper mounting for his telescope involved various aspects of physics. Allan accepted the challenge of developing his own mounting. He worked out the necessary weights for properly balancing and adjusting the telescope and succeeded in doing a superb job.

To introduce Allan to other areas of science we mutually built a small chemistry laboratory in the basement so he could experiment with chemistry. He devoted some time to that but continued to spend most of his time with astronomy. He got interested in plotting sun spots and would rush home at noon and go out and record spots on 3" X 5" cards and later developed the necessary statistics to measure changes over time. He also wanted to grind and polish a fairly large mirror which could later become a part of a complete telescope. Grinding and polishing a mirror is a very delicate process requiring a dust-proof area. Allan and I therefore took a corner of the laundry room in the basement and built a dust-proof cubicle. He developed a strong proprietary interest in that cubicle. He got a padlock and kept the door locked when he was not working on the mirror. That entire operation was great experience for him. The mirror was eventually finished but never incorporated in a telescope.

When Allan entered high school he wanted to go out for football. Neither Dorothy nor I were enthusiastic about that prospect but did not try to dissuade him. His coach was Weeb Eubanks who later became the head coach of a leading professional football team. Unfortunately or fortunately, Allan's "career" in football was dashed when early in his first season he broke his collarbone. He chose not to return to football after the break healed.

Adult Diversions

The Ping Pong table in the basement was used frequently. Dorothy developed no interest in the game, but Allan and I played often. Also, some of the faculty people came down for occasional games. I became fairly proficient and could hold my own in faculty competition. One time when my publisher visited the campus, he was invited to have lunch with us in our home. After lunch, I suggested that we might have a game of Ping Pong if he cared to play. He acquiesced and we retired to the basement to play. I soon recognized that I was completely out of my league. After two games, I had accumulated not more than four or five points per game. My publisher friend then informed me that he had been Illinois state champion at one time. This was a sobering but educational experience.

There was an episode associated with the new fireplace in my study that demonstrated my sometime tendency to dramatize a situation. I had an appointment with a colleague who was to come to my home study to go over some college matters. I had built a fire in the fireplace and thrown some chemicals on the logs to create various colors in the fireplace. They appeared at their most brilliant state when my colleague arrived. He expressed amazement at the colored flame and asked how that came about. On the spot I created a fictitious story. I commented that a well-known former professor of chemistry at Miami who had died a year or so earlier was a very research-minded individual. I stated that the professor had embedded various metallic shavings, such as copper and iron, in young trees to test the hypothesis that the tree would absorb these into the wood and create special color effects if and when the wood was used in fireplaces. I indicated that the professor had left instructions that when the trees he had so treated were cut down that at least part of the trees would be cut for use in fireplaces and the results of their use carefully noted by the user and reported to the chemistry department. I indicated that I had been fortunate enough to obtain a few pieces of the fireplace wood from these trees and would be filling out reports for the current researchers. I was somewhat astounded to note that my colleague was taking me seriously, but I had gone too far to make a correction so we got down to the business at hand. The next day when I went to the campus I was asked by several people about the professor's firewood. My colleague had passed the story along to others as real. He believed the whole thing. I was embarrassed.

Sharing Assets

The sharing of assets described here was entirely involuntary. They were purloined by others.

There were three incidents during the depression years in Oxford when I had personal items stolen from my office in Irvin Hall. The first theft was rather trivial—only a pen and pencil set on my office desk. Several months later my overcoat was stolen from my office. That occurred in early December when the weather was already winterish and when an overcoat was essential.

I was moved to report the latter theft in a short story published in the student newspaper.

> I have come up with a new method of measuring the growing depth of the economic Depression. Some months ago I had a pen and pencil set stolen from my office. Two days ago my overcoat was stolen. It seemed obvious that the pen and pencil set was not stolen because of economic need. The overcoat, however, is another matter. It must have been taken by someone who is in dire need of clothing that protects against the winter weather and without means to obtain appropriate clothing. I, too, am suffering from the Depression but I make this pledge to the individual who took my coat: If you can demonstrate a greater economic need than that which I have, I will make the coat a gift to you.

Two days later my overcoat was delivered to the men's restroom in Irvin Hall where I retrieved it. There was no note, but I assumed—and I think rightly—that the individual was guilt laden and that the newspaper article moved him to return the coat.

Another time at Oxford I had my wallet stolen. It was on a Saturday during a football game. I did not attend the game because our budget did not include that "luxury." A colleague and I decided to go to the gymnasium during the game and play some handball. I had changed my clothes and placed them in my locker, closed the door, but did not lock it. My wallet was left in my clothes. After the game and after getting dressed my wallet was gone. Obviously, someone had lifted it while we were playing handball. This was a real blow as I had planned to go uptown to pay utility and other bills with cash instead of with checks. Those bills remained unpaid for some time.

Years later, when I was on leave of absence to serve as visiting professor at Harvard, I had my wallet picked from my pocket in the Atlanta, Georgia, railroad station. I had spent two days in Atlanta interviewing advertising executives of business firms who were using radio as a means of advertising their products. Dorothy and Allan were still living in Oxford until Allan's school was out. I was boarding the train in Atlanta to go to Cincinnati where Dorothy was to meet me and I would then spend the weekend in Oxford. This was during the war years and rail traffic was extremely heavy. In boarding the train in Atlanta, the person behind me bumped my back with his suitcase. I thought nothing of it at the time. After getting on the train, I went to the lounge car to read the newspaper before going into the diner for dinner. When I was ready to go in for something to eat, I reached for my wallet and it was not there. I had the total sum of sixty-nine cents in change in my pocket, certainly not enough for an evening meal. Hence, I went on a "fast" until I arrived in Cincinnati the next morning. Fortunately, Dorothy had enough money on her so that we could have a good breakfast before driving on to Oxford.

Our Life during Temporary Assignments

We lived in our new home from 1938 until 1943 when we moved to Boston. We rented to others until the spring of 1944 when we returned to reoccupy the place. Our stay in our home in Oxford was again shortened because of the job I had taken in Chicago. I traveled to Chicago on July 4, 1944, to start work in my new job on July 5 and to seek a place to live. Allan had enlisted in the Navy, hence was not at home, and Dorothy was to stay in Oxford until I found a place in Chicago. Finding such a place was not an easy task.

I found temporary quarters in a small room in the Allerton Hotel but was informed that I could have the room only until the national political nominating convention would open in Chicago. I had called every conceivable apartment rental agency in Chicago and was informed they would put my name on a waiting list but that the prospects of finding anything were meager. I therefore spent my evenings visiting apartment buildings and asking the person on the desk if there were any apartments for rent.

The first week of such effort resulted in drawing a blank at each apartment building. Later, however, when I had gone through the routine at an apartment building and was told that there was nothing available, the elevator operator stopped me and said she had heard me say that I was looking for an apartment. She said she would take me to the twelfth floor because somebody was moving out the next week but she could not tell me the name. She took me to the twelfth floor and let me off, and I was on my own.

I went to the apartment door and knocked. A voice from within the apartment asked who was there. I had not thought that far along and I was stumbling along trying to answer when the voice again asked who was it. I said "You do not know who I am, but I am looking for an apartment to rent." The lady opened the door and I told her my problem and she invited me in to talk about a sublease. The elevator operator had told me that the occupant was leaving within two or three days and that this had apparently been a fairly recent decision.

This turned out to be correct as the lady indicated she was leaving for a short stay in Mexico and she could let me have the apartment within the next four or five days. I signed a lease on the spot without a specific expiration date. It was agreed that if she needed the apartment I would vacate on one week's notice and that I could cancel my lease with the same short one week's notice. I moved in that weekend.

I had not inspected the apartment very carefully, but recognized that it was fully furnished, that it had white shag carpeting, and appeared to provide comfortable temporary living facilities. I was amazed, however, when I actually moved in to find that no attempt had been made to clean or prepare the apartment for a new occupant. Unused food was still in the refrigerator, the bed was unmade, and the white shag rug was extremely dirty. All of this was very much out of harmony with the basic quality of the apartment house, which was located in Near North Chicago four blocks away from the Drake Hotel.

I now had a place which would permit Dorothy to join me. I did not want her to come, however, until I had the apartment completely cleaned and respectable for family occupancy. I got some help to do that, but did most of it myself using several cans of Glamorene to clean the carpeting.

I now started seeking permanent housing and finally succeeded in getting a furnished house that would be available the first of September. This was located eight blocks north and three blocks west of the Edgewater Beach Hotel.

The location of our new residence was ideal considering the transportation problems during the war. I used my automobile very little. I could walk three blocks to a bus stop which picked up passengers for the eight blocks to the Edgewater Beach. There was an express bus from there to the Wrigley Building on North Michigan Avenue where I had my office. The Wrigley Building was the point of origin for the return bus after work. It likewise was an express to the Edgewater Beach. Two blocks west of our house was the Chicago Transit Electric Line. I could also use that, which was partly surface and partly subway, but it was not as convenient as the bus that took me directly to my office. Dorothy, however, used the Electric Line often when she would go downtown to shop or to concerts at the University of Chicago campus since the line carried on south of the Loop to the university.

We were fortunate to have university families whom we knew who provided us with interesting social companionship. We had a pleasant year in Chicago, but the pull of university life was irresistible and we returned to our home in Oxford in the spring of 1945 so that I could fulfill a one-year obligation to Miami before moving on to another university.

Selling Our Oxford Home

It was not long afterward that I accepted the position at the University of Illinois and thus we would be leaving Oxford permanently. That meant our home would be for sale. I was in a quandary to know what would be a legitimate price to ask a potential buyer. The war had brought substantial inflation so it was obvious that the price in 1946 should be higher than our 1937-38 cost. I tried to use a research approach in arriving at a figure. I took the government figures on changes in the cost of living and particular components such as building materials and wages. I took the original cost, subtracted a figure for depreciation, applied the inflation percentage, and arrived at what I considered to be a reasonable price to ask a potential buyer. I then ran an advertisement in the paper. Two days later, a professor called and asked to see the house. After his thorough inspection, he asked what the price would be. I told him how I had arrived at an asking price and quoted it to him. He said, "I'll take it." Three days later a party from Hamilton, fourteen miles away, called and offered to pay 22 percent more than I had asked the professor. Obviously, that offer was rejected because I had already agreed to sell at the lower price. We moved to Urbana, Illinois, in the summer of 1946.

From the 1922-23 Graceland College *Record-Acacia:*

Charles H. Sandage

Business Manager

"Sandy" has the wonderful talent of being able to make friends and collect money. And what is still more wonderful, he has the faculty of being able to keep both. A Business Manager with these two attributes needs no other recommendation. He is a hard worker and has helped materially in making our publication possible.

Charles H. Sandage   Lamoni, Iowa
    Niketes
    Lambda Delta Sigma
    Business Manager Record-Acacia.
  "Then he will talk—good gods! how he will talk."

Graceland Junior College graduates "Sandy" Sandage (left) and his friend, Bill Ely, during the summer of 1923 before leaving Lamoni, Iowa, for his first teaching assignment in Dunlap, Illinois.

191

A Ford roadster (below right) was Sandy's first automobile, pictured here in 1925. A year later, in July 1926, Sandy and Dorothy Sandage (above) proudly show off their infant son, Allan. Two-year-old Allan inspects flower gardens (below left) in Lawrence, Kansas, with his father during Sandy's tenure at the University of Kansas.

A deep-sea fishing trip off the coast of Maine in 1936 netted quite a catch for the Sandage family and friends (above). In June 1937 during a summer sabbatical at a New Hampshire farmhouse (left), Sandy sported a nine-day growth of beard for this snapshot with Dorothy.

During his years at Miami University in Oxford, Ohio, Sandy envisioned the destruction of forty acres of woodlands for an airport as a marketing challenge, which provided firewood to anyone willing to chop it down and cut it themselves.

Whether working in his home library (above) with his ever-present pipe or with a group of advertising students in a graduate seminar (below), Professor C. H. Sandage placed tremendous value on education and the teaching profession.

Sandy congratulated Allan on his induction into Phi Beta Kappa in 1948.

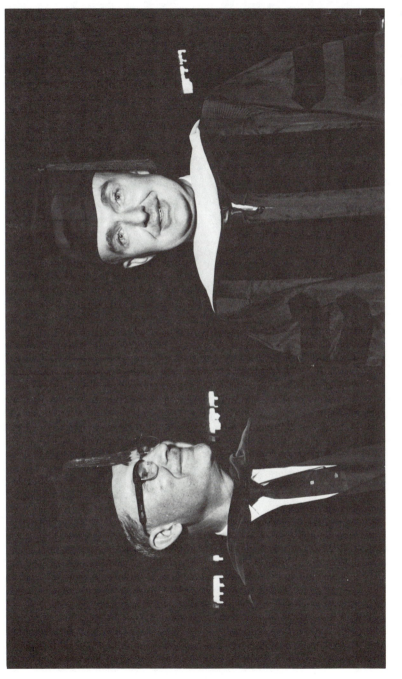

An obviously proud father, Professor C. H. Sandage placed the cowl around Allan's neck during a University of Illinois ceremony when Allan received an honorary doctorate.

197

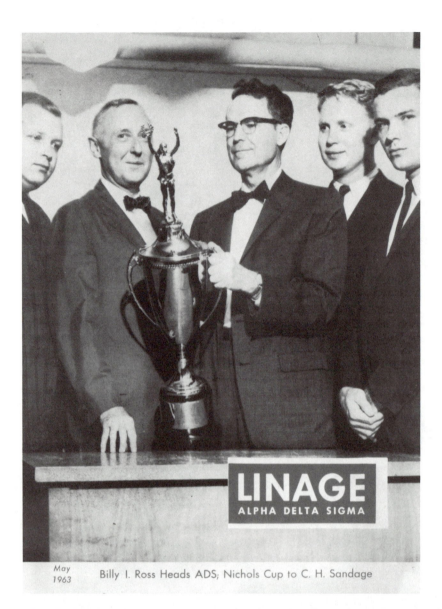

May 1963   Billy I. Ross Heads ADS; Nichols Cup to C. H. Sandage

Alpha Delta Sigma, the national professional advertising fraternity, awarded Professor C. H. Sandage its Nichols Cup in 1963 at its convention in New York City for "outstanding service to advertising education."

In June 1965 at the annual convention of the Advertising Federation of America in Boston, Professor Sandage addressed the prestigious gathering (above) after receiving the AFA Gold Medal (below) for his achievements in advertising education.

The University of Illinois honored Professor Sandage at his retirement in May 1968 at Allerton House (above) with a major symposium, "Frontiers of Advertising Theory and Research." Dr. Sandage addressed the gathering of leading national advertising figures.

During his "emeritus" years, Dr. Sandage received minor fame in regard to a stop sign in his neighborhood (left). Graceland College honored him (below) with an honorary doctorate.

Induction into the American Advertising Federation's "Hall of Fame" in March 1985 at New York City's Waldorf Astoria Grand Ballroom brought appreciative smiles from Professor Sandage (above, right) and his fellow inductees, Thomas Adams and James Fish. Later (below), Sandy and his second wife, Elizabeth, admire the certificate.

Drs. Charles H. and Elizabeth Danner Sandage

PART IV
UNIVERSITY OF
ILLINOIS, URBANA

Chapter 9

Getting Established in Urbana

The housing situation in the spring of 1946 was extremely tight. Little or no home building had been done during the war, and the return of service personnel to civilian living created much pressure. It therefore seemed appropriate to start early to find housing in Urbana so that we might be settled there in time for the opening of the university in September.

We spent a weekend in Urbana in the early spring to look for houses to buy or rent, and we traveled the outskirts of the community to see if there might be one, two, or three acres that could be purchased and permit building our own home. We were in the hands of a good real estate agent, but he could show nothing that was at all adequate. On our second day of searching, however, the agent said there was a lot that just came on the market that might interest us. It was one of eight one-acre lots in a small ten-acre development. Three houses had already been built, but this was the only one of the remaining lots available for purchase. We did buy the lot and thought if necessary we would build a large garage and live in it until the house was completed. That, however, became unnecessary when a large, furnished house close to the university campus became available to rent. We signed a lease for that house to run for at least nine months and possibly later if the owner, who was on leave of absence from the

205

university, was not ready to return at the end of nine months.

Our rented house was available the first of June, and we planned to move in about that time even though it was three or more months until school started. We would have to store most of our own furniture until we built the house on the lot we had purchased, although we were able to have some of our own things in the house we were renting. We engaged a trucking firm to transport all of our things from Oxford but had items divided into three groups: (1) things that we would have in our rented place; (2) things that would be put in public storage; and (3) items that would be delivered to my office at the university. The trucking people were instructed to load items so that it would be easy to deliver them expeditiously.

The trucking firm could not give an exact date when they would pick up our things in Oxford or when they would be delivered in Urbana. I had agreed to attend a meeting in Illinois and give a talk in June and had expected that we would have moved before the time of that meeting. Unfortunately, we were informed by the trucking company that they would not be able to move us until about the time of the meeting and would not give us a specific date but that they would arrive sometime within a span of four days. It therefore seemed necessary for me to go to Illinois alone to attend the meeting and Dorothy stay on in Oxford to await the arrival of the moving van. The trucking people gave us a schedule sometime between a Thursday and Monday and stated that there was a possibility they would arrive in Urbana on a Saturday or Sunday.

Fortunately, I would be free to accept the truckers anytime during that period. I learned, however, that it would be necessary to pay the truckers before they would unload the furniture, that they would not accept checks, and that they must have cash. The total trucking cost would be much greater than any cash I would have on hand so I needed to select a local bank, open an account, and withdraw $400 or $500 in cash.

The closest bank to where I would be living was the Busey National Bank. I went to the bank, indicated my wish to open a checking account, and was turned over to one of the officers. I was able to write a substantial check for deposit because of the sale of our Oxford home, but indicated to the officer that I needed $400 in cash. I also said I recognized that in many respects this would be a loan since it would take a few days for my Oxford check to be cleared. The officer demurred and said how did he know I had any money in the Oxford bank. I had already explained that I was to be a professor at the university and had given him substantial identification. The officer's reaction disturbed me to the point were I thanked him with obvious disgust in my voice, stating that we were planning to make Urbana our home, that we had even purchased a lot in south Urbana. The officer immediately changed his expression and said, "Oh, you have property. That's different." But I left that bank and went to the First National Bank in Champaign. The officer there was most cordial, was satisfied with a minimum listing of credentials, accepted my deposit, and let me withdraw $400 in cash. That became our bank for many years.

Moving Frozen Food from Oxford

Moving more than 200 miles in changing permanent residence involved more than transferring furniture from one house to another. In this case, it also involved transferring perishable food.

Remember that this move was made in 1946 after a long war and rationing of many food items, especially meat. In 1946 there were few, if any, home freezers for the storage of perishables. Instead, the more common method was frozen food lockers located within the community, operated on a rental basis as a service business. We had such a locker in Oxford and it contained some precious meat. It was my plan to rent a locker in Urbana, pack the Oxford locker's contents in our automobile with dry ice, and place it in an Urbana locker after the 200-mile trip. Unfortunately, there was no locker space available anywhere in Urbana or Champaign. I put my name on a waiting list to get a locker but needed a temporary storage place until such space was available. I knew that the College of Agriculture at the University of Illinois had a sales operation and freezer facilities but, of course, none for rent. I could not resign myself to losing our precious cache, so I went to Professor Bull, who was head of the meat department in the university sales division. I explained my dilemma pointing out that I was to be a new full professor and would it be possible for him to find space to preserve our Oxford perishables until we could obtain a locker downtown. He agreed to do that and that problem was solved.

Building Our New House

We soon commissioned an architect to start planning a house that we could build on our new lot. Plans were completed by late fall and a local contractor was engaged. He was to start work as early in the spring as weather would permit. He indicated that he would have us in our new house by the first of September. He did not anticipate difficulties in obtaining materials. We were not to get into our new house until October. It would have been later than that had I not been able to help in getting supplies delivered. There was no plasterboard available in Champaign-Urbana at the time it was needed. I called the firm in Oxford that had supplied materials for our Oxford home, found that they had plasterboard and would let us have enough for the Urbana house. Our contractor then sent a truck to Oxford to pick up the necessary material.

The architect had specified Anderson windows for the house. The local Anderson dealer had indicated that the windows would be delivered in time to put in place as soon as the carpenters were ready, but they did not come as promised. Both the architect and the builder pressured the supplier but to no avail. I called the factory in Minnesota and found that the window frames were already manufactured but the windows were not finished and they wanted to ship both at the same time. Actually, if the builder had the window frames he could install these and plastering could be done even though there were no windows in the frames. The manufacturer was persuaded to ship the frames immediately and send the windows at a later date.

Sometime in the spring of 1947, our landlord, who was on leave of absence, wrote and indicated his intention to return to Urbana and wanted us out by June 15. We found the house of a public school teacher who would be away for the summer, so we moved from one house to another for that period. We obviously had to be out of the second house by early September when the public schools opened. Unfortunately our new house was not yet ready. We found a couple who had an apartment who were to be away during the month of September. They let us have their place until the first of October at which time we were able to move into our almost completed new house. We then began to feel that we could settle down and start living a normal life.

Allan

Allan was mustered out of the Navy in August 1946 after almost exactly eighteen months. He had enlisted as a seaman in a special electronics program after he had passed the necessary examinations to qualify for that program. He had previously qualified for all of the requirements for the Naval ROTC program at Miami University except the physical examination. He was sent to Cincinnati to take his physical and was rejected because he had flat feet. Apparently the Navy could never tolerate a flat-footed officer but that was not a qualifying factor for a seaman.

A tour of duty in the Navy moved him from the Great Lakes to Biloxi, Mississippi, to Treasure Island and San Diego. His work in electronics, radio, and various aspects of communication was educational even though quite different from the academic offerings in a university, which he had enjoyed very much. He was, therefore, ready to return to a university campus when he got out of the Navy. He was indeed fortunate to be mustered out at a time when he could almost immediately register for the fall semester. The question then arose as to whether he should return to Miami University where he had finished two years of college work or apply for admission to the University of Illinois and live at home since we had moved to Urbana. This was not an easy decision for him to make. As parents who had been deprived of his presence for eighteen months, we had looked forward to having him with us again. We could try to persuade him to transfer to the University of Illinois, but we believed it was very important to leave the decision to him. He was counseled to consider such factors as the quality of instruction, social environment, and pros and cons of living at home. It was rather clear that he would be majoring in physics or mathematics because those were the areas that would be most valuable to his interest in astronomy.

There was also some astronomy offered at Illinois. How much of a factor that was in Allan's final decision I do not know, but he did decide to transfer to Illinois and live at home. He was therefore involved in our somewhat nomadic living his first year, the progress in the building of our new house, and helping convert it into a home. Upon his graduation from the University of Illinois he was elected to Phi Beta Kappa and had his name engraved on the Bronze Tablet. He had decided to go to graduate school to major in astronomy and made applications to the University of Chicago (with its Yerkes Observatory), Harvard University, and the California Institute of Technology. He was accepted at all three schools and offered fellowships or graduate assistantships at each. He chose Cal Tech primarily because the school had a newly established department of astrophysics and also because it would be the home of the Palomar Observatory with its 200-inch mirror.

Allan eventually received his Ph.D. degree from Cal Tech and an appointment as a research astronomer with the Hale Observatories. He divided his observational time among the observatory on Mt. Wilson, the one at Palomar, and a new one in Chile which he had a major hand in developing. He spent one year at the observatory in Canberra, Australia, and lesser time in

South Africa and England. His research work in astronomy was eventually recognized by having many honors bestowed on him, the most recent (1991) and most prestigious, the coveted Crafoord prize, which is the equivalent of the Nobel prize, and is administered by the Swedish Royal Academy of Science. Others included the gold medal of the Royal Astronomical Society, Rittenhouse medal, Pope Pius XI gold medal of the Pontifical Academy of Science, and the U.S. National Medal of Science. He was the Fulbright-Hayes scholar in 1972 and has been awarded many other prizes and medals. In addition he received honorary doctorate degrees from Yale, University of Chicago, University of Illinois, University of Southern California, Miami University, and Graceland College.

Chapter 10

Evolution of Advertising Education at the University of Illinois

My challenge at Illinois was to develop a program in advertising education that would be recognized as a worthy member of the university family of individual intellectual disciplines. I had cut my eyeteeth on the subject at Miami University and sharpened my interest in applying research to test the impact of various aspects of advertising on business and society.

My first task was to build a unified curriculum and faculty. It was recognized that any curriculum should emerge from an underlying philosophy that tied individual courses together to provide a cohesive structure.

The University of Illinois had been offering courses in various aspects of advertising for a number of years. Some courses were offered in the College of Commerce and others in the School of Journalism. There was some interaction between the college and the school in their respective advertising offerings only in the case of one course, that being the basic, "Introduction to Advertising." That course was cross-listed with a general understanding that one-half of the sections offered would be taught by Commerce faculty and one-half by Journalism faculty. The director of the School of Journalism believed that a closer coordination of work in the two units would be beneficial. I was employed to try to bring about that coordination. I, therefore, had a joint appointment, which thus gave me faculty status in both Commerce and Journalism.

There was no legislative approach toward coordination and such would not have been appropriate at that early stage. I approached the problem on the basis of voluntary cooperation. I brought together as a group all individuals who were teaching any courses in advertising in either Journalism or Commerce. We had more or less regular meetings to discuss the basic nature of advertising not only as a tool of business but also as a significant part of our economic and social structure. We raised questions as to whether it could or should be viewed as an area of inquiry worthy of having classification as an academic discipline. In other words, did it or should it have a philosophical, economic, and social base on which to build a worthy and effective advertising curriculum?

The division of courses between the two academic units tended to fractionate rather than unify the area. Courses dealing with the creation of advertisements and the selection of media for distributing them were housed in Journalism, and courses dealing more with management housed in Commerce.

It was our objective to have those who were teaching advertising become a cohesive group dedicated to focus their scholarship on understanding, evaluating, and communicating the many-faceted aspects of advertising. The attention I had given to the study and evaluation of advertising during my Miami years led me to recognize its institutional aspects as well as its professional aspects. I used architecture as an example to guide us in the development of a curriculum for students who wished to major in advertising. The architect first considers the function his structure is supposed to serve. He develops complete plans and blueprints to guide the masons, carpenters, and bricklayers in building the structure. The professor of architecture places major emphasis on concepts, function, and purpose but does not ignore the importance of the strategy of putting a building together and the kinds of workmen needed to build the complete edifice. In similar fashion, professors of advertising might well give substantial attention to the functions which society has assigned to or expected individuals to perform.

From a societal point of view, the overriding function seemed to view advertising as the institution of abundance. High-level employment would seem to be a goal of society in order to provide consumers with purchasing power. High-level employment, however, could not be sustained without high-level consumption. Advertising would be a potent force in bringing that about. It would do this by calling the attention of consumers to the existence of want-satisfying products and using persuasive messages directed to consumers.

We did not depend entirely on members of the advertising teaching staff for curriculum ideas. We thought that it might be helpful to solicit input from practitioners. I therefore organized a two-day "retreat" to be attended by carefully selected practitioners and all of our advertising faculty. Practitioners invited included a representative from a Chicago department store, a national advertiser, a newspaper executive, a broadcast executive, a research director of a consumer goods manufacturer, an advertising agency, and the advertising press. The meeting was held at Allerton Park, guaranteeing isolation and concentration on discussing advertising curriculum matters. Each practitioner had to be alerted well ahead of time concerning the purpose of the meeting. Each was urged to come prepared to discuss the functions being performed by the advertising in his company and what he sought in advertising personnel they hired.

We had tape recorders in our meetings and participants knew that their comments were being recorded. We promised to send them a manuscript of all proceedings at a later date.

In some respects our two-day "retreat" was a fiasco and in other respects it was a huge success. In general, the practitioners had not done their homework. They chose to devote most of their comments to what they thought we ought to be teaching and very little to their own operation. We eventually sent each participant a copy of the transcribed tapes, asked their reaction, and whether they would recommend that we publish the results in some form. The response was interesting. Most expressed wonderment and chagrin at what they had said. We were urged not to publish the results.

The results of the retreat would seem to have provided little or no help to the advertising faculty. In reality, it provided great help. It dramatized the fact that curriculum building was the responsibility of professional educators. In general, practitioners had a very narrow view of advertising education. Their thinking was primarily at the level of advertisements, their creation and placement, with little or no attention to the economic, social, and institutional aspects of advertising. We had to conclude that we must develop a curriculum that we believed to be important and then try to get it approved by our colleagues in Journalism and Commerce.

The curriculum we eventually developed was composed of specific advertising courses and a number of nonadvertising courses designed to broaden the horizons of the advertising student. Some of the strictly skills courses tangential to advertising but required of advertising majors were eliminated as requirements but left as electives. Other more general courses to be taught by the advertising professors were added and included these courses: "Consumer Behavior," "Advertising Research Methods," "Media Strategy," "Campaigns," and "Advertising in Contemporary Society." Courses not carrying an advertising label included as requirements were in the areas of psychology, statistics, market research, economics, and journalism. The recommended curriculum was to provide a major or area of concentration for students whether in Journalism or Commerce. All advertising courses were thus to be cross-listed.

There were parts of our recommended curriculum that disturbed faculty members both in Journalism and Commerce. The Journalism faculty questioned the suggested removal of some skills courses from the required list and were skeptical about adding nonadvertising courses such as marketing and statistics. Over time these objections were overcome. Help came when a new book by Clyde Bedell titled *Let's Talk Retailing* was published. I had it circulated among Journalism faculty members who had objected to reducing the number of journalism courses required. The point our advertising faculty members were trying to get across was that an advertising practitioner needed to know a lot about the functions and work of those for whom advertisements were to be created. Thus, how could someone who wanted to join the advertising department of a retail store hope to be effective if he did not know a lot about retailing. The Commerce faculty chose to shrink and modify our recommended curriculum but include a segment of it as a part of its marketing major. This resulted, however, in having the major focus of advertising education centered in the School of Journalism.

Graduate Program in Advertising

A graduate program in advertising was introduced in the School of Journalism the fall that I arrived on the campus. Graduate work had been approved for various areas in the School of Journalism before the fall of 1946, but there was no advertising faculty member who had Graduate College status. My appointment included membership in the Graduate College faculty.

The development of the graduate curriculum for advertising students was worked on at the same time that we were developing an undergraduate curriculum. Some of the senior advertising courses such as "Media," "Creative," "Campaigns," and "Advertising in Contemporary Society" carried graduate credit if the student had appropriate prerequisites. If such students had not had the appropriate prerequisites, they would be required to take those before or concurrent with some of the graduate courses. We added two major courses open to graduate students only. They were "Advanced Principles in Advertising" and "Advertising Research Methods." We also required the student to design and implement a research project culminating in a thesis to be approved by the advertising faculty.

The first master's student in advertising was Harry Gray. He was an older student newly mustered out of the army and had reentered the university, from which he had received a bachelor's degree, to work for a master's degree. He chose as his research project a study of the student market. The objective was to provide the college newspaper with factual data concerning the size and character of student purchases. Such information should be very valuable in informing business firms of the kind of market that could be delivered by the college paper. That first advertising graduate student set a high standard and excellent example for the many graduate students who were to come into the program.

Eventually advertising students could obtain a Ph.D. degree in communications with advertising being the area in which their research for the dissertation would be done. This Ph.D. program was a part of an interdisciplinary program under the auspices of the College of Communications. The School of Journalism was the immediate ancestor of the College of Communications, but advertising had a significant influence on that evolution.

Members of the advertising faculty felt that the term "journalism" described an area of study separate and different from the area of advertising. Effort, therefore, was applied to getting a broader umbrella-type word for the school or college name. Thus the name "College of Communications" came about with advertising, journalism, and broadcasting as separate areas of concentration and later departments, each having equal status under the word "communications."

The interdepartmental doctoral program attracted over the years many candidates with major interest in advertising. Their doctoral dissertations made substantial contributions to a greater understanding of the social and economic aspects of advertising and added to the literature in the field. There was great demand for such graduates by other universities who were developing academically oriented programs in advertising. The Illinois philosophy of advertising education was thus exported throughout the United States and to some foreign countries.

Working with Practitioners

Attempts were made to involve members of the advertising industry in the advertising education program at the University of Illinois. The initial attempt in such involvement was the "retreat" held at Allerton House. That effort ended in disappointment but we looked ahead with hope for an opportunity to approach involvement in some other way. That opportunity presented itself in 1951. This came about through an article in *Advertising Age* authored by Earle Ludgin, head of a leading advertising agency in Chicago. The article reported on a speech he had made in which he severely criticized the nature of advertising education in our universities. The Ludgin article gave me the opportunity to present the Illinois philosophy of advertising education and to challenge members of the advertising industry to cooperate in furthering that kind of education. A copy of my reply as printed in *Advertising Age* is given here.*

Ludgin Comments on Advertising Education Challenged by University Spokesman

Appearance in these columns October 8 of a speech by Earle Ludgin, president of the Chicago advertising agency of that name, detailing what happened when his son decided to seek a job in advertising, has created an unusual amount of discussion in advertising and aca-

---

*"Ludgin Comments on Advertising Education Challenged by University Spokesman," *Advertising Age* (November 12, 1951).

demic circles, much of which has been mirrored in the Voice of the Advertiser columns of *Advertising Age*. The following piece, which was also addressed to that department, is presented here because it raises many questions about advertising education, and presents some thoughtful arguments for cooperation, which will be of interest to all advertising people.

By C. H. Sandage
Chairman, Division of Advertising
University of Illinois

Earle Ludgin's research into the advertising training programs in American universities, which appeared in these pages October 8, was not worthy of the head of a highly respected advertising agency. It would appear from the *AA* story that Mr. Ludgin made his evaluation of the advertising in our universities on the basis of a casual examination of one textbook. Surely he would not recommend that kind of research to a client of his who wanted an advertising campaign built upon fact rather than hunch.

But perhaps Mr. Ludgin's purpose in speaking as he did was primarily to arouse the interest and thinking of both advertising practitioners and educators concerning the importance of sound, professional training for future advertising men and women. If that was his purpose, then I believe that he will find, if he delves more carefully into the subject, that many universities are doing a far better job of teaching advertising than his personal experience has indicated.

While the number, type and content of advertising courses in our colleges and universities vary widely, I am convinced that all good schools aim at one fundamental objective with their advertising students: To develop well-rounded individuals with a sound, basic education and some specialized knowledge of advertising methods and practices, rather than to turn out advertising technicians or specialists.

Let me cite the educational program at the University of Illinois as reasonably typical, although of course there are variations from school to school. Illinois provides a "major" in advertising for students who wish to make advertising their career. This major is elected primarily by students registered in either the college of commerce or the school of journalism and communications. Election of this major is made at the beginning of the junior year. By that time most students have had work in economics, psychology, sociology, political science, English and history. Some have had work in accounting, physical science, agriculture, home economics, and fine arts. Additional courses in these fields can also be taken during the student's junior and senior years.

The amount of time which the advertising student will devote to specific courses in advertising will average about one semester of work out of eight. It is not the purpose to turn out a narrowly trained person, but rather to provide students with a fundamental understanding of the economic and social order in which they live, cultivate their powers of analysis, assist them in developing systematic methods for solving problems, and equip them with enough technical knowledge in their chosen field to permit them to become effective apprentices or interns in the advertising industry. With such a combination it is believed that graduates will enter the field of advertising with the philosophy of a professional person and contribute to the material progress of their chosen field. Of course the advertising program places some emphasis on the techniques employed in the advertising business, but always with the purpose of those techniques in mind. They are means to an end, not an end in themselves.

Specific instruction in advertising is built around a core of five courses, with three other courses which may be elected by the student but are not required. In addition to these specific courses in advertising, all students must have certain courses in economics and marketing to meet the requirement for graduation.

A careful analysis of the content of each of these courses would indicate that they meet the specifications suggested by Mr. Ludgin for a balanced program of instruction.

Qualifications for Teaching

The quality of the faculty to teach courses in advertising is as important as the courses themselves. We believe we have at Illinois an advertising staff that is eminently qualified to practice the fine art and science of teaching advertising, and that other good schools can make the same statement without qualification. Teaching is a profession and requires professional talents. It is vital that advertising teachers know their subject matter, but it is equally vital that they know how to communicate with students and to stimulate student imagination and powers of analysis.

The Illinois faculty—like all other good faculties—has had experience, but not so much experience of one narrow type as to dull or kill their sense of perspective and objectivity. They continually seek to keep informed of current developments and, through attendance at conventions, inspection of current plant practice, and personal conferences with leading practitioners, keep their finger on the pulse of the industry.

There are ten members of our advertising staff, and all of them have had good formal training which qualifies them for the profession of teaching. In addition, every one of them has had practical experience in advertising or closely related fields. It is also interesting to note that in the past three years three of our men have served summer internships with leading newspapers under the program sponsored by the Newspaper Advertising Executives Association. A large number of books, bulletins and magazine articles have been produced by members of this staff. Several, also, are frequently called upon by the advertising industry to serve as professional consultants.

The cry of Mr. Ludgin and others for more practical experience for teachers is perhaps unrealistic. Advertising agency personnel specialize in telling manufacturers and retailers how to operate a part of their business.

Not many agency men have had years of recent experience in the manufacturing or retailing businesses whom they serve. Instead of considering that a handicap, agency men rightfully list it as an advantage, since they can offer a more realistic and effective kind of service when they operate with the perspective which the detached position of an independent counselor provides. The teacher of advertising should be no less an independent functionary than is the agency practitioner.

A Chance to Help

Advertising practitioners, however, can help improve the present high standards of teaching in our leading colleges and universities. This can be done, not so much by making part-time or "hobby" teachers of advertising men, as by developing an organized method whereby teachers can spend several of their summer weeks in actual work residence in advertising offices. Newspapers, as we have indicated, are already doing this; others might follow their lead.

Schools can also invite practitioners to the campus for staff seminars and talks with students, and many do. At Illinois for example, we inaugurated an organized program of that sort last year. The Illinois course in "Current Advertising Developments" is limited to, but required of, all advertising majors during their last semester in residence. That course meets 16 times during a semester and from 12 to 14 of those meetings consist in having leading advertising practitioners explain their own advertising operations.

Some speakers believe that they should give the students a complete advertising education in 50 minutes, but we are generally successful in getting speakers to talk about their own specific operations. Mr. Ludgin has a standing invitation to serve as one of those speakers.

Furthermore, the University of Illinois will be delighted to serve as host to any group who will sit down and study the program of education for advertising seriously. One such meeting has already been held at Illinois. This is an open invitation for practitioners to initiate another and to invite educators to meet with them.

Pleads for Realism

In our thinking about advertising education let us be realistic and modern. Let us not judge current education programs from the perspective of our office chair, the cursory examination of a beginning survey textbook, or the status of advertising education when current senior practitioners were college students. Teaching, like advertising, is dynamic and changes, too.

And while we are speaking of realism, does Mr. Ludgin honestly believe that we should studiously avoid bringing to the attention of modern students of advertising any references to untruthful and exaggerated advertising that are made in editorials in *Advertising Age*, *Tide*, *Printers' Ink*, and *Advertising Agency*, the speeches of Fairfax Cone at Four A's conventions, the actions of leading newspapers, and the work of advertising organizations? Would he not prefer that such students be trained to assume the responsibilities suggested in the codes of the profession and be ready to recognize and help "unfrock" the charlatan and quack?

Close to 100 students of advertising will be graduated from the University of Illinois next June. These men and women will be seeking employment with retail stores, various advertising media, manufacturing concerns, agencies, and service institutions. Current practitioners can give further help to college and university training in advertising by accepting such fine young men and women as interns for the final polish required before they are ready for full membership in the profession. The record of many of our former advertising graduates will attest to their good training and superior worth. And certainly other schools can say the same.

Earle Ludgin accepted the challenge to come to the university and speak to our advertising students. He became an avid supporter of our program.

Other activities developed from the *Advertising Age* article and Ludgin's visit to the campus. We worked out a program with the Central Region of the American Association of Advertising Agencies (AAAA or "4 A's")—a two-way relationship. Advertising agencies would make available to any university a three-member team to visit the campus for a day and evening. A number of universities accepted their offer. In our program at the University of Illinois, the agency team listened to and evaluated student presentations of some of their work. The team in turn presented to students a review of the development and execution of a complete campaign for one of the agency's clients. The visit was topped off with a meeting with all the members of the advertising faculty at a dinner and post-dinner seminar in which practitioners and faculty exchanged views, critiques, and suggestions for various aspects of advertising education. Advertising agencies not only provided teams to visit campuses but also provided summer internships to young advertising faculty members who might be short in field experience. In addition, the Central Region of the Four-A's invited advertising educators in their region to attend their regional conventions.

The team operation as provided by advertising agencies was not the only use we made of outside speakers. We not only brought to campus individual advertising men and women but also academic and consumer critics. For example, we had people like Colston Warne, president of Consumer Union, and Esther Peterson, the U.S. government's full-time consumer advocate. We attempted in all cases to provide our students with all aspects of advertising—good, bad, and indifferent. We never lost sight of the basic function of advertising and its potential, if not actual, role to serve as a consumer benefactor. I took the opportunity to present the consumer benefactor element to practitioners whenever possible. I was included in a meeting of practitioners one year when speakers were criticizing the consumer movement and its presumed anti-advertising bias. I suggested that in many respects advertisers and advertising agencies were basically consumerists. Their function was to help consumers maximize their satisfactions. They were to call the attention of consumers to products and services that would meet a need or help solve a problem. They should have grasped the opportunity to spearhead and help shape the direction in which the consumer movement might go. While it might be a little late, they still would find it appropriate to get on the side of the angels and support the basic concepts of the consumer movement.

Visits of practitioners to the University of Illinois campus eventually provided not only moral and intellectual support, but also financial contributions.

Philosophy of Advertising Education

The new relationship with the Central Region of the 4-A's brought an invitation for me to speak at one of their annual meetings. I used that opportunity to present the philosophy of advertising education as we were developing it at the University of Illinois. The essence of that speech was later printed in the *Journalism Quarterly*. It is reproduced here because many people reported that it had a significant influence on introducing changes in the approach to advertising education in many universities.

A Philosophy of Advertising Education

There are today many teachers of advertising in American colleges and universities. Some have been teaching advertising courses a long time while others are relative newcomers. There has, however, been little exchange among us on matters dealing with basic educational philosophy as related to either specific advertising courses or a full curriculum in advertising.

My own philosophy of education in the field of advertising is to minimize strictly skills courses and to place more emphasis on the "why" of advertising in its business and social environment.

Advertising is a broad field. It is concerned with people, their motivations and satisfactions. It is concerned with products and how to get them distributed with benefit to both the seller and buyer. It is concerned with the dissemination of ideas that are not necessarily product oriented. It is concerned with broad economic matters such as full employment, high level consumption and human standards of living. It is concerned with communications—the art of translating the language of business into the language of the consumer. It is concerned with the organized message carriers. It is concerned with research and progress toward reducing still further the areas of ignorance that surround our field.

Advertising is also concerned with skills, but only as those skills contribute to the solution of problems and the furtherance of broad-gauge objectives. The practitioner who concentrates on skills only and forgets the basic purpose of his creation is apt to be merely an artisan and not one who can or will contribute much to the progress and growth of the profession of advertising. He is more like the bricklayer than the engineer.

A university should be concerned with training future leaders. This cannot be done if we become preoccupied with training youths for their first jobs. Emphasis should always be placed on teaching the student rather than teaching a course or subject.

If we place emphasis on teaching the student, we will attempt to sharpen his ability to think and to solve problems. We will look upon thinking as an instrument of action and a basic tool for solving problems.

If we are good educators I believe we will follow the practice of the good creative advertising practitioner. We will seek to determine the real needs and wants of our students, and key our educational curriculum to the intellectual and emotional raw material which these students bring to us. We will not be misled by surface wants of students but rather seek to minister to basic needs and desires.

Our students will react to one appeal more than to another. The self-interest appeal is perhaps the most potent of all in moving one to act. Advertisers spend a great deal of time and money in research and observation to determine what their consumers want most. They then translate the merits of their products in terms of that want. Universities might well do the same thing and utilize the power of self-interest in motivating students in their search for knowledge and understanding.

Many universities during the past two or three decades have had a large number of young men and women come to them and say that what they want most is an education to prepare them for a career in advertising. Some universities have said to those students, "We have no curriculum in advertising, but you should not take work in advertising anyway. What you should really take are courses in philosophy, literature, mathematics, economics, French, English and theology."

Other universities have welcomed such students and have attempted to utilize the human want factor to make a broad educational program more meaningful and beneficial to the student. The student who can say that he is majoring in advertising at the university will often be more highly motivated in his study of psychology, sociology, anthropology, literature, mathematics, and philosophy than will be the student who takes such courses for their own sake. One is studying for a purpose; the other may be studying only for a degree.

In building a university curriculum for the advertising student it would probably be wise to provide relatively few specific courses with an advertising label. Schools that have an advertising curriculum might limit specific advertising courses to a range of 10 to 12% of the student's total university program. Those courses should be a mixture of "why" and "how." They might best be offered during the student's last two years of college work and be taken along with work elected from such areas as the humanities; sciences—both social and natural; and business.

The maximum figure of 12 percent of the student's college time devoted to strictly advertising courses is certainly not great. We might look at this percentage as the additive, the TCP, the catalytic agent in the entire college program. *Its presence increases the total learning of the student because it adds significant purpose to his total educational program.*

In attempting to sharpen the student's ability to think and to solve problems we do not, as educators, set up special courses labeled "Thinking" and "Problem Solving." Instead, emphasis on these fundamental educational objectives is found in many courses. Certainly courses in philosophy and mathematics have no monopoly on thinking and problem solving. Major advancement in the ability to solve problems is achieved when there is a need or a desire to solve a problem.

This force can be utilized for the advertising student by giving him problems that are oriented to advertising. This will elicit more reading and more thinking than if some problem were developed that was totally unrelated to student interest. An advertising student might easily learn more English and psychology in a course in advertising copy than a liberal arts student would learn in specific English or psychology courses if the latter student had no real motivation for learning.

A university curriculum for young men and women who wish to enter the field of advertising should not be designed to turn out polished practitioners at the end of four years of training. The program suggested here holds specific work in advertising to a small percentage of the total. Furthermore, it is recommended that such work be heavily weighted with the why and philosophy of advertising and that training in specific advertising skills would seem to be necessary, but only as an aid to communication and to problem solving—and to shape the rough diamond for future polishing by the buffing wheel of practice.

Polishing is a job for industry to do. We should not expect universities to prepare skilled artisans for a first job. Let us help students to develop a philosophy of advertising, sharpen their powers of analysis, and give them enough training in specific skills so they will be apt pupils when we turn them over to their employers in the field of advertising.

There were various opportunities for myself and other members of the advertising faculty to write articles for professional journals and the advertising business press. Also, invitations were frequently received to speak before advertising groups. One of the groups that invited me to speak at its annual convention in New York was the Association of National Advertisers. The topic of my speech was "A Positive Approach to Advertising."* It was well received. One leading practitioner wrote the president of the university to express his reaction to and evaluation of the speech. A copy of his letter to the president is included here.

Dr. David D. Henry, president
University of Illinois
Administration Building
Urbana, Illinois

Dear Dave:

It will be no surprise to you, I'm sure, to have me report once again of the fine job Dr. Charles H. Sandage is doing for the University of Illinois in the advertising world.

---

*This speech, "A Positive Approach to Advertising" by C. H. Sandage, is reproduced in its entirety in Appendix A.

231

Monday it was my pleasure to sit with some 400 of the largest advertisers in the United States and to hear Sandy, as the principal and final speaker at a two-day convention, deliver one of the soundest addresses I have heard in my twenty years in this business. Sandy has without question done more than any single man anywhere in the United States to set up the basis for understanding between the advertising practitioner and our higher educational system. In the effete East, I think they find it a little odd that someone from the University of Illinois, astraddle of the Middle West, should have such a clear understanding of the problems, the responsibilities, and the goals of a completely commercial occupation.

Long ago I became convinced that the success of my own business was largely dependent on the kind of people we were able to attract and to hold. I'm sure this must be equally true of the University. That being the case, Sandy is a magnificent representative of the University and in his field brings it a distinction fully equal to that some of our great professors of chemistry, engineering, accounting and other fields have done in the past.

With best regards,

Yours very truly,
Wm. A. Marsteller

That speech was printed in a number of publications and over time was included in several books of readings prepared by different professors of advertising. It was also reformatted, illustrated, and published (with permission) by an East Coast advertising agency and distributed widely by that agency.

In one part of that speech I commented that universities generally followed the practice of providing professors sabbatical leaves during which time they could concentrate their full time on some aspect of their field other than teaching. I suggested that industry might give some of their senior advertising people occasional sabbatical leaves and offer them as potential short-time teachers of advertising on a university campus. A number of people in the audience talked with me after the meeting and indicated a desire to do just that. The eventual result was that Cluett Peabody and Company gave its director of advertising a one-semester leave on full pay to accept an offer from the University of Illinois to be a visiting professor of advertising. Other arrangements were made from time to time cementing relationships between the academic and the professional.

Financial Aid for Graduate Students

The advertising program at the University of Illinois was attracting an increasing number of students interested in enrolling in the advertising graduate program. A number of the talented and promising students did not enter the program because there was no financial aid specifically available for advertising students. I found that most departments on the campus had scholarships or assistantships available for their graduate students. In some departments 100 percent of all graduate students had some type of special financial assistance. I set about to try to develop funds for graduate students in advertising.

I had known James Webb Young from my Miami days. He was an outstanding individual with a rich background in advertising agency work and a national reputation for excellence. He had been the moving force in organizing the War Advertising Council, which continued as the Advertising Council after the war. I invited him to the Illinois campus to speak to our advertising students and was able to offer him $250 to pay for his transportation. He suggested that we keep the $250 for departmental use. This we did and set up a special account in the business office, labeling it the "James Webb Young Fund." Later he, with G. D. Crain, Jr., publisher of *Ad Age*, and I had lunch in Chicago at which time they both agreed to serve on an industry committee to raise funds to support graduate students in advertising. From that small beginning the fund grew to a level to permit giving full tuition and $2,000 to $3,000 per year financial assistance for twelve to twenty graduate students annually. As of 1990, the principal in the endowment fund had reached several hundred thousand dollars. A number of industry people continue to make annual contributions to the fund.

A significant number of graduate students who received a Ph.D. degree from the University of Illinois were in high demand by universities throughout the country because of the philosophy and nature of the educational program at Illinois. The Illinois graduates or members of the Illinois advertising faculty were hired by other universities to head or become important members of their advertising programs. This included North Carolina, Georgia, Northwestern, Michigan State, Minnesota, Tennessee, Washington State, University of Washington, University of Oregon, Indiana University, Southern Methodist, University of Texas, University of Florida, San Francisco State, Southern Illinois University, University of Wisconsin, and the University of Oklahoma.

The importance of the University of Illinois as a leader in advertising education was recognized on several occasions by awards given to me as symbolic of that leadership. The Gold Medal conferred annually by *Printer's Ink* and the Advertising Federation of America was conferred on me at its Boston convention in 1964. In 1984 I was elected to the Advertising Hall of Fame as an advertising educator, an uncommon award to education.

Advertising and Freedom of Speech

The view of advertising as held by people in general was that it served only to promote commercial products and services. That was too narrow a view, in my opinion. I had included in the early editions of my advertising textbook the idea that advertising could be used to explain and sell ideas. This point of view was developed and became a part of the philosophy of advertising education that became known as the "Illinois School of Advertising Thought." It was my position that the institution of advertising could be used to implement freedom of speech. I held that freedom of speech was a hollow freedom unless those who "speak" could have access to modern methods for distributing such speech.

I presented this viewpoint in speeches in various places and in short articles in academic and professional journals. The essence was given in a speech before the convention of the Association for Education in Journalism in August 1958. That speech is reproduced here.

Using Advertising to Implement the Concept of Freedom of Speech

Freedom of the press is a right claimed by every journalist. It is a right that has been recognized by every government of free people. It has been woven into the legal fabric of states and nations so that all may know this right of free man and so that it might serve as a warning and restraint to governments that may be tempted to curtail such freedom.

But the basic freedom from which freedom of the press emerged is the freedom of speech. It is no accident that the American Constitution and the constitutions of most states where press freedom is enunciated place freedom of speech before freedom of the press. Thus, the pertinent part of the first amendment to the Federal Constitution reads, "Congress shall make no law...abridging the freedom of speech or of the press." The English Bill of Rights of 1689 emphasized freedom of speech but made no mention of press freedom. Sir William Blackstone emphasized the primary position of freedom of speech when he said, "Every free man has an undoubted right to lay what sentiments he pleases before the public; to forbid this is to destroy freedom of the press."

The basic logic back of press freedom is that man shall not be denied this means of "laying what sentiments he pleases before the public." If man could reach as many people with equal effort and effect from the town square soap box, as he could by means of the press, there would probably be no need for upholding freedom of the press.

Actually the press afforded a means for implementing freedom of speech. It provided the vehicle for distributing one's thoughts and ideas to the many rather than to the few. If a person wished to publish his own paper and use it to carry his own personal speeches or messages it was his right to do so. That many chose to employ this method in our own early national history to disseminate personal views is attested by the numbers and character of publishing ventures. Newspapers were largely personal undertakings. The owner was usually also publisher and editor. There were sufficient numbers to provide competition and representation of divergent points of view. (The owner needed relatively little capital to inaugurate his publishing venture.) The editor had only his own conscience to answer to in directing the character of his editorials.

In recent years this situation has changed radically. Relatively few communities have newspaper competition. Capital requirements for newspaper operation have increased many fold. The complexities of operation have dictated the separation of ownership, general management, and editorial writing. Numbers have decreased substantially and divergences of points of view have narrowed. Under such circumstances the press no longer affords a ready means for letting "free man lay his sentiments before the public."

This development strikes a cardinal blow at the efficacy of freedom of speech in a democratic society. The soap box as a platform for reaching today's mobile and diffused population is wholly ineffectual. Space provided by publishers in 'letters to the editor' columns is under the control of publishers and cannot meet the test of affording either freedom of speech or freedom of the press for the lay citizen.

How, then, can the "crackpot," the non-conformist, the critic of the present order, the dreamer for a better world, the little man who has been crowded out of the formal council chambers get his ideas before the electorate? How can he let his voice be heard? How can he break through the tight controls of the modern press? How can we recapture this essential ingredient of a healthy democracy?

There is a way and it is immediately at hand. It is to be found in the institution of advertising. That institution has many facets, one of which is to serve as an instrument of communication. This facet of advertising could be used, by anyone who has sentiments to express, as a method to have his voice heard. Its use would require relatively little money when compared with the cost of setting up a personal publishing venture.

The modern publisher is an operator of two distinct enterprises. One consists of providing the public with news, entertainment, analysis, and personal views through editorial material. The other consists of selling white space to those who wish to buy it for purposes of presenting their own messages to readers of the publication. The latter he refers to as advertising.

It is true that the great majority of buyers of white space from publishers have used it to promote the sale of material goods and services. This use has been so predominant that we are prone to view advertising as dealing wholly with affairs of business. In fact, the historian, David Potter, has characterized advertising as being the institution of economic abundance.

One cannot quarrel with the Potter label for advertising, but we must add that advertising is also an institution of communication. True, its communicating function has been confined largely to informing and persuading people in respect to products and services. On the other hand, it can be made equally available to those who wish to inform and persuade people in respect to a city bond issue, cleaning up community crime, the "logic" of atheism, the needs for better educational facilities, the abusive tactics of given law enforcement officers, or any other sentiment held by any individual who wishes to present such sentiment to the public.

The institution of advertising can be used to make the freedom to speak vastly more available than has been true in recent years. Adherence to the old concepts of implementing freedom of speech can only curtail and largely destroy the effective communication of the lay citizen with various publics. The newer concept of using advertising as a communication vehicle for the lay citizen can make each purchaser of a two-inch column of space his own editor and publisher. The freedom to speak is meaningless unless there is effective machinery for distributing speech to those whose ears one wishes to reach.

Two operational procedures would help in furthering a development along the lines suggested here. One is to have all teachers of advertising and advertising practitioners emphasize this use of advertising. The other is to recognize publishers as common carriers in respect to the advertising aspect of their operations. Only by this latter procedure can we have true freedom of speech through advertising without the restrictive power of the publisher as licenser. Publishers should have no logical basis for objecting to common carrier status for advertising. Freedom for the press was fought and won on the ground that freedom of speech meant freedom to print and publish without government restriction. Freedom for the advertiser of ideas from restrictions imposed by the publisher (beyond those encompassed by established common carrier regulations) is likewise essential to true freedom of speech. But even without formalizing a common carrier status for publishers great strides can be made, through the institution of advertising, toward giving a broad base to freedom of speech in democratic America.

Journalists and governmental agencies generally have been reluctant to recognize advertising, even advertising devoted wholly to the dissemination of ideas, as speech protected by the first amendment to the constitution. They ardently attempt to protect their positions as gatekeepers to control what is permitted to flow to or be kept from the public. The United States Supreme Court, however, has been inching its way toward recognizing commercial (advertising) speech as being on a par with any other speech and hence free from journalistic or governmental censorship. Guaranteeing freedom of access to the various media of communication awaits further evolution.

It has given me great satisfaction to see advertising accepted at many universities as an academic discipline that attracts the efforts of scholars to devote that scholarship to the discipline. I am proud that the University of Illinois has been instrumental in providing scholars to many colleges and universities in the field of advertising. I retired from the university in 1968 but my interest in advertising education has not diminished. The advertising program on the Illinois campus has continued to be a strong one and viewed as a model for the guidance of other universities.

Chapter 11

Organizational Structure

It is one thing to develop a philosophical framework for an advertising education program and quite another thing to implement that philosophy. Effective implementation involves not only the assembly of a capable faculty but also an administrative structure that provides an environment that enhances the application of scholarship in the discipline of advertising. Attention was therefore given to the development of an effective administrative structure.

Thus, during my first year I was able to unify faculty members in both Commerce and Journalism who taught any courses in advertising. We were able to get courses cross-listed and duplication eliminated. However, the system was awkward because of the different philosophies in the two schools. The difficulty was somewhat intensified during my second year because of the arrival of a new dean of the College of Commerce.

President Stoddard was an innovator and believed that the College of Commerce needed a "progressive" new head. He appointed the young, dynamic Howard Bowen with instructions to "modernize" the College of Commerce. The new dean arrived at a time when student enrollment was burgeoning and hence had the responsibility for adding new members to the faculty. His appointments, for the most part, could be classified as "new thought" scholars who leaned toward Keynesian economics and "New Deal" business philosophy. This resulted in a conflict between the older established faculty and new additions. This conflict was especially strong in economics and to a lesser degree in marketing and advertising.

The dean, in one of his talks, referred to advertising as the "prostitute daughter of the business family." Most faculty members interpreted that comment literally and took it somewhat out of context of the dean's total statement.

I was a relatively new faculty member but had not been appointed by the new dean. It was therefore easy for both the anti- and pro-Bowen factions to court my support and vote at faculty meetings. Actually, Bowen's basic economic and business philosophy was not substantially different from my own. He basically was a free enterpriser with a consumer orientation. His "prostitute daughter" comment was not indicative of his basic attitude concerning advertising. He thought advertising was an important part of marketing and would like to have advertising centralized on the campus, but as a part of marketing.

The College of Commerce did not have a strong departmental structure. There was no separate marketing department, but there was considerable pressure to establish one. There was an area of concentration or unified curriculum for students wanting to study marketing, but no department. The recognized head of the marketing area was Professor P. D. Converse. He had authored a widely used textbook on marketing and had made substantial contributions to the American Marketing Association. He was not, however, research oriented, and he generally lacked imagination and philosophical leadership.

Dean Bowen was not unwilling to accept a marketing department but did not want to appoint Professor Converse to head it. He called me into his office and offered to recommend me to be head of a new department. There was some hope that such a move might also bring most of advertising into the college and department. I was flattered by the dean's offer, but declined. I emphasized that P.D. Converse was "Mr. Marketing" on the U of I campus and was recognized nationally in marketing circles.* I indicated that if I accepted his appointment it would exacerbate conflict and destroy the opportunity to develop a harmonious working unit. I urged him to appoint Professor Converse as first department head and be patient. Professor Converse was nearing retirement age and the dean would have an opportunity to appoint someone more to his liking in a relatively short time. The dean did not follow my recommendation and he never established a marketing department. The anti-Bowen group eventually succeeded in forcing his resignation.

The organizational structure of advertising within the overall educational bureaucracy on the University of Illinois campus was an important factor in my thinking. I considered advertising education to be a combination of philosophy, theory, and skills to research, test, and implement. As such, it was worthy of being recognized as a separate and distinct academic discipline.

I pleaded this case before the faculties in both the School of Journalism and College of Commerce. There was great resistance. I presented briefs in support of my case. Both the marketing faculty in Commerce and

---

*I never told anyone about the dean's offer to me as long as Professor Converse lived. The dean had not made his offer public.

the Journalism faculty wanted to control advertising. It did not matter that marketing had fought to become independent of a department of economics and that journalism had fought to become independent of a department of English.

In my "crusade" I pointed out that advertising as a separate discipline could not and should not forget or forsake its heritage. One might say advertising education was sired by Commerce and dammed by Journalism. In addition to that filial relationship, it was recognized that advertising had genetic ties to psychology, philosophy, sociology, economics, and English. Advertising, however, was no longer a child and was striving to establish its own identity as an independent and responsible adult. The full development of advertising education at Illinois was undoubtedly slowed because of the absence of an organizational structure that would provide unity. Progress toward complete unity, however, was made.

It was earlier pointed out that those teaching advertising courses, whether in Commerce or Journalism, met as a unit to discuss objectives and various aspects of education in advertising. We tried to consider it an emerging academic discipline but encountered constraints. Individual members were still legally, and to considerable degree intellectually, tied to either marketing or journalism. Students interested in majoring in advertising would not feel they had an academic home labeled advertising. They were either marketing or journalism students with advertising merely as an area of concentration. What we needed was a faculty who dedicated its scholarship to the study of advertising as such and then students could be advised and taught by real advertising educators.

We succeeded in moving in that direction by establishing a major in advertising, both in the College of Commerce and the School of Journalism. I also was able to get the name of the School of Journalism modified by including the name "Communications" in the title. The school also was officially labeled a college. (Sometime later the word "journalism" was dropped from the title and it became the College of Communications.) At the same time, advertising became a division having equal status with journalism and broadcasting.

I thought the designation of advertising as a division within the college was helpful but that a unification of an advertising faculty by and within one college would be beneficial. I, therefore, made proposals to both Commerce and Journalism/Communications for placing all advertising courses and faculty in one or the other unit. I expressed no preference but rather stated that the unit in which the advertising instruction and faculty should be housed be chosen on the basis of which unit would provide the best environment for the development of advertising as an academic discipline. Such recommendations were shelved and, thus, essentially rejected by each college. I then drew up a proposal to establish advertising as a department having quasi-independent status. All advertising courses would be allocated to the department and cross-listed in each college. All advertising faculty would be given joint appointments but remain financially tied to one or the other college. I suggested a unique, but probably unworkable, administrative plan in which a joint committee of the two colleges be appointed to handle and administer college and university matters, such as budget, curriculum approval, etc. These recommendations were also rejected.

We had a faculty concentrating their teaching and research efforts in the field of advertising. They increasingly felt handicapped by being continually tied to their "parents' apronstrings." Without departmental status new course proposals, changes in curriculum, budget matters, or special assignments affecting advertising were, in essence, controlled by Journalism/Communications faculty on the one hand and Commerce faculty on the other hand. We, therefore, continued to work for academic recognition in the form of departmental status.

If a department were to be established, it was obvious that it should be in one or the other college. We submitted our recommendation for department status to each college. Journalism/Communications rejected the request but Commerce responded by offering departmental status for advertising if all advertising courses, whether in Journalism/Communications or Commerce at that time, were transferred to the department, and if all of the advertising faculty in Journalism/Communications would follow the department to Commerce. University statutes included a provision for the transfer of a unit of instruction from one college to another, but such transfer could not be made without the approval of the college from which the unit was to be transferred. The advertising faculty would therefore need to petition the College of Journalism/Communications to permit transfer to Commerce. A petition for such transfer was prepared, signed by all advertising faculty in Journalism/Communications save one, and submitted to the college faculty. Our petition was denied. This turned out to be a favorable situation for advertising. We could present a strong case to the J/C faculty that because they would not permit us to accept departmental status in Commerce, they were essentially obligated to establish an advertising department within their college. After considerable debate, approval was granted by the J/C faculty and eventually approved by top university officials and the board of trustees. Thus the University of Illinois in 1959 officially recognized the area of advertising as a legitimate academic discipline. Now students interested in advertising could feel they had an academic home. It also placed additional emphasis on the opportunity and responsibility of faculty members to devote their scholarship to this particular area. They could not ignore that challenge.

The establishment of an advertising department did not, however, provide complete unification of advertising instruction and faculty. Some courses and some faculty remained in Commerce, but that situation was to change. The Carnegie and Ford Foundations were soon to issue reports on their study of education in colleges of business administration. In those reports recommendations were made for modifying curricula in such colleges. Both reports recommended concentration on the broad aspects of business administration and the reduction or elimination of courses that might be viewed more narrowly. Advertising was one of the areas considered as a somewhat narrow specialization. The University of Illinois College of Commerce and Business Administration, along with many other such colleges, was influenced by the Carnegie and Ford reports. The influence on the U of I resulted in transferring all advertising to the College of Journalism/Communications.

Chapter 12

My Research at the University of Illinois

My belief in the importance of research as a foundation for developing advertising strategy and as a guide for those who implemented strategy, obviously influenced my emphasis on research on the evolution of advertising education at Illinois. If advertising was to serve society in general and business in particular, it was important to know the purpose of business and the function of advertising. My view of the purpose of business was to serve the needs and wants of consumers. To me, the function of advertising was to operate as a middleman or translator of the want-satisfying quality of goods and services in terms of the language, beliefs, and psyche of the consumer. Thus, research would not only be helpful but often essential in determining target audiences, the characteristics of these audiences, and the media of communication available to reach them. In some respects the nature of my appointment at the University of Illinois mirrored the duality of advertising. I became a sort of middleman to sense the needs and functions of each area and develop a unity of purpose.

My joint appointment provided me with two offices— one in Gregory Hall in the School of Journalism and one in McKinley Hall in the College of Commerce. My research activities were also divided. I was fortunate in my College of Commerce connection to be granted a research fund by the Bureau of Business and Economic Research, which I could use to support research of my own choosing. I used the funds to follow up on my measurement of radio listening that I had started at Miami University. At Miami, I had developed and employed a diary to be used by individuals in recording their listening to radio programs. That instrument had permitted me to collect data that would allow analyzing radio audiences by rather minute demographic groupings.

I selected two counties in Illinois, namely Champaign and McLean. I wanted to use one county to measure listenership during the winter and the other county to measure listenership during the summer. I used the individual diary method in the study and secured a sufficiently large sample to permit segmentation by location (urban, village, farm), age, and sex. The results of that research were published in a Bureau bulletin with the title, "Qualitative Analysis of Radio Listening in Two Central Illinois Counties."

Much emphasis had been placed by the radio industry, as well as by commercial agencies serving that industry and advertisers, on the measurement of radio listening. Major attention had been given to measuring total listening. Radio had been viewed primarily as a mass medium; hence agencies engaged in checking listening had been content with merely counting numbers. Only minor attention had been given to classifying listeners by sex, age, or cultural groups.

There was a need for greater understanding of the kind of people who listen little or much and of those who listen to specific program types. The purpose of this study was to place greater emphasis on individual differences in listening than on the extent of listening.

The selected counties contained an urban center of about 40,000 permanent residents, several villages, and an extensive farm population. Each is the site of a state educational institution. Students enrolled at those institutions were excluded from the survey. Individuals rather than families represented the base used for analysis of listening. This procedure permitted a more detailed inspection of factors that might have a bearing on listening than would otherwise be possible. Listeners were grouped according to sex, area of residence, age, and education. Group comparisons could thus be made for average hours of radio listening and types of programs selected.

The results of the study highlighted significant differences in radio listening by different demographic groups. It provided evidence that different kinds of programs assembled different types of listeners. In the case of listening to different kinds of musical programs, the research showed the distinct influence of education. Thus, the listenership by women with differing levels of education showed that only 1.5 percent of the women with grade school education listened to classical music; 2.2 percent to semiclassical; 4.8 percent to popular; and 11.8 percent to folk music. At the other end of the scale, results showed that of women with a college education, 6.5 percent listened to classical music, 11.4 percent to semiclassical; 11.1 percent to popular, and 3.9 percent to folk music.

The value of this research to advertisers might be illustrated by the difference in listening to the specific program "Harvest of Stars" by different demographic groups. The program was sponsored by International Harvester and advertised products for farmers. Thus, comparison of listening by occupation or location of residence should be of value to the advertiser. Our research presented listening data by three separate places of residence: urban, village, and farm. Our sample had approximately the same number in each of these three categories. Our research produced the following results for the program:

Listening by Women to "Harvest of Stars"

Place of Residence	Champaign County	McClean County
Urban	5.6%	4.9%
Village	*	*
Farm	*	2.1

The music on "Harvest of Stars" was semiclassical in nature. The advertiser thought it was a very clever approach to advertising for International Harvester. The association of the company name with what at least in the mind of the advertising creative person meant harvesting "quality" music, would be phenomenal. The only trouble was that farmers preferred folk to semiclassical music. The distribution of the printed bulletin that carried the results of this research brought increased recognition to the College of Commerce for its research to improve business practices.

Advertising Experiment Station

My advertising textbook, first published in 1936, placed emphasis on the importance of research that might provide insights into the needs, wants, and aspirations of consumer groups. It, at least theoretically,

---

* Less than 1 percent.

could measure the effectiveness of advertising to draw people to the product or service being advertised and culminate in a purchase. My research at Miami of Ohio was devoted primarily to measuring consumer buying behavior and the use of various media of communications. My work at the Institute of Transit Advertising attempted to measure the actual sales effectiveness of specific advertising efforts.

When I came to the University of Illinois I conceived the idea of organizing what I termed an "advertising experiment station" for purposes of testing the effectiveness of advertising to move consumers to the marketplace. I had noted the work in the field of agriculture through the various experiment stations established in Land Grant colleges. The agriculture experiment station at the University of Illinois had its famous Morrow Plot. This was a one-acre area on the campus that had been used for many years to test and measure the effect of various kinds and amounts of inputs on the production of different farm products. One section of the plot was devoted to continuous corn year after year without adding any fertilizer or organic material. Other sections of the plot measured the effect of adding certain kinds of fertilizer at different rates of application, and still other sections on the effect of crop rotation.

I thought academically we needed our own advertising Morrow Plot. I developed a proposal for the establishment of such an advertising experiment station at the university. It was modeled somewhat after the research I had done at the Institute of Transit Advertising and included the establishment of consumer panels, members of which would keep diaries of purchases of specific commodities. By the discrete use of such panels the effect of various "fertilizers" of the market by different kinds of advertising could be measured. Thus, one panel might research advertising via magazines, another via radio, and still another by direct mail. A fourth panel would be used as a control, thus receiving no advertising "fertilizing" input.

I had discussed this concept with fellow educators in other universities, and several indicated an interest and willingness to join a consortium in which all members would be focusing on the same objective. The results of such research should provide data from which generalizations could be drawn. This would add to the literature in the field of advertising, but perhaps even more importantly, could lead to improvements in advertising practice.

My proposal was submitted to the university's Graduate Research Board with a request for a monetary grant which I deemed sufficient to finance such a station at the University of Illinois for three years. It was my belief that such a station would be self-sufficient from business contributions after three years. The value to business would be recognized by enough concerns to attract the funds necessary to continue the work after the developmental period.

It was a distinct disappointment to have my proposal rejected by the research board. They received the request at a time when there was great demand for research in the hard sciences and all available monies went to them.

The director of the School of Journalism, Fred Siebert, was sympathetic to my interest in research. After the turndown by the Graduate Research Board, Siebert and I worked together to develop a research program that would be applicable to and could be supported by the school as a whole. We had our plans fairly well developed, but our hopes were suddenly and unexpectedly destroyed by an announcement from the president of the university, George Stoddard. The morning papers reported the approval by the U of I Board of Trustees of a new academic unit, namely the Division of Communications and the appointment of Dr. Wilbur Schramm as its dean. Under the division were to be a number of university units including the School of Journalism and an Institute of Communications Research. This meant that any research in the school would now be subject to the approval of the Institute of Communications Research. It did not mean that individual faculty members would be prohibited from seeking funding for their individual research from other sources, but anything that was to be funded would be under the direction and supervision of the Institute.

There was some hope that the new Institute of Communications Research would give significant attention to research in the field of advertising. That hope was stimulated when I was appointed to or accepted by the Institute as a member of its faculty. Also, I was included as a member of a group participating in a Blue Ribbon workshop on communication research that the new dean assembled in the early days of the Institute. I recall that Paul Lazarsfeld was a member of that group. I had known Dr. Lazarsfeld and had exchanged research ideas with him on previous occasions. He had experimented with the use of a citizen panel to explore attitudes and actions on political matters. He knew of my use of panels in the marketing and advertising field. I recall that he urged our new dean to recognize and take advantage of the work I had been doing. Unfortunately, the word "advertising" was emblazoned like a scarlet letter on my forehead and that was enough to rule out any of the kinds of research that Seibert and I had been contemplating.

There was, however, an unexpected opportunity in the early days of the Institute to develop some research that had some of the characteristics of my vision for an advertising experiment station. That involved another exploration in the field of broadcasting, but in this case emphasis was to be placed on measuring the actual effectiveness of specific kinds of advertising.

The basic purpose of that research was to test various methods of promoting or advertising listening to the radio station WILL, the university's educational station. The stimulus for funding that research was somewhat accidental. There was an important visitor on campus who was a specialist in broadcasting. A small group including the university president, the director of the School of Journalism, the director of the recently established Institute of Communications Research, and myself had lunch with the visitor. Much of the discussion at the table involved programming on commercial radio stations, and disappointment was expressed with the quality of such programming. Several wished the government could provide quality programming and have its own stations to distribute such programming. After listening to such comments, I suggested that they might look in our own backyard; the U of I in fact did operate a government station and had complete control over programming. I suggested that it was not enough to provide quality programs. Quality programming would have little or no effect if people did not listen. I suggested that the university might well devote an important part of its broadcasting budget to building an audience to let people know that such programs existed and in essence promote or advertise programs to the public. Apparently my comments struck a responsive chord with the university president because we walked out of the luncheon together and he asked me how much money I would need to follow through on my suggestions. I named a figure, and he said that I could start tomorrow, which I did.

The nature of that research was to again select a representative sample of families with radio sets and have individuals within the family keep diaries of their listening. We had members of the research panel of families keep a diary before any promotional effort was employed. This would establish a base against which future listening could be measured after promotional effort had been applied. We would then experiment with different methods of promoting listening.

Our first promotion consisted of distributing to pupils in a sample of public schools of Champaign County mimeographed or printed material describing WILL programs. Those pupils were instructed to take the material home with them and give it to their parents. When we tabulated the results from diaries after that public school type of promotion was completed, it showed no significant increase in listening to WILL. We hypothesized that our message and method of promotion were the weak elements in the operation and not necessarily the character of programs on WILL as the cause of low listening. Our measurement of listening did indicate that very few people tuned into the WILL programs. We decided to try another approach. We produced an eight-page brochure with illustrations, color, and a detailed description of four specific programs. We had WILL mail our brochure to one-half of our consumer panel that was keeping listener diaries.

Our contact with the listener diary keepers was under a name completely foreign from WILL so theoretically the panel members would not know that we were responsible for the distribution of brochures. Splitting our panel into two segments, with one segment receiving the promotional material and the other not, at least theoretically provided a rather accurate measure of the effect of promotion on listenership.

The brochure did more than list and give a short description of the types of programs aired by the station. Instead, considerable detail was given on only four programs. One such program was labeled "For You at Home." It consisted of news directed to housewives. The person behind the microphone was Jessie Heathman. Two pages in the brochure devoted to a discussion of that program were designed to make Jessie Heathman a personality whom people would enjoy having in their homes. A photograph of Jessie was included to help the listener visualize the visitor in her home. The "Chamber Music Hour" was another program detailed in the brochure. The copy describing that program included interesting glimpses of two great musicians whose works were frequently aired. Those two musicians were Franz Joseph Haydn and Johann Sebastian Bach. The actual copy describing Haydn was as follows:

> You would have enjoyed knowing the jovial, 18th-century musician, Franz Joseph Haydn. Everybody called him "Papa." He got his nickname because he had a fatherly way with music and with anyone connected with music.
>
> He liked to play musical jokes. For instance, in his *Farewell Symphony* each player had a lighted candle on his music stand. Then, one at a time, they blew out their candles and left the stage. Finally only two musicians were left. And when they, at last, blew our their candles,

the symphony was over. Or take his *Surprise Symphony*. The music begins softly and simply, and practically lulls you into repose, when suddenly—BANG! The whole orchestra hits a loud, sharp chord.

"Papa" Haydn wrote more than symphonies, though. Many of his compositions were for his patron, the Austrian Prince Nicholas. These were played by strolling string ensembles, and when the musicians came into a room, conversation would stop and everyone would sit back to enjoy the relaxing strains of Haydn's melodies. And these compositions were written for just such an intimate audience—the audience of a room, rather than of a concert hall. Now we call such compositions "Chamber Music."

Bach was presented in a similar way.

The results of this research were printed in a bulletin titled "Building Audiences for Educational Radio Programs" and issued in 1951 as the first research publication of the Institute of Communications Research. Our theory was substantiated in that listenership was increased on the average three- to five-fold, not only for the four programs that were described in our brochure but audiences were drawn to other programs as well. This bulletin was distributed rather widely to educational radio stations around the country. This brought invitations to me to speak at some of the meetings of educational radio operators. I was surprised and disappointed at the general reaction to advertising the programs offered by educational radio stations. While there were exceptions, the basic position was that the responsibility of educational broadcasting stopped at the microphone. They continued to seemingly glory in hiding their light under a bushel. To engage in advertising would cheapen their efforts, they felt. They would continue to be satisfied to program only to the "elite" who were already sufficiently sophisticated to seek out their offerings and needed no urging from others to do so.

Graduate Student Research

The completion of the WILL promotion research ended my personal research that was university funded. I continued to be active in research funded by commercial interests but did not abandon my interest in the purely academic. That interest was met primarily by supervision of master's theses and doctoral dissertations by the large number of graduate students with concentration in advertising. We were fortunate in having advertising as a basic part of the interdisciplinary doctoral degree offered by the Institute of Communications Research. Over the years, there were almost as many Ph.D. candidates concentrating their research in advertising as there were in all other areas of communications.

One student research project grew out of my personal annoyance with messing with little envelopes of Sanka (decaffeinated coffee) at restaurants when I did not want to drink regular coffee with my meal. In our home we used vacuum packed, ground, decaffeinated coffee which we brewed in our kitchen just as we did regular coffee. I wondered why restaurants could not do the same and serve decaffeinated coffee in the same way in which they served regular coffee. One of our graduate students accepted the challenge to test the commercial feasibility of that approach.

We first developed a questionnaire designed to determine the beverage-drinking habits of families with their regular home meals. We asked individual family members to indicate what hot drinks they served and used in their own homes. If they used decaffeinated coffee at home but did not order it in restaurants we asked why. Answers to the latter question indicated several negatives including embarrassment in ordering a "sissy" drink, nuisance in mixing one's own drink at the table, and inability to get a refill at the table similar to what was available for regular coffee.

We were able to get two restaurants willing to work with us in an experiment. We supplied each restaurant with cans of decaffeinated ground coffee ready for perking. Each restaurant agreed to brew the decaffeinated coffee in the kitchen and serve it from distinctly labeled carafes in the same manner as that used for regular coffee. We asked each restaurant to keep an accurate record of the number of cups of both regular and decaffeinated coffee ordered by patrons with that record covering the two weeks preceding the introduction of the regularly brewed decaffeinated coffee. At the end of the two weeks each restaurant owner started offering brewed decaffeinated coffee in the same manner as regular coffee. It was advertised by placing a tent card on each table with the statement "We now serve kitchen brewed decaffeinated coffee in carafes like regular coffee." We asked each restaurant operator to then keep an accurate record of the consumption of decaffeinated coffee for the next two weeks.

The results were startling. In one restaurant the increase in consumption of decaffeinated coffee was nine-fold and in the other twelve-fold. These results may sound unbelievable but only because the base for comparison was extremely low. In other words, all of the negatives flowing from the little envelope method of serving Sanka meant relatively few people ordered that beverage. By correcting such negatives the increase in consumption was tremendous.

The results of this experiment dramatized the value to business of being guided by serving the needs and wants of consumers. Unfortunately, many business firms are slow to accept that truism. This is illustrated by the reaction of General Foods to the results of this experiment. Top management at General Foods was informed of the results of this research and they sent a mid-level executive to Urbana to discuss it with me. We had recommended in our report that makers of Sanka supply restaurants with hot plates and carafes clearly labeled Sanka for serving the brewed beverage. The General Foods executive was the manager of the company division responsible for serving institutions (hotels, restaurants, etc.) rather than retailers. The gentleman rejected our recommendation because, as he said, major increases in the sale of Sanka to institutions would reduce their sales of Maxwell House to institutions.

It was almost twenty years after the results of this simple "experiment station" project were known that industry finally began serving decaffeinated coffee in the manner recommended in the report.

Another interesting primarily student project dealt with religion. One of our students wondered whether the concept of serving the needs and wants of consumers could be applied in the field of religion. The student was a regular attendee at church and asked herself whether her minister was actually serving the needs and wants of his parishioners. She developed a questionnaire to determine what churchgoers would like to get from their ministers. She also surveyed the ministers of different churches to determine what they were giving their parishioners. Her objectives were to correlate what the ministers were giving with what the parishioners indicated they wanted. Again the results were startling. The one outstanding finding was that a large majority of parishioners in most of the churches involved in the study wanted their ministers to devote much more time to presenting and interpreting the Bible than whatever it was they were giving.

Journal of Advertising

Major student research in advertising was done by doctoral candidates. Their dissertations covered many aspects of advertising. Some were primarily historical, some were essentially theoretical, and others experimental. The research of many of the graduate students became a part of the advertising literature in the form of journal articles or monographs.

Seeing that scholars who concentrated their scholarship in the field of advertising shared that scholarship with others was an abiding interest of mine because I believed that the institution of advertising was a vital part of society and worthy of inclusion in the educational hierarchy as a separate and distinct discipline. It needed the enrichment of scholarly thought and research investigation to sustain and enhance it.

Attraction of scholars to the field could be helped if there was a realistic opportunity to have the results of scholarly effort published and made available to others, and not so incidentally to feed the ego of the scholar. The academic journals available for the distribution of such were in the fields of marketing, economics, psychology, and journalism. There were no academic journals carrying the name "advertising," edited by advertising scholars, and distributed to academics interested in advertising. I therefore devoted considerable time to promoting the idea of a journal of advertising and to seeking financial support to get such a journal initiated.

I presented my idea at conventions of journalists and marketing people. The marketing people felt that because advertising, in their view, was essentially marketing there was no need for a journal of advertising. Journalists urged advertising people to submit their materials to their journal, *The Journalism Quarterly*. But their publication was edited and articles refereed primarily by journalists, and it did not have room to add many advertising articles.

One place where I got a favorable reaction was from a representative of the Hearst Foundation who kept assuring me for at least two years that funding would be forthcoming. Because of that assurance, I did not devote much time to cultivating other areas for possible support.

Aside from funding, the development of the concept was enhanced by the Academy of Advertising embracing the idea and appointing a journal committee, naming me chairman. When it appeared that the Hearst money would not be available to support the journal, the Academy Journal Committee was strong in its position to not give up hope, and hope we kept. It seemed logical that the University of Illinois should also encourage and perhaps support a journal of advertising. After all, the University was universally recognized as we developed a solid and academically viable program in advertising education. That leadership also carried with it responsibility. The university, therefore, provided funds to underwrite the publication of a series of "Occasional Papers in Advertising." The idea was to have these "Papers" provide a prototype for a journal. Such should, and it was hoped would, broaden and stimulate interest in the eventual establishment of a true journal of advertising. The first issue of *Occasional Papers* appeared in January 1966, and I served as its editor. Three additional issues appeared during the next four years. The Academy Journal Committee did yeoman work in keeping the journal idea alive and in getting the eventual journal established. Special recognition should go to Daniel Stewart for that accomplishment. The first issue of the *Journal of Advertising* appeared in 1972 with Daniel Stewart as its editor; I was listed as honorary editor. The *Journal* was named as the official publication of the American Academy of Advertising and financially supported by it. It has provided a stimulus to scholarship and made significant contributions to the literature in the field.

Chapter 13

Work Ancillary to Academic at Illinois

During most of my working life I have had more than one job. These generally consisted of writing books or journal articles, serving business firms and government agencies as a consultant, or providing marketing and advertising research services. My university work always took precedence, even though my other jobs provided information and experience of substantial benefit to my teaching. These jobs helped to bring an element of realism to the classroom and tested various hypotheses that evolved from my teaching.

I have earlier referred to some of these "outside" jobs. I mentioned my work with the Greenhills development outside Cincinnati, the time spent as a division chief with the U.S. Bureau of the Census, my research as a visiting professor at the Harvard Graduate School of Business Administration, and my work as director of research at the Institute of Transit Advertising. Those all occurred before my move to the University of Illinois.

Shortly after joining the University of Illinois faculty, I became a consultant to a young advertising agency in Chicago, headed by William Marsteller. I served in that capacity for ten years and was involved with a number of minor research projects during that time. One of these projects was designed to measure both the value received and credibility attached to the editorial and news content of industry business publications by readers of such publications. The hypothesis to be tested was "the higher the benefit and credibility, the greater the benefit as a medium to carry advertisements." The results of this research tended to support the hypothesis and was used by the agency in selecting the particular medium to recommend to its advertising clients.

Dr. Theodore Peterson, a member of the U of I Journalism faculty and a national authority on magazines, was an important contributor to that research.

Federal Communications Commission

In the mid-1950s I was asked by the Federal Communications Commission (FCC) to become an advertising and marketing consultant as a member of the committee or team selected to study broadcast networks and make recommendations to guide government regulation. Congress had appropriated funds to support such a study, hence this was work mandated by the United States Congress. The study was known as *Network Broadcasting: Report of the Network Study Staff to the Network Study Committee.*

An announcement of my appointment to the FCC Network Study Staff was released to the press on January 13, 1956. Shortly afterward, meetings were held between the study staff and a number of network officials. The purpose of these meetings was to permit the networks to acquaint us with their operational practices and problems they considered they faced. After two of these early meetings each member of the staff, whether a permanent member or a consultant, was asked to prepare a memorandum covering his or her view of the practices, problems, and areas each thought should be examined in detail by the staff.

During the next several weeks I submitted two major memorandums. In these I discussed in some detail the problems of scarcity of broadcast channels, the reluctance of networks to develop affiliation with UHF stations; the unfair advantage possessed by VHF stations and their affiliation with networks; and the special position held by noncommercial educational stations. I presented suggested models that might be considered as possible solutions to a number of problems recognized or perceived as inherent in the current situation.

My memorandums specifically, and that of others in a general way, provided a sort of blueprint to guide discussion and research. The work of this committee covered a period of three or more years, requiring periodic trips to Washington as well as time spent at home wrestling with various problems. It also required some field research interviewing broadcast personnel at the station level.

One problem that smaller stations appearing on the fringe of metropolitan stations viewed as critical involved the practice of networks being able to clear various specified time periods on affiliated stations for programs sponsoring advertisers wanted distributed in said station's market area. If the advertiser did not want to have its sponsored program carried by all of the network's affiliated stations, it could pick only those markets it wished to cover. The crucial problem was that the affiliated station not selected by the advertiser was denied the right to carry the network program. I had the specific responsibility to study and analyze that particular problem and to recommend possible solutions. I interviewed a number of station personnel where the problem appeared to be acute. At the conclusion of my research I presented the following report:

Control of Television Program Distribution

The Federal Communications Commission and the Congress have been debating for a long time what to do with or how to regulate television stations and networks. The debate continues without much progress. The Department of Justice is also becoming concerned with this medium of communication.

Television is a powerful medium. It has achieved a public following of tremendous proportions. This achievement has been accomplished with a minimum of government regulation. In many respects television has been permitted to grow like Topsy. It would seem that some basic changes in the philosophy of regulation are sorely needed. However, there appears to be little in the recent actions and pronouncements of the FCC that would suggest any basic changes.

True, much time and effort have been devoted to studying, discussing, and issuing reports on matters such as the power of television networks, what should be done about option time, whether competition in program production should be encouraged, how a favorable climate for program competition might be provided, and whether the must-buy practices of networks should be abandoned or modified. Positive action has been taken on only one of these areas of discussion, namely, the must-buy practices of networks.

Other items of concern to the industry and ones which cry out for solution include the paucity of VHF channels, the competitive disadvantage of UHF channels, the proper position and power of advertisers in TV operations, the place that educational television should hold in the total industry, and the excessive profits to licensees of choice channels that encourage situations like the Channel 10 scandal in Miami.

There is no disposition to discuss all of these problems here, but rather to single out one television operating practice that is seldom mentioned or discussed but which grievously limits the ability of many of those stations serving smaller communities to operate in the public interest. The practice in question is that which grants to advertisers the almost absolute power to determine what communities will have access to what programs. This is especially true in the case of network programs and advertiser-sponsors.

Perhaps an example will best illustrate the power which networks have permitted advertisers to exercise over the distribution of network programs. The XYZ television network develops or contracts for a half-hour program to be offered to its 160 station affiliates. We shall call this program "Playhouse 80." It is first distributed as a sustaining program because no advertiser is willing to sponsor it until some measure of audience size is available. As a sustaining program, it is carried by 150 of the 160 network affiliates. After four weeks the program achieves a high audience rating and the network is able to sell it to an advertising sponsor.

The network urges the advertiser to buy time on all 150 of the stations carrying the program. However, the advertiser wishes to reach only the top 60 markets in the country and thus will contract only for time on the 60 stations serving those markets. The network agrees to this provision. This means that 90 of the network affiliates that have been carrying "Playhouse 80" are not included in the advertiser's line-up of stations from which time is purchased.

One would think that those 90 stations could continue to carry "Playhouse 80" on a sustaining basis if they so desired, but such is not the case. Instead, the network permits the advertiser to prohibit any station on which time has not been purchased to carry that program.

You might ask why advertisers would prohibit stations from which time has not been purchased to carry the network program in communities where the advertiser has chosen not to distribute its commercial messages. The advertiser answers that to do so would reduce the overall audiences of those stations that do carry the advertiser's commercial messages. For example, station A in Chicago is one of the 60 stations in the advertiser's coverage areas. Station B in Rockford, 80 miles away, is also an affiliate of the XYZ network. There are,

271

however, many homes in Rockford that can tune in station A from Chicago if the program there is more desired than a program broadcast from a Rockford station. If the advertiser were to permit station B in Rockford to broadcast "Playhouse 80," some families who otherwise would tune in station A from Chicago would tune in Station B in Rockford to receive "Playhouse 80." This would thus reduce the total number of families that would be exposed to the commercial messages of the advertiser.

The manager of station B in Rockford is thus forced to discontinue his broadcasting of "Playhouse 80" even though a great many people in his community object strenuously to this action and even though the station manager believes that the interests of the people in his community are to be best served by offering them "Playhouse 80." This practice of networks gives effective ownership and control of programs and their distribution to advertisers. This would seem to be in contradiction to the oath licensees took, to operate in the public interest, when they were granted a television channel.

It is proposed here that some specific action be taken, and soon, to place the control of program distribution in the hands of station licensees. This could be done rather easily by including as a condition of the network-station affiliation contract that any station affiliate would have access to any and all network programs whether sponsored or not. If an advertiser chose not to purchase time on a given station affiliate, the program would nevertheless be available to that station if it wished, and the cost not to exceed any additional line charges necessary to pipe the program into the station. The advertiser's commercial messages would, of course, be deleted from programs broadcast over stations not included in the advertiser's combination of stations. Sale of these vacated spots might be prohibited or, if allowed, then the distribution of income might be negotiated by the network, advertiser, and station.

Surely this would not be an unreasonable regulation. Surely stations should have access to the programs of their network. Much testimony has been given by leaders in the television industry that a network affiliation is a practical necessity for the profitable operation of most television stations. It is pointed out that network programs help build audiences because of the superior character of those programs. Network affiliated stations that are denied such programs are usually those in greatest need of them. Most VHF stations have some kind of network affiliation, but for many this is a hollow achievement. Neither the network nor the station can be assured of having a network program aired in a community served by the station affiliate—only the advertiser can assure this.

This situation is particularly anomalous in view of the power granted a network to option time on affiliated stations when stations are not guaranteed access to those programs. A network—operating in the interest of advertisers—can commandeer a station's time, but the station—operating in the interest of the people—cannot commandeer its network programs.

The point of view expressed here should in no way blind us to recognition of the tremendous debt which the television viewing public owes to the financial support which advertisers have brought to television. The growth of the television industry has been rapid and fruitful. While many might wish that more top quality programs were available on television, it is probable that progress in quality programs has been substantially enhanced by advertisers. It is not at all unlikely that leaders in the advertising field would support the basic arguments and suggestions made here. They too, perhaps as much as network and station operators, are mindful of the public interest.

It should be obvious that advertisers must be able to obtain value from their television efforts equal to their monetary outlay for time and talent. One of the factors the advertiser uses in calculating value is the cost per thousand viewers of his commercial message. If a television station affiliated with a network were permitted to carry sponsored network programs (but not sponsored over that station), the advertiser might have his total audience reduced. This would thus increase the cost per thousand persons exposed to the advertiser's commercial message. If this increased cost exceeds the predicted advertising value, such cost could be reduced by a reduction in the time charges by those favored stations on which time is to be purchased. A look at the profit and loss statements of those television stations most commonly included in an advertiser's station schedule would reveal an ample cushion to permit rate reductions.

If the proposal suggested here to guarantee access to network programs by station affiliates is not activated soon, it is possible that some more drastic measure will eventually be needed. It is possible, for example, that advertising sponsorship of programs would be entirely eliminated. If this were done, programming would become entirely a function of the television industry—station licensees and their network partners. Advertisers would then become interested in purchasing time in terms of the size and character of the audience delivered. Networks might still clear time on affiliated stations for commercial messages, but these messages might be found within the "Playhouse 80" program on one station, the "Jack Penny" program on another station, and the "Steve Sullivan" program on another.

In any event the television industry is too vital an element in American life today to permit it to continue to grow like Topsy.

I added grist to the committee mill on other issues, but most of my recommendations failed to get into the final report. The one that was fairly radical, but which I think would have served the public well had it been adopted, dealt with the struggle to sustain and stimulate the growth of UHF television. That was one reason why the FCC and others were interested in the growth of UHF: the limited space on the broadcast spectrum for VHF outlets. UHF broadcast stations had a great handicap on at least two counts. Most owners of TV sets had instruments that would receive only VHF signals. Viewers who wished to tune in a UHF station either needed to buy a new TV set or have their VHF set equipped with a converter. That problem was being met in part by government requiring TV sets manufactured after a specific date to be capable of receiving both VHF and UHF signals. The other and maybe even more difficult problem was attracting a sufficiently large audience to a UHF station to cause advertisers to buy time on the station. Without advertising revenue such stations could not exist.

Established VHF stations had already built a substantial number of viewers, and most such stations had developed an affiliation with a national network. These networks provided a valuable source of quality programs of a nature to attract large audiences. It was a rare situation for any VHF station not to have a network affiliation. Those so-called independents were located in large metropolitan areas where they could operate without benefit of a network.

Very few UHF stations were able to obtain a network affiliation, thus the majority did not have access to the popular programs provided by national networks. That plus the paucity of home receivers equipped to bring in UHF signals placed the UHF station at a great disadvantage.

I proposed to the committee and urged it to adopt a play that would stimulate the growth of UHF and provide some pressure for VHF to provide the kind of service Congress and the FCC had emphasized as being highly desirable. My proposal was to prohibit national networks from having any VHF station affiliates while encouraging networks to affiliate with any number of

UHF stations. This proposal if adopted would, I thought, guarantee the success of UHF by providing them with popular national network programming and stimulate the manufacture and purchase of UHF receiving sets. In addition, it would make VHF stations independent community-oriented outlets. They were already strong and could remain strong without the national network affiliation. In fact, many might increase their strength because they were receiving a relatively small portion of the advertising revenue associated with network-created programs.

My proposal was too radical or speculative to be accepted. I did have the opportunity to discuss the proposal orally with two FCC commissioners whose response was that advertisers would not accept the plan. I thought it strange that I was officially listed as the advertising and marketing consultant and my recommendation was rejected at least in part because advertisers "would not like it."

Most of my other consulting and research work was done through the Farm Research Institute. That is a part of my life that might best be reviewed in a chapter of its own.

National Advertising Review Board

The elements of ethics and truth in advertising were problems that concerned leaders in the advertising industry. Their interest gave rise to the establishment and growth of Better Business Bureaus. It also placed the practice of advertising under the scrutiny of the Federal Trade Commission (FTC) with its regulatory powers. Leaders of thought in the industry placed emphasis on the importance of having advertising practitioners maintain a high degree of ethics and truth in their creative work. Such emphasis led to a program of self-regulation and the establishment of the National Advertising Review Board (NARB). Members of that board were drawn from advertising agencies, advertisers, and the general public. I was appointed as one of the persons representing the public on the board and served in that capacity for several years.

The NARB functioned somewhat like a jury. Complaints brought before the board involved such matters as untruthful or unethical advertising or advertising practices that could result in misleading consumers. Such complaints could be made by lay citizens, competitors, or other concerned persons. The "jury," after hearing all evidence, would issue a report including recommendations for discontinuance, modification, cancellation of such advertising, or that the complaint was unjustified. If the report included a recommendation for modification or discontinuance, the accused offender could accept and implement the recommendation or choose to ignore it. If the latter choice was made, the entire case would then be turned over to the FTC, which would be given all the evidence collected in the hearings.

One of the cases brought before the NARB while I was a member involved two major national advertisers where one claimed that the advertising of its competitor's product was untruthful and misleading and thus injurious to the complainant's product. That case lasted two complete days. The accused and the accuser each had lawyers, research specialists, top officials, and expert witnesses pleading the case before the board. After two days of hearings we issued our report which included recommendations to the accused to modify its advertising. The accused accepted the recommendation and made modifications.

This is cited here to indicate the significant movement toward professionalism in the practice of advertising by American business firms. The development of such self-regulation naturally grew from the recognition that credibility in the mind of the consumer was an essential factor in the effectiveness of advertising.

American Association of Advertising Agencies Education Foundation

The development of advertising education, particularly at the University of Illinois, and the attention given it in the trade press and academic journals may have been the stimulus for the American Association of Advertising Agencies to establish its Education Foundation in 1967. John Crichton was executive director of the 4-A's. He and his board of directors thought such a foundation would help improve the image of advertising both on college campuses and with the public in general. The foundation would solicit development of an endowment fund, the income from which would be used in various ways to support and further advertising-related education.

Early announcement of the formation of the foundation was given prominent notice in the trade press. There was considerable attention given to and discussion about the selection of members to serve on an advisory board to the governing body of the foundation. Crichton took the position that the advisory board membership should come primarily from nonadvertising people. He thought that professors of political science, history, sociology, and economics would be appropriate and effective members. For the most part, such members would be chosen from persons who had been vocal in their negative criticism of advertising. For example, Dr. John Galbraith topped Crichton's list of potential board members. He studiously excluded any advertising educator from his list.

It seemed to me quite appropriate to have negative critics of advertising on such an advisory board, but quite inappropriate to exclude anyone who was focusing his major educational effort in studying, researching, and evaluating both the institution and instrument of advertising.

My feeling on that matter was sufficiently strong to make it an issue, and I expressed my point of view in a letter to Crichton. He was not receptive.

During that period I had frequent business meetings as a consultant to the advertising agency, Dancer, Fitzgerald & Sample. I called John Crichton and asked for a personal meeting with him in his office sometime when I would be in New York. He reluctantly scheduled such a meeting. In that meeting I pleaded my case primarily on the grounds that it was highly inappropriate to exclude anyone representing advertising education. His "ploy" of loading the advisory board with anti-advertising educators would generally be viewed as a propaganda operation rather than any attempt to further real advertising education. I suggested that such an approach might backfire and raise questions of sincerity. I asked him to present my position to his governing board but to emphasize that I was not at all personally interested in membership. What I was asking for was that the advisory board not be loaded with anti-advertising people and that at least one member from the area of advertising education was essential.

He did bring my position before his board and it was accepted.

Even though I had emphasized that I had no personal interest in being the advertising education representative, Crichton's board insisted that I be that representative. I thus joined people like the president of a liberal arts college, the dean of a school of business in a major university, an economist in a social research organization, and a research-minded historian. We laid the groundwork for a program designed to give financial assistance to scholars who had research projects, the results of which would increase one's understanding of the impact of advertising on society. We solicited applications from such scholars and included in our solicitation a request for a detailed presentation of the proposed research. The advisory board had at least quarterly meetings to review proposals and eventually to evaluate the results emanating from such research. I served on that board for several years and was delighted that the principle of having an advertising educator on the board was firmly established. Such representation has been continued.

American Marketing Association

The American Marketing Association (AMA) was a national organization created from a merger of the National Association of Teachers of Marketing and Advertising (NATMA) and the American Marketing Society (AMS). The former was composed of educators whereas the latter was composed of marketing practitioners and professionals. I had been a member of NATMA and was thus also a charter member of the American Marketing Association. I had served on the national board of directors and also as vice president of AMA before coming to the University of Illinois.

In addition to the national office, AMA had local chapters designed to serve the interests of local members. Shortly after arriving at the U of I the national office of AMA suggested that a Central Illinois chapter be organized. One of the functions that such a chapter could perform as an aid to the national organization was to provide a facility for initiating and awarding honors to be known as the P.D. Converse Award. A generous donor had provided funds to underwrite the cost of such awards.

Three or four of the professors of marketing and advertising at the university had been or were officers of the national organization and hence were in a position to spearhead the organization and development of a local chapter. I was one of these people. During the course of my service on the university faculty and for years following I was an active member and frequent officer of the local chapter.

Champaign-Urbana Advertising Club

It seemed appropriate as part of advertising education in Champaign-Urbana to bring students and practitioners together occasionally. Some members of our advertising faculty, including myself, initiated the establishment of the Champaign-Urbana Advertising Club. The club held regular monthly meetings at which time some local or imported advertising practitioner would speak and provide a period for discussion. The club became affiliated with the American Federation of Advertising (AFA). Occasionally a representative of the national organization would be brought to the campus and also provide a program for the local Ad Club. The club also served as a representative of AFA to award the AFA Silver Medal to any local member deemed to meet all criteria established by AFA and worthy to receive such an award. Two of our faculty members eventually received this honor.

Better Business Bureau

In addition to providing some leadership in the establishment of an Advertising Club, I explored the possibility of establishing a Champaign-Urbana Better Business Bureau. The national Better Business Bureau and local bureaus in many cities had been in operation for a number of years. Local bureaus were organized and financed by local business firms and communication media. It seemed eminently appropriate that the university with its commitment to providing an effective program in advertising education could lead efforts to establish a local Better Business Bureau. The community was fortunate in having in its midst H. J. Kenner, who was the author of a book titled *Truth in Advertising* and had served as the full-time director of Better Business Bureaus in three different cities. He had retired from active work and had chosen Champaign-Urbana as a place to live in his retirement.

Kenner and I had several discussions concerning the potential for a Champaign-Urbana Better Business Bureau. He indicted a willingness to serve as an initial manager and to guide and train an understudy if such a bureau were to be established. We got together some materials dealing with purpose, organizational structure, and financing. I called on local media and retail establishments to test the extent of interest in such a project. A major retailer and official of the local newspaper called a meeting of persons with potential interest in such a venture. At that meeting Kenner, along with others, discussed the pros and cons. After two or three such meetings the idea for a local Better Business Bureau was rejected. A majority of those involved thought that the local Chamber of Commerce could perform the same functions that a Better Business Bureau would be involved with. It was also recognized that it would be difficult, if not impossible, to adequately finance another organization that in some respects paralleled the Chamber of Commerce.

Even though the attempt to organize a local Better Business Bureau failed, the concept of local self-regulation of advertising practices became a significant part of the work of the Chamber of Commerce.

PART V

POST-ACADEMIC YEARS

Chapter 14

Not All Work

Before moving to Illinois my professional life was somewhat nomadic, having taught in ten different institutions: a high school in Illinois; part time as a graduate student at the University of Iowa; two positions in evening colleges in Cincinnati and Dayton, Ohio (part-time second jobs); as an adjunct professor at the University of Pennsylvania while employed by the U.S. Government; in summer school at the University of California at Berkeley; as a visiting professor at Harvard Graduate School of Business Administration; and four full-time appointments, at Simpson College in Iowa, the University of Kansas, Miami University of Ohio, and the University of Illinois.

My personal and family life, therefore, were also nomadic and included at least nine different geographic locations where Dorothy, Allan, and I pitched our tent. These were located coast to coast with Boston/Philadelphia on the east and Berkeley, California, on the west. During those years we had built and owned one home but lived in it only four years. Our other abodes during that period were either apartments or rented houses. The house we had in Berkeley was located about two-thirds of the way to the top of Grizzly Peak and directly in line with San Francisco Bay and the Golden Gate Bridge. The apartment we had in Cambridge (Boston) was a high rise on the Charles River.

In some respects this type of living, particularly on

the front end of one's life, is in itself very educational. It was, I think, beneficial in that respect for all three of us. It particularly broadened the horizons of a young, inquiring Allan with his visits to museums, planetariums, astronomy observatories, national parks and Lincoln trails. That was, fortunately or unfortunately, capped with his eighteen months in the U.S. Navy. That took him to many different stations and a different kind of life.

Allan returned from the Navy just as we were getting settled in Urbana, Illinois. We had him as a resident member of the family for only two years after which he left for California and graduate work at Cal Tech. That left an empty nest which probably gave some stimulus to travel for his parents. With Allan now away from home, Dorothy and I were left on our own for travel and leisure time. We made frequent trips to California to see our son. We visited many of the national parks in the West, took different routes to and from California, and visited the University of Idaho in Moscow, Idaho, one summer when I was teaching a short course.

We became close friends with a couple in Urbana who liked many of the same things we did. We often would spend two or three weeks together in northern Wisconsin during the summer. Woodruff and Minaqua, Wisconsin, became almost second summer homes for us. Dorothy and I traveled one summer through parts of Canada and New England where we renewed our previous visit in the New Hampshire mountains.

Dorothy and I took two short holidays on the water. One was a cruise on the Caribbean visiting Puerto Rico, St. John's, and other islands, and the other was to Bermuda. That latter trip was for me part work and part pleasure. I was attending and a participant in a market research convention held on the ship to and from Bermuda. This was very pleasant during the trip to and the stay on the island. Unfortunately on our return trip we ran into a terrible storm which lasted almost all the way back to New York. It was so severe that the majority—at least 70 percent—of the passengers were so sick that they did not leave their cabins. Dorothy was one of those. She vowed that she would never go on a ship again. Her previous experience with ocean travel was when she was three years old and traveled all the way from the Philippine Islands to San Francisco.*

I took a sabbatical leave from the University of Illinois in 1966, immediately after I retired as head of the advertising department. After my sabbatical year, I was obligated to return as a member of the faculty for one year after which I made my retirement complete. By the time of my sabbatical leave, we had been in forty-eight of the fifty states (all but Hawaii and Alaska). We added Hawaii to the list, leaving Urbana for that idyllic state the day after my successor as head of the advertising department took over. We both wanted to see Hawaii and I wanted to avoid any temptation to look over the shoulder of my successor and relieve him of any feeling that he should seek my advice or counsel. We spent two weeks in Hawaii. On our return we picked up our car, which we had stored in Los Angeles, and traveled back to Urbana, taking in new sights on the way. We had

---

* Actually, she had been born in the Philippines when her father was a U.S. Government official charged with the responsibility of developing an educational system for the Philippines. Both she and her twin sisters were born while her parents lived in the Islands, but her mother died shortly after the birth of the twin girls. After their mother's death, all three were returned to the States and lived with relatives until their father was transferred back to the States. After his remarriage the family was then brought back together as a unit.

earlier started the practice of spending one or two weeks in Florida during the winter and continued that until Dorothy's untimely death. It was discovered in September 1970 that she had developed cancer. She underwent surgery shortly after that and seemed to be recovering, but unfortunately the disease spread throughout her body and she died later that year.

After Dorothy's death I did some traveling but for the most part buried myself in work. I drove to California to visit my son and his family and friends who had moved there from Urbana, then drove across the continent to Boca Raton, Florida, to attend a meeting of the education committee of the American Association of Advertising Agencies of which I was a member, then back to Urbana to continue my life as a bachelor. I did some writing during that period, gave a lecture at the University of Missouri, and went to Washington, D.C., to attend a meeting at the White House when Allan received the National Science Medal presented by President Nixon.

The advertising faculty at the university continued to invite me to both its academic and social meetings. It was during one of these social meetings that I met and was attracted to a Ph.D. candidate and part-time member of the advertising faculty. Her name was Elizabeth Danner. She had previously been a public relations employee for a major manufacturing company, an advertising representative of *The Denver Post*, and holder of both a bachelor's and master's degree in advertising from the University of Colorado. She had come to Illinois to work for her Ph.D. in communications (advertising).

While I was attracted to her she apparently was attracted to me even though she was some twenty-eight years my junior. This mutual attraction eventually resulted in marriage in July 1971. Our exchange of vows was quite private, a mutual preacher friend performed the normal religious ceremony witnessed only by Dorothy's brother, George, his wife, Lois, and Elizabeth's son, David. My son, Allan, could not be present but he telephoned his congratulations and good wishes shortly after the ceremony. Thus, while my remarriage may have seemed to some to have occurred improperly soon after my loss of Dorothy, the new marriage had the encouragement and support of Dorothy's family, my son, and Elizabeth's son and daughter, Diana. The latter, like Allan, was not able to attend the ceremony.

Elizabeth had spent the previous year teaching part-time and working for her doctorate degree. Because of her new life as my wife, she chose to shelve her graduate work and not to take it from the shelf to complete such work until a few years later.

Because I was not now teaching and she was free from schoolwork, we did some traveling. That included a motor trip up the Michigan side of Lake Michigan to Mackinac Island, across the Sault into Canada, on to Ottawa, Montreal, and Quebec City, then down through the White and Green mountains, a short stay at Cooperstown, and back to Urbana. Although I was no longer teaching, I still attended some of the meetings of my professional organizations with Elizabeth also attending since most of these were also her organizations. These meetings and vacation jaunts took us to such places as San Diego; Birmingham and Point Clear, Alabama; Norman, Oklahoma; and Brownsville, Austin, and San Antonio, Texas. One of our short historic trips was down through Kentucky and back to Illinois on the Lincoln Trail. Included on the trail was

Tell City, Indiana, where we spent a little extra time because that was the birthplace of my father. This route had been covered years earlier when Allan was a small boy and he got a little history lesson along with the rest of us.

Now that I had a second family it encouraged travels to places that might not otherwise have been included. Elizabeth's family was centered primarily around Independence, Missouri, central Kansas, and the Denver-Colorado Springs area. My family was centered around southern Iowa and southern California. The location of our respective families meant that we learned many details about the area between Urbana, Illinois, and southern California, much of which Elizabeth had never seen.

It seems that the normal practice of professors immediately after retiring is to engage in extensive travel, both domestic and foreign, thus leaving their established homesite for an extended period of time. This rather normal practice was not followed by me. I had actually done more traveling before than after my retirement from the university, although in each case there was extended travel within the United States but for short periods of time. I had established a small market-research company while still at the university and continued to operate it on a somewhat expanded scale after my university retirement. Also, Elizabeth had removed her graduate work from the shelf, took up part-time teaching again, and completed her work for the doctorate in communications. That plus my market-research business kept us both physically and mentally active, and I am sure added to our personal enjoyment.

Chapter 15

Corporate Board Memberships

In the spring of 1965 I was eating lunch alone at the Red Wheel restaurant on West Springfield Avenue in Champaign. An acquaintance and fellow Kiwanian came in, saw me, and joined me at lunch. During the course of our meal he told me of his success in raising capital to start a holding corporation and an insurance company, with the holding corporation owning a majority of the insurance company stock. The names of the new corporations were Holding Corporation of America (HCA) and Thomas Jefferson Life Insurance Company of America. The name of my luncheon companion was Quenton L. Snook. He invited me to become a member of the board of directors of the insurance company. I thanked him for the offer and promised to get back to him within a short time with my decision.

I had very little knowledge of Snook's background and activity and wanted to do some checking of his history. My research was fairly extensive. I found he had his supporters and detractors. The net result, however, indicated he was honest, trustworthy, and a superb salesman. He seemed to have put together a combination of a holding corporation and operating insurance company that was adequately capitalized and gave promise of providing both social benefit and financial reward if properly managed. I agreed to accept membership on the board of his insurance company and was appointed as chairman of the investment committee. We had a much greater capitalization than was common or legally necessary for the organization of a new insurance company. There were, therefore, substantial sums to be invested.

I reviewed the regulations pertinent to investment guidelines in the placement of investments for the company. I maintained a judicious mix between bonds and equities, but in all cases selections carried approved rating symbols. Whether it was luck or judicious selections, the result produced sufficient income to create a reportable profit by the company even in its first year of operation. This was unique in the history of new insurance companies. The fact that Snook had raised significantly more capital than was legally necessary was a major factor in making such profit possible.

Government regulation of insurance companies recognized the fiduciary responsibility of board members and officers to protect persons who purchase insurance policies. Investments were required to meet government quality standards, although there was a wide range of the kinds of securities allowed.

Decisions concerning investments during the first several months of operation were made entirely by our investment committee. It seemed to me that this was too much of a risk for the committee to assume because we had no historical credentials to support our investment expertise. We, therefore, recommended to the full board that we select a financial investment counselor so that we would have legal support for our investments. The Trust Department of the Continental National Bank in Chicago was selected as our counselor.

We learned much from the advice of our investment counselor, not all of which was highly beneficial. The bank assigned one of the top members of its trust department to counsel us. We found that our counselors were addicted to the popular concept of the time that investments in equities should be confined to the so-called "Top 50" corporations. I personally disagreed with that philosophy but other members of the board differed with me and voted to commit some of our funds to stock in two of the "Top 50" companies. Unfortunately for the reputation of our investment counselors, we followed their recommendation to purchase shares in two of the "Top 50" when stock prices were near a cyclical peak and we were never able to recoup our original cost. In general, our investments were highly successful. Partly because of the success and partly because of the large original capitalization, the company showed a profit in all of its early years of operation. This was extremely unusual for any newly organized insurance company.

Snook sought my advice and counsel on many matters and assigned an office in the headquarters building to me. He used the telephone frequently to confer with me when I was in my Farm Research Institute office. He insisted on having a second telephone line installed in my FRI office to provide reasonable assurance that he could always get through.

Many discussions in the office and by telephone revolved around personnel matters. He seemed to have trouble with the position of sales manager. Snook would bring in a new man as sales manager and theoretically give him reasonable freedom to operate the office, but he found it impossible to adequately delegate authority along with responsibility to any sales manager. This resulted in frequent turnovers in that position, dissatisfaction among the salesmen in the field, and conflict within the board. It also brought rebellion on the part of most sales people, who organized a meeting in which they called for Snook's resignation.

Snook had protected his legal control over both the holding corporation and the insurance company by issuing special "B" stock to be held by himself and which would give him absolute authority to nominate members for election to the board. Such election, however, would be called only once a year. In the interim, the standing board could dismiss him as president or any other office and thus, at least momentarily, deprive him of any administrative authority.

There were two of us "outside" or non-officers as members of the board. We counseled and together recommended that we employ Booz Allen & Hamilton, a business management consulting firm, to make a study of our management problem and recommend a solution. The board approved our recommendation.

The Booz Allen study recommended that Snook be appointed as chairman of the board, resign his position as president, and that another be brought on as president and chief executive officer. This was harsh but realistic advice, although it was rejected by Snook. The next approach was taken by the HCA board, which dismissed him as president and CEO and offered to buy him out. The board had found an individual, Victor Sayyah, in Chicago with a highly successful management history and with sufficient capital to underwrite a buy out. After considerable negotiation, Snook agreed to the sale at a figure that would give him a very high price for his ownership position. The purchase of HCA also meant the ownership of a majority of the stock in the insurance company. Therefore, Snook could then also be relieved of his position as chairman of the board, president, and CEO of Thomas Jefferson Life. It also meant that the insurance company board would also be involved in the buy out of the holding corporation board.

By that time I had become recognized as the leader, if not the chairman, of the insurance board. Negotiations for buy out therefore meant that I was strongly involved in these negotiations when there were joint board meetings held. Papers were all drawn for the transfer of ownership and a date set for signatures. That meeting was to be held about two o'clock on the specified day with all parties involved in exchanging signatures to be present. At 1:30 Snook's lawyer called to inform the joint boards that Snook had changed his mind and was not going to sell, although he had already agreed in writing to sell and the papers were on the table to be signed. I took action that may have been extralegal but which brought success. In the absence of the insurance board chairman, I, as a member, called a special meeting on the spot of those board members who were present. I placed before the board a motion to dismiss Snook as president of the corporation. That motion was passed. I then called Snook's lawyer stating that he was no longer president, that he had signed papers to sell his property, that he had agreed to be present to affix his signature on the final papers, and that if he did not appear to do that he would subject himself to serious legal action. That brought Snook to the table and the transfer of ownership was made.

Regardless of my action in respect to Quentin Snook, I had great respect for his ability as an entrepreneur, his vision and success in founding two new corporations, and ability in raising more than adequate capital to ensure that success could not be denied. His forte was in plowing new furrows; that expertise did not carry over in the art of management.

After the buy out, there was a slight reorganization of the holding corporation and I was added as a member of its board of directors. A short time later I was named as chairman of the board.

The holding corporation needed to borrow $1 million to consummate its buy out of Snook's controlling interest. It could offer as security a contract with Victor Sayyah in which he agreed to purchase sufficient shares of stock on a periodic basis sufficient to service the debt and retire a portion of the principal. There were various sources that might loan to HCA but a local source was preferred. Because I owned a small amount of stock of the Champaign National Bank and had a close relationship with its officers, I was asked to help in soliciting a loan from that bank. I arranged for a meeting with the chief financial officer, myself, another member of the board, and Mr. Sayyah. I introduced Sayyah to the financial officer and explained the nature of the security which he would provide. After detailed discussion the loan was arranged. An interesting episode associated with that meeting is worthy of mention. The financial officer, after being introduced to Sayyah, asked, "Do you mind if I call you Victor?" Sayyah astounded the financial officer by saying "Yes, I do." I mention that episode primarily because it seems to me that in the 1980s and early 1990s there seemed to be a fad, fashion, or contrived practice both in sales letters and telephone solicitation for the writer or solicitor to first-name the prospective customer. I believe this is not good sales practice and certainly not by the bank official then. Fortunately, in the case of the bank, after an embarrassing few minutes we got down to serious business and consummated a loan.

Victor Sayyah was an excellent manager and operator. He developed a cohesive sales force but placed major emphasis on expanding operations through acquisitions. In the first few years of his operation several insurance companies were purchased and became subsidiaries of the holding corporation. He sought out a top-quality, experienced insurance executive from a successful competitive operation and persuaded him to accept the position of president and CEO of all our operations. Corporate headquarters were moved from Champaign to Englewood (Denver), Colorado. Satellite offices were established in Toronto, Boston, and Dallas. Ross Perot's EDS Corporation was given a $1 million contract to develop a special computer system for insurance companies which would tie together all offices and use the same record system in all instances. This increased operating efficiency substantially.

Sayyah's enthusiasm for expansion eventually carried him outside the field of insurance. He became interested in the entertainment field and especially the casino type of entertainment. I received a telephone call at my home one Sunday morning from him. He said he was calling from Las Vegas, Nevada, and that he had with him our president and the representative from the legal firm in Chicago that served as our legal counsel. He said he had just completed the purchase of the Aladdin Hotel and put down $1 million of earnest money to seal the sale. He indicated he needed board approval and did he have my affirmative vote. I asked him if he had checked with other members of the board and he said yes, he had left me until the last. I asked him what their reaction was. Well, they all approved. I indicated that a decision to enter into an operation of that size and character should not be made without a thorough investigation. I indicated that I did not wish to make a decision by telephone and recommended that a special meeting of the board be called where we could consider all of the pros and cons of such a purchase before signing any contracts. Realizing that he could not get my approval by telephone, he acceded to calling a special meeting.

At the special meeting additional details of his contractual arrangement were discussed. He and his legal counsel had, in fact, created a separate corporation chartered in Nevada. That corporation was buying the Aladdin, and it would be the board of directors of that corporation that needed to approve the purchase. I asked for the names of the board members and was told that they were the same as the members of the HCA board. I asked how such persons could become members of the board if not asked if they were willing to be members. Because I had never been asked, and certainly never agreed to be a member, I had no power to vote yes or no. I did, however, have power to vote yes or no on whether HCA would become the owner of the Nevada corporation. The legal aspects of the operation, however, were of little concern as compared with the nature of the casino business. Would not that business be in distinct conflict with the business of insurance? We had developed a strong and favorable position in the insurance field. We were asking people to save money as a protection against future poverty. We urged people to postpone current satisfaction that they might experience greater satisfaction in the future. Now, with the casino business as part of our operations, we would be asking people to gamble their savings away on slot machines. It was eat, drink, and be merry today and forget tomorrow versus planning and working for a safe today and a pleasant tomorrow. I urged our board to reject the purchase of the Aladdin Hotel, and the board approved that action. However, it took more than twelve months to recover the $1 million that had been placed in escrow as earnest money to seal the agreement to buy.

My relationship with Victor Sayyah was almost always pleasant and with admiration for his expertise. I could generally approve his actions and recommendations. However, I tried always to operate as an independent outside director, believing that it was my responsibility to serve the interests of all stockholders and not just the holder of sufficient shares to control the corporation. I, as well as any other board member, could be voted out at an annual election, but as long as we were members we were legally obligated to operate as overseers and policymakers in a manner which we felt could be in the best interest of all stockholders.

Sayyah recognized my attitude and position and occasionally would comment that he wished I were younger and had been with him years earlier to help keep him always traveling on a straight road. However, I will mention two or three more experiences which brought me into conflict with him.

Sayyah had purchased a two-engine Lear Jet airplane for corporate use. The purchase had the approval of the board. Its ownership and operation added substantial expense, which seemed to be justified because of the frequent travel of officers on corporate business. It was not long, however, until it seemed that Sayyah was the only officer who used the plane to any significant degree. The independent members of the board became concerned that he was often using the plane for personal trips that had nothing to do with corporate business. We had the audit committee check the logs to determine the character of use. The findings raised enough questions to warrant discussion by the full board. After such discussion, the board voted to order the sale of the airplane. He agreed to the decision but suggested that he could probably be more effective than others in finding a buyer and asked for a period of six or eight weeks to permit him to seek a buyer.

I must report that he located no buyer, found various excuses for keeping the plane, and apparently continued to use it for some personal trips without compensating the company for such use. That and other nagging developments caused me to write a letter directly to him expressing my concern as a director for some of his activities as an officer of the corporation. A copy of that letter is reproduced here.

February 7, 1980

Mr. Victor Sayyah
HOLDING CORPORATION OF AMERICA
7730 E. Belleview Avenue
Englewood, CO 80111   (this was actually sent to his
                                        home address)

Dear Victor:

This is both a personal and business letter. It will deal primarily with HCA matters. Its primary thrust is to examine the responsibilities of directors and to consider gray areas where actions of directors may be questioned.

In broad terms a corporate director is a representative of stockholders. He is held responsible for protecting the rights and property of equity investors. He contributes to the establishment of a policy framework within which management operates. Failure to adhere assiduously to the mandates under which a director functions, whether through negligence, fear, self-serving, or indifference, may subject him to a charge of misfeasance.

Your position as a director is somewhat unusual in that you are also the major and controlling owner. Yet you, like the rest of us, must represent the interests of all stockholders. There are times when this quite naturally creates a conflict of interest for you. When such occurs it places an extra burden on other directors. They are all interested in helping you reach your financial goals, but only by concentrating their efforts in maximizing the profits of HCA. To the extent that this is accomplished, minority stockholders gain along with you.

I believe it is not only wholesome but also essential that the board review those areas in which a conflict of interest may exist. Where such does seem to exist I believe we should take action to resolve such conflict. This will be a protection to you and to all board members.

1. Ownership of the Lear Jet;
2. Your future compensation;
3. Perquisites such as an automobile;
4. Conflict between our press release regarding your resignation from officerships and management committees and your appointment as investment officer;
5. Major "investments" in selected stocks;
6. Unilateral action between you and an outside party purporting to bind the company without prior board or executive committee approval.

Victor, please recognize this letter is written with the warmest of feelings toward you. It is also written because I take my board responsibility seriously.

Some of the questions I have raised and positions taken in the past no doubt have been an annoyance to you. I do not wish to create conflict in the board. I do believe it is necessary for the board to consider matters such as those raised here. Could you and I have a personal talk before the next board meeting to compare notes and evaluate the significance of various problems as I see them? If you are to be in Chicago or St. Louis before February 25, maybe you could fly to Urbana for a personal meeting. If not that, could you arrive in Urbana early February 25 so we could have a discussion before the meeting on February 26 and 27?

Warmest personal regards

C. H. Sandage

After my February letter, Sayyah, Jack Gardiner, and I met in a special personal meeting in St. Louis to discuss various matters mentioned in the February 7 letter. It was a frank discussion, but it resulted in no solution to matters where significant differences existed. After that meeting and with serious analysis and evaluation of the various concerns I had in respect to board member response, I tendered my resignation as chairman and member of the HCA board and its corporate subsidiaries. My letter of resignation follows.

March 12, 1981

Mr. Victor L. Sayyah
P.O. Box 668
23077 Pawnee Road
Indian Hills, Colorado 80456

Dear Victor:

In 1965 I accepted the invitation tendered by Q. L. Snook to become a member of the Board of Directors of Thomas Jefferson Life Insurance Company of America. Mr. Snook had demonstrated great ability in founding the Holding Corporation of America and TJL, with the former holding a controlling interest in TJL. It was personally both rewarding and challenging to serve on the TJL Board.

304

It is well known that during the first 10 years of TJL's operation internal dissension, personality conflicts, and high personnel turnover created severe management problems. Even though the Company had never suffered a financial loss it seemed prudent to develop changes in management and perhaps ownership. Thus Mr. Snook chose to sell his interest in both TJL and HCA. It was shortly thereafter that HCA purchased your IRA, effected by an exchange of stock, which resulted in your becoming the controlling stockholder of HCA. I was asked to serve on the HCA Board as well as to continue on the TJL Board.

I thought then and I think now that it was fortunate for both companies when you assumed a major leadership role. Your breadth of vision, management skills and dedication to growth were attributes needed by the fledgling companies. The boards of the two companies believed that minority stockholders would be best served by having a person of your quality and ability direct the affairs of the companies even though you owned a majority of the shares of HCA. They reasoned that whatever prosperity came from your leadership would flow to all stockholders in proportion to shares held.

I have served with you on the boards of HCA and subsidiaries for the past six years. During that time the companies have prospered beyond expectations. Your skills in personnel selection brought in a team capable of handling the management details needed in operating the substantial number of acquisitions consummated within a relatively short period of time. Your decisions have not all been successful. There have been some failures, but the net results have been phenomenal.

With such success, and with ownership of 60-70 percent of HCA stock, it would seem natural for you to think of HCA as YOUR company. Concomitant with such thought is the temptation to operate the companies as a single proprietorship and lose sight of the fact the 40-30 percent of the company net worth is owned by stockholders other than yourself. Thus, recognition of the tremendous contribution made by those stockholders in providing the great pool of original capital might fade into the background of your memory. Successes of the last six years resulted from a combination of that capital base and your personal ability. We should always keep in mind the relative contribution of each entity in that combination.

Were the company in fact a single proprietorship there would be no place for a board of directors. Since the company is a corporation with multiple ownership, a board of directors is mandated. In the case of a corporation such as HCA where one stockholder owns a majority of the stock, there is probably greater pressure and responsibility on a board than where ownership is highly diffused. Such a board must be eternally vigilant that it not lose sight of the rights of minority stockholders. That is not to say that the board should not concern itself with the rights of the major stockholder, but rather that care must be exercised to avoid what might result in undue dominance by such stockholder to the detriment of minority interests. Perhaps that is why the SEC has been emphasizing the importance of having a majority of board members independent of management.

All of the above leads me to share with you some of my thoughts that have been formulating over the past year or more. Some of these have been expressed in board meetings and some in conversation, but I record them here to permit you to give them whatever consideration you wish.

Up until the Aladdin affair you concentrated your efforts in developing HCA as a force in the financial services industry. When the HCA Board voted to withdraw from the Aladdin proposal you resigned your posts in HCA and announced your desire to pursue other business interests. Even so, you seemingly continue to view HCA as YOUR company and therefore consider it your prerogative to guide or dominate the decision-making process.

In your other business interests you have established your own personal corporation and entered into partnership with others to develop programs outside the financial services area. There is certainly nothing wrong with that, but it does place extra responsibility on you and the HCA Board in respect to possible conflicts of interest. Can one determine whether proposals brought to one entity for approval will result in undue enrichment to another entity? Does this not create unusual problems in determining whether assets or personnel in one company are used for the primary benefit of another personally interlocked company? This could be especially true when you professedly view HCA as your company and by implication, reject the concept that HCA is a PUBLIC corporation. The fact that you are the investment officer of HCA multiplies the prospect of conflict.

As a board member I have accepted the responsibility to serve the interest of *all* stockholders to the best of my ability. It does not necessarily follow that what is good for you is always good for the other owners. I believe my concept of serving all stockholders in a public corporation is incompatible with your view that HCA is your company. It is unlikely that this difference in philosophy will be resolved. Thus, after careful consideration, I have concluded that the interests of all concerned will be best served by my withdrawal from the company. Therefore I am tendering my resignation, both as chairman and as a member of the Boards of Directors of HCA, Inc. and each of its subsidiaries.

Sincerely,

C. H. Sandage

After my letter of resignation addressed specifically to Victor Sayyah with copies sent to each member of the board, I wrote a detailed letter to Jack Lewis, secretary of the corporation. That action was taken because of various troubling matters that I felt obliged to address while I was still responsible as chairman and board member. That letter is also given here.

March 16, 1981

Mr. Jack Lewis, Sec'y
HCA Board of Directors
7730 E. Belleview Avenue
Englewood, CO 80111

Dear Jack:

I am writing you as Secretary of the Board of Directors and will send a copy to Mr. Gardiner as Chief Executive Officer of the Corporation.

Some may consider it inappropriate that I write now since I have submitted my resignation from the Board. However, I am still a Board member until my resignation is accepted. I am also a stockholder and even in that capacity it is appropriate that I write.

My resignation letter was dated and mailed March 12. On March 14 the Chairman of the Audit Committee showed me two reports of the Internal Auditor, one dealing with attorneys' fees billed to HCA and the other the company airplane log. These were brought to my attention because of my position as Chairman of the Board. Those reports must be carefully evaluated and definitive action taken by the Board, keeping in mind the Prudent Man Rule to which we are all subject.

In respect to attorneys' fees, those related to the Integrated Resources case raise a serious question of conflict of interest. This is especially relevant since the legal fees associated with Integrated were approved by Mr. Sayyah who is not a general officer of the company. But even if he were, how could he appropriately make the decision when the question involved both the company and Mr. Sayyah personally? It would seem prudent for the Board to mandate that no company officer or employee be permitted to use the company attorney as his or her personal attorney. This question should be resolved before any action is taken on any matters involving HCA and Mr. Sayyah's personal interests where Mr. Wimmer has served as counsel to both parties.

The Flight Authorization Log reveals a number of extremely questionable items. They are items that cannot be effectively and prudently dealt with after a first reading. I am confident Board members would wish to have the Internal Audit report and Flight Authorization Log in hand days before dealing with them in a group meeting.

However, I wish now to comment on some of the items in the Log. Aside from the very serious question of whether many of the flights were primarily personal in nature there are perhaps even more vital elements to consider.

1. When Mr. Sayyah was the only *company* person using the plane the authorizing officer was Mr. Sayyah. When other company personnel flew with Mr. Sayyah, or alone, the authorizing officer was Mr. Gardiner, the Chief Executive Officer. Did the CEO delegate to Mr. Sayyah the power to authorize his own flights or did Mr. Sayyah assume that power?

2. There were eight flights in 1980 in which the stated business purpose was related to the Aladdin affair. How many flights for the same stated purpose were made in 1979 is not at hand. The Board needs to relate the costs of such flights to the pledge made by Mr. Sayyah to the Board in June 1979 that he would personally see that HCA lost nothing on the $1,000,000 he had pledged and caused the company to pay in the Aladdin case. Presumably that pledge would place the cost of getting the $1,000,000 returned to HCA on the shoulders of Mr. Sayyah.

3. A substantial number of flights were made by Mr. Sayyah and non-company associates to Nassau,

309

Las Vegas and Reno with the stated purpose to investigate potential investment opportunities. At least nine such trips were made to the Bahamas with non-company associates except that Mr. Wimmer was on one such trip.

Mention is frequently made of an Airport Hotel in Nassau, the Down River Hotel, and Jockey Club in Las Vegas. All of this interest in hotel financing seems particularly strange after the Aladdin experience. Of even more vital concern is the fact that the Board was never informed of such activity by Mr. Sayyah. Presumably he also failed to discuss such interest with the company Investment Committee.

The conflict of interest factor looms large when it is noted that on such trips he was often accompanied by persons who were seemingly investors in or owners of hotels. Questions might be asked as to whether any such trips were related to potential or actual investments by Sayyah Corporation and/or whether such trips contributed to the formation of a partnership Mr. Sayyah has entered into with another party, such partnership having heavy interests in hotels.

The problems facing the Board that have grown out of past actions must be resolved in a prudent fashion. And what of the future? The company is once again faced with the question of what to do with the airplane. That question seemed to have been resolved months ago when it was agreed by all board members that the plane would be sold. Apparently when sale was imminent such sale was aborted. Now is the time to take positive recorded action to sell the plane. If from time to time the company needed special custom plane service it would be much less expensive to use the service of a company like Executive Jet Aviation, Inc. of Columbus, Ohio.

I have stated before my opinion that matters flowing from the internal audit are too important to be included on the March 23 Board agenda. A special meeting limited to consideration of these matters would seem to be more prudent.

Presumably my resignation will be brought before the Board March 23. If the Board chooses to not accept my resignation I would call such a special meeting to be held, preferably in Chicago, at an early date. Whether my resignation is or is not accepted I ask that this letter be brought to the attention of all Board members and hopefully included as a matter of information in the corporate records.

Sincerely,

C. H. Sandage
Chairman of the Board

cc: Mr. Gardiner

My letter of resignation created a great disturbance with Sayyah and Wimmer, the legal counsel. The latter called me and urged me to withdraw my resignation. He indicted that if my resignation were accepted, it would be necessary to provide the SEC with a complete statement of reasons for the resignation. He said that would be unnecessarily damaging to the corporation. I agreed to withdraw my resignation *if* a special meeting of the board were called and action taken on matters that gave rise to my resignation. It was agreed that such special meeting would be called for that purpose. It was convened in Chicago at the offices of Lord, Bissell and Brook, the corporate legal counsel.

At that meeting the board resolved all of the issues I had raised. I wished to place in writing as a matter of record my understanding of action taken by the board and the formal withdrawal of my resignation. That statement is included here.

March 25, 1981

Board of Directors, HCA, Inc.
7730 E. Belleview Avenue
Englewood, Colorado 80110

Gentlemen:

By letter of March 12, 1981 I tendered my resignation as a member of the Board of Directors of HCA, Inc. and as a member of the Board of Directors of each of its subsidiaries. I tendered my resignation for the reasons set forth in my letter of March 12, 1981 sent to Victor L. Sayyah. After March 13, 1981 I reviewed certain reports of HCA's Internal Audit and commented thereon as set forth in my letter dated March 16, 1981 to Jack E. Lewis, Secretary of HCA.

Victor L. Sayyah and HCA's management responded by arranging, at my request, a Board of Director's meeting of HCA in Chicago on March 23, 1981. At this meeting the Board addressed each of the concerns I had noted in my earlier letters. Specifically, the Board took the following action:

1. The Board adopted a policy that in transactions in which both HCA, Inc. or a subsidiary and a director, officer or principal shareholder had a material interest, HCA and each director, officer or shareholder shall be represented by separate counsel;

2. The Board adopted a policy that as to all trips involving the company plane, a contemporaneous record must be made setting forth the purpose of the trip, HCA's involvement, the persons contacted, the relationship to HCA's business involvement and the nature of the business discussed;

3. The Board agreed to establish specific investment guidelines indicating what type of investments HCA and its subsidiaries might be interested in pursuing.

4. The Board adopted a policy that if the Investment Officer developed an investment opportunity within the parameters of HCA's guidelines, he would offer that opportunity to HCA or one of its life insurance company subsidiaries;

5. The Board adopted a policy that the Investment Officer could investigate but could not bind HCA or any of its subsidiaries to any loan or investment (except routine projects and sales of bonds and stocks within the parameters previously established by the Board) without the advance approval of the Investment Committee or the Board;

6. The Board decided to sell the plane, authorizing the Investment Officer to attempt to sell the plane within the next sixty (60) days, and if not sold within that time, to list the plane for sale with Gates Lear Jet in Denver.

After thorough discussion and questioning of Victor L. Sayyah, the Audit Committee was completely satisfied that there was not personal use of the plane except for that use which had been personally charged to Victor L. Sayyah. The only remaining concern was the lack of adequate documentation in said case.

Victor L. Sayyah agreed that if as a result of the Internal Revenue Service audit of HCA's Federal income tax returns for 1975, 1976 and 1977 any expenses reimbursed to Victor L. Sayyah by HCA should be determined to be personal, Mr. Sayyah will reimburse the Company.

After thorough discussion the Audit Committee and the Board were satisfied that the legal fees in connection with the negotiations for a sale of HCA to Integrated Resources were properly charged as between HCA and Victor L. Sayyah.

Accordingly, I am completely satisfied. All of my concerns have been addressed and, in my opinion, properly dealt with by the Board. I, therefore, withdraw the tender of my resignation and will remain as a director of the HCA and its subsidiaries until the 1981 annual meeting of the stockholders.

Sincerely,

C. H. Sandage

It was apparent that Sayyah's interests were developing beyond the areas of insurance. It was difficult for him to operate with the constraints placed upon him by an active board of directors. He soon, therefore, accepted an offer from Robert Shaw, who controlled the ICH Corporation and subsidiary insurance companies, to buy all of his interests in HCA and its insurance subsidiaries. Sayyah was handsomely rewarded financially, as were minority stockholders in his properties.

My intimate association with the policymaking and operational aspects of business corporations came to an end with Sayyah's sale of his properties. I had spent seventeen stimulating and satisfying years in what must be called an avocation. During part of those years I was still a professor at the University of Illinois. That experience, I think, was beneficial and certainly not detrimental to my academic responsibilities. After my retirement from the university, I limited my professional activities to my association with Snook/Sayyah insurance operations and the management of the Farm Research Institute, a market-research company that I had originated, owned, and operated as an adjunct to my teaching for many years.

Chapter 16

Farm Research Institute

Let us go back to 1945. I had returned to Miami University after spending more than a year in Chicago as vice president and director of research of the Institute of Transit Advertising. Sometime in the fall I was invited by the Indiana Farm Bureau Cooperative Association (IFBCA) to come to Indianapolis to speak to their management and sales people about marketing.

At that meeting I pointed out that the function of business was to produce goods and services that would meet the needs and wants of consumers. It seemed to me that the IFBCA represented a special type of business because it was, in fact, owned by farmers, the people they were supposed to serve. To implement the function of meeting needs and wants, it behooved business management to know a great deal about consumers and their needs and wants. I indicated there were systematic methods of research which, if used, would provide beneficial information to management.

The IFBCA apparently liked what I had said and invited me to return for another meeting with its people. After two such sessions management asked me to help them organize a market-research department whose function would be to collect information from actual farm families and present that information to management in a form that could be used both to shape policy and develop action. I agreed to work with them to that end.

In the spring of 1946, a young graduate from Purdue University, Richard Smoker, was employed to serve as the first director of market research. I was placed on the payroll to serve as a consultant to work with him in organizing and developing plans of action for the new department.

Shortly after the establishment of the market research department, I moved from Miami University to the University of Illinois in Urbana, but this move did not disrupt the working relationship that had been established with IFBCA. There was no significant difference in the traveling time from Oxford, Ohio, to Indianapolis compared with that from Urbana, Illinois, to Indianapolis. During the summer of 1946, Dick Smoker and I jointly developed two specific research projects in which we personally visited a sample of farm families to collect answers to questionnaires we had created. One questionnaire dealt with the use of various media of communication including farm magazines and publications of the IFBCA. Another questionnaire dealt with the purchase of different commodities and the respondent's intentions for future purchases. Also included were questions dealing with their likes and dislikes concerning specific commodities and their attitudes toward the quality of products and services rendered by various suppliers.

The results of these early surveys impressed management to the extent that they wanted to have continuing contact with the people that constituted their basic market, namely, farm families in Indiana. They asked me to recommend the best way to accomplish this.

The cost of collecting information from farm families by using personal interviews was very great. This was especially true in the case of farmers because of the amount of travel that would be required. In my research with the Institute of Transit Advertising, I had organized panels of housewives to get them to answer questionnaires or to keep records to supply information related to their purchases of various consumer products. I thought that approach would be especially valuable and cost effective in the case of farmers. I therefore recommended that a representative sample of farm families in Indiana be selected and invited to become members of a panel whose function would be to supply information related to the needs and wants of farm operators.

It was emphasized that in order to maintain the objectivity of the research and the avoidance of bias in respondents' answers to questions IFBCA could not be the contact with panel members. Management agreed with that line of reasoning. As a result, this provided the stimulus for establishing the Farm Research Institute. It was to be an independent research organization that could and would serve various clients. It would organize panels, be wholly responsible for developing policy and relationships with panel members, assure that all communication with panel members would be objective to guard against respondent bias, and would never discuss with a respondent the name of the client for whom information was sought.

It was recognized that the cost of establishing a panel would be prohibitive if it had to be absorbed in only two or three field studies. It was pointed out that if a minimum of six projects per year and at least a two- or three-year operation were guaranteed, the cost of organizing and operating a panel of farm families in Indiana could be justified. IFBCA agreed to meet these minimum requirements and thus became the stimulus for the establishment of the Farm Research Institute and its first client.

Some of the first studies were very revealing. Our early work was done shortly after the close of World War II. There had been shortages of many commodities but that was gradually being relieved. Management was guessing on what items would be most in demand and the quantity that should be ordered to meet that estimated demand. The home freezer was one such commodity. Management had somewhat nervously ordered a freight carload of home freezers with the hope that they would be able to sell all of them. We made a study designed to measure the demand for various items including home freezers. The results of our study indicated that at least four carloads of home freezers would be necessary to meet the demand. Management was not willing to accept our findings completely but did double their order. The result was a quick disposal of both carloads and a reorder to essentially meet our forecast.

In another study, farm equipment was the subject of our inquiry. We asked questions about farm grain combines. We found that Indiana farmers would not buy a combine that was more than twelve feet wide. One important reason for that was the width of gates on farms, most being twelve feet or less. When we presented our results, management said we were wrong because they knew from their internal records that eighteen sixteen-foot combines had been sold to Indiana farmers. One could hardly dispute the accounting records of the company, but I did ask whether their records showed the sale to farmers or to IFBCA retail outlets. Management followed up on that question and found that not one of the sixteen-foot combines had been sold to an Indiana farmer, but that the local retail outlet had made deals with Kansas dealers where there was a large demand for sixteen-foot combines and had thus disposed of their IFBCA inventory. Other examples of research findings of equal value to management could be given, but it is sufficient to say that IFBCA is still a client of FRI in 1991 when this is being written.

Establishing a Panel in Illinois

The value that IFBCA management was receiving from the market research developed by their department in cooperation with FRI did not go unnoticed by other farm cooperatives. An officer from a New York-based farm cooperative visited us at Urbana to see what we were doing and see how it might be used in New York. A sister organization that served Illinois also visited us and asked us to do the same thing for them that we had been doing for IFBCA. This was in 1950, the year we accepted the invitation of the Illinois Farm Supply Company (now Growmark, Inc.) to organize a farm panel in Illinois and operate it in the same manner in which we were operating the one in Indiana.

We followed the same practice we used in Indiana to build the Illinois panel. We took a road map of the state and marked for each of the 102 counties two or more crossroads two or more miles away from any city or town. We employed a professional personal interviewing firm to take the road map, have an interviewer start at the marked crossroad, turn right, stop at the first farmhouse and invite the occupant to become a member of our panel. If said occupant refused, the interviewer was to stop at the next house and the next until a recruit was obtained. The interviewer was then to skip three farmhouses and continue the process of invitation. After a quota (which varied by size of county) was obtained on that road the interviewer was to move to another marked quadrant in the county and repeat the process. Each party that accepted our invitation filled out a questionnaire we called a Personal Data Sheet, the contents of which provided extensive demographic information. This information could then be checked against the U.S. Census of Agriculture for purposes of determining the statistical validity of the sample.

Illinois agreed to the same type of contract we had with Indiana in respect to minimum number of studies and years of operation. Again, as was true of Indiana, Illinois was still a client in 1991. The only difference was that in mid-1985 FRI added panels in Iowa and Wisconsin to cover the states which had been added to the territory served by the Illinois cooperative.

Illinois had done some market research before FRI entered the picture but had not formally organized a market-research department with a director until our contract with them. I mention that because the individual who had done some market-research work had become a significant member of the management group and voiced some skepticism concerning the accuracy of information reported by members of our panel. The skepticism was dissipated after several months of operation. The cooperative had developed feed mills for the production of livestock feed, particularly for swine. The potential demand for swine feed would vary according to the number of animals to be marketed. The time between farrowing and marketing the finished animal was approximately six months. The general practice of swine producers was to time the breeding of sows so that farrowing would occur in early spring and produce finished hogs six months later.

320

The government issued forecasts of the probable pig production several times during the gestation and farrowing periods. We decided to experiment with our own forecasting procedure and asked the swine-producing members of our panel to give us the number of breeding sows they had, when they expected pigs to be born, the number per litter expected, and the average percentage of pigs lost at birth. From those data we projected our forecast. We released our findings about the time the government pig crop report was issued. There was a significant difference between our figures and those of the government. Our management critic let us know that he was disturbed. The second government report provided figures somewhat closer to ours. The third government report, issued many weeks after ours and their first report, was almost identical to ours. After that our validity had been established with management.

Testing the Hypothesis of Bias

The use of panels was generally criticized by academicians and most orthodox market-research people. The basic negative was the claim that fixed or continuous membership in a research panel would result in bias over time. I wanted to test the theory because if continued membership in our farm panels resulted in bias, then we could not depend on the basic accuracy of our findings. I thought I had an ideal method for testing the hypothesis of bias.

I did the testing with the Indiana panel. That original group consisted of about 300 members. The second or third questionnaire we sent to that original panel was designed to measure the attitude of farmers toward farm cooperatives. We included in our questionnaire chain stores along with farm cooperatives. This was done so that respondents would not suspect that we had a particular or peculiar interest in farm cooperatives as such. The questionnaires were mailed out in the late 1940s when chain stores were much in the news and criticism of their adverse effect on independent business firms was substantial. The questionnaire used was highly objective in nature.

Sixteen months after that questionnaire was used we added approximately 300 new members to our panel. The first questionnaire mailed to the new members was identical to the one mailed to our original panel. We also mailed that same questionnaire to our original panel at the same time it was mailed to the new recruits. Two years later we added another significant number to our panel. The first questionnaire we mailed to that group was the identical chain store/farm cooperative questionnaire. Also, at the same time we mailed the questionnaire to our original panel and our second expanded panel. Thus, the oldest segment of our then-current panel had received and answered it three times. The second segment had answered it twice, and the newest segment answered it once. If there had been a bias built in over time, there would have been a significant difference in the answers given by each of the three segments. If there had been a difference in the answers of the original panel between their first answers and their third answers, it could not be claimed to be the result of bias if their answers to the third round matched with the answers of the new recruits. The only conclusion, if that had occurred, was that there had been a change in the total population, not a change because of membership in the panel.

To make sure there would be no bias in our statistical analysis, I had Dr. Robert Ferber, a nationally known statistical expert and author of a textbook on statistics, analyze our data in every appropriate way to test for bias. His conclusions were "no bias." The results of that test were carried in an article published in the April 1956 issue of the *Journal of Marketing* under the title "Do Research Panels Wear Out."

I make a distinction between panels used only to measure habits, general buying behavior, attitudes, and opinions and panels used to measure differences in taste, flavor, texture, and other elements of new or competitive products. In the case of the latter, one might be testing a product that had never been experienced by consumers or a product whose characteristics had been changed. Such action or experience would mean that 100 percent of all members of that panel would have experienced something new which would have been experienced by only say 2, 4, 10 or X percent of the universe of people in that market group.

Our specialization of market research in the field of agriculture and our pioneering use of fixed panels to collect information on the attitudes, interests, and buying behavior of commercial farmers created an interest in other research firms to learn what we were doing. The Doane Agricultural Service in St. Louis, Missouri, became quite interested in our work. Officers of Doane came to Urbana to study our operation. They expressed a strong interest in developing a nationwide fixed panel patterned after FRI. They wanted me to work with them in developing such a panel. I agreed to serve as a consultant and was placed on the Doane payroll to function in that capacity. I served as their consultant for two years helping to get their countrywide panel established and in operation. The Doane panel is still in operation as this is being written (1991). They have never been a competitor to FRI because we limited our efforts to the Midwest and maintained sufficiently large samples that would permit analysis of data by individual states which Doane did not do.

Expanding Panels into Iowa and Wisconsin

Our Illinois farm cooperative client absorbed into its operation a farm cooperative in Iowa and Wisconsin sometime in the 1960s. Illinois asked us to develop panels in these states to supplement what we were doing in Illinois, but at that time we chose not to expand our operation. We did help a professor from Purdue and his partner, who was with the marketing division of the Iowa Department of Agriculture, organize an Iowa panel under the name Agricultural Marketing Research (AMR). These two men operated that panel for a few years but found it unprofitable, eventually abandoned the operation, and AMR was dissolved.

After the failure of AMR, we helped a professor from Bradley University move in to fill the void left by the demise of AMR. A new Iowa panel was developed and also one in Wisconsin. They were operated under the name Scotti Bureau. Most of the business for the Iowa and Wisconsin panels was generated by FRI clients. We therefore felt a responsibility for monitoring the service provided by Scotti Bureau. The Bradley professor moved from Illinois to Tampa, Florida, and with that move the service deteriorated. It was then decided to discontinue our cooperation with Scotti Bureau.

After both AMR and Scotti Bureau failed to render the kind of service needed, FRI decided to organize and operate Iowa and Wisconsin panels. We opened an office in Des Moines in 1985 and appointed Lyle Kreps as a vice president of FRI and manager of the Des Moines office. He had a full-time position as director of market research for *Successful Farming*, a Meredith Company publication, and operated the FRI-Des Moines office on a part-time basis. Kreps left Meredith in 1989 to become director of the Des Moines Grand Prix. With that move it became necessary for him to cancel his relationship with FRI. We then closed the Des Moines office and moved its entire operation to Urbana.

Multiplicity of Clients

FRI early established itself as an independent research organization. The Indiana and Illinois farm cooperatives provided the stimulus to get us started. Our work with them brought FRI many other clients. They included companies such as American Cyanamid, Ceba-Geigy, Standard Oil, major livestock feed companies, the U.S. Department of Agriculture, research professors in colleges of agriculture, state government agencies, and various communications media serving the farm market.

FRI Research as an Adjunct to Teaching

It was never my intent to devote full time to the operation of FRI; my great love was teaching, and research became an adjunct to that. I never let it keep me from devoting full time to my university responsibilities. In many respects I looked on FRI research as a substitute for what I had hoped to do as university-sponsored and financially supported research.

Even though the research done under the FRI label had distinct academic value, I chose to judiciously separate its physical operation from my university office and work. Instead, the FRI office was maintained in my home for the first fifteen years of its operation, my spacious study becoming the focal point of FRI operation. My wife, Dorothy, assumed responsibility for keeping records and handling correspondence with panel members. We had a secretary who worked half time.

During the first decade or so of our operation we not only prepared questionnaires and collected data from our panels but also did all of the tabulations and wrote the reports for clients. These were days long before the personal computer. All of our tabulations were then done by hand using 17 x 22-inch size graph paper. That work was done by housewives we employed on a part-time basis and sometimes by students who needed some extra money. In 1965 I also brought into the company on a part-time basis a professor and colleague, Dr. Arnold Barban. He assumed responsibility on certain research projects and carried them through to completion. He was a part of FRI for eighteen years until he left the University of Illinois to join another university.

A few years before my retirement from the university, we moved our office from my home, first to an office on Lincoln and shortly thereafter to an office building located at 2003-B Philo Road in Urbana. We had about 650 square feet of space in our new offices, which permitted us to spread out and enjoy the luxury of uncramped facilities. We remained in that office for twenty-four years, from 1966 to 1990, and occupied about 15 percent of the space in the entire building—its first occupant, by the way. The turnover in tenants of other parts of the building was rather frequent until the winter of 1990 when Carle Clinic leased the entire building except our offices. The building was L-shaped and our offices were in the elbow of the L. Our landlord told Carle that he would not let them have our space because we had been his original tenant and that we could stay there as long as he was the landlord. I recognized that our space would be very beneficial to Carle and that if they should purchase the building we would probably be forced to leave. I therefore went to Carle and asked if they would like to have our space. They expressed great interest in it. I agreed to let them have it if we could find adequate space somewhere else. We did find such space at 1717 Philo Road and offered to release our space to Carle. They demonstrated their appreciation by paying the cost of our move to our new office space.

My wife, Elizabeth, received her Ph.D. in communications from the University of Illinois in the spring of 1983. She had been a part-time lecturer in the advertising department while doing her graduate work.

Now that Elizabeth had received her doctorate and I was eighty years old, I gave serious consideration to retiring from FRI. I could completely liquidate FRI, sell it, or find someone who would manage it and I retain ownership. Elizabeth expressed some interest in becoming a part of FRI, and that became an important element in my thinking.

I had always operated FRI as a single proprietorship. It occurred to me that it would be much better to organize FRI as a corporation. I employed a lawyer to draw up the necessary papers and FRI became a corporation in January 1984. With Elizabeth's interest in becoming a part of FRI, she became a stockholder along with me in the new corporation. The two of us constituted the board of directors. I was listed as president and treasurer; she was listed as a vice president and corporate secretary. She continued her part-time teaching at the university until June 1984 and then became a member of the FRI staff. FRI had never done its own computer work, preferring always to farm it out to specialists. Now that Elizabeth was interested and capable in that area of expertise, we equipped our office with a computer and Elizabeth became the director of that work.

It became apparent that if we ever wanted to sell FRI the fact that we were now a corporation would make it easier to attract buyers. In addition, FRI's computer capability provided a dimension to the operation that would increase its value to potential buyers. Also, with Elizabeth being much younger than I, her expertise and interest in FRI might be continued with any change in ownership or management.

I am a realist and recognized that time is finite, that sooner or later FRI would be either nonexistent or would be owned and/or managed by someone else. There was one vital aspect of FRI that I considered personal. It dealt with a long-established practice of paying members merit points for completing questionnaires sent to them. The accumulated value of merit points was substantial. I did not wish to transfer that liability to someone else who might choose not to or not be able to redeem those merit points in the future. I therefore wrote all panel members in January 1984 explaining that I was eighty-one years old, that I might be retiring, and someone else would then own or manage FRI. I explained that I was assuming a personal responsibility for the merit point credit they had on our books and asked if they would try to redeem all points by at least December 31, 1985. Many people did do so but many did not. I wrote to those who did not redeem points and again urged them to meet the December 1985 deadline. This brought forth some additional redemptions but there was still a substantial liability on the books. I then wrote to that group indicating that if they did not redeem points by December 1985 I would contribute equivalent dollars to a charitable organization to be used for scholarships to students of agriculture. This would be done in recognition of the contribution of farmers who had helped FRI in its research.

This is being written in 1991 and obviously I did not retire or sell when I first started thinking about it. I still recognize that time is finite but that we should make the most of it while alive and well. To me, "making the most of it" means striving to make a positive contribution to some aspect of life.

Relationship with Panel Members

Every attempt had been made to develop a warm, personal relationship with panel members. This has been true with the first panel and all that followed. All contacts with panel members are made by mail, with a personalized letter going out with each questionnaire. Usually some comment of a nonbusiness nature is included in the letter. It may be mention of something that has happened to myself or my family. Reference might be made to crop conditions, attendance at farm meetings, what panel members did at Thanksgiving or at Christmas, or where they took their vacation, if any.

We often included some questions we call "Special Questions" with a regular client study to cover these and other matters of a personal nature. For example, when the U.S. Surgeon General first announced the health hazards associated with use of tobacco, we asked our panel members (1) whether they use tobacco;

(2) if they did use tobacco, in what form (a) cigarettes (b) cigars (c) pipe (d) chewing; and (3) whether the wife used cigarettes. We could and did report the results of that survey to our panel members. (We would never report to members the results of client studies because of the possibility of developing bias.)

Our tobacco questions were repeated every four or five years. This permitted us to chart the downward trend in the use of tobacco by farmers. In our original study, slightly more than 40 percent of the men reported use of tobacco. The sixth study, reported twenty-three years later, showed a decline of use to 18 percent. The major change was in the use of cigarettes, but there was a decline in the use of all other forms except chewing tobacco. That did not go down until the 1988 study which showed an 11 percent reduction from the study four years earlier. This decrease in the use of chewing tobacco must have resulted from the news and other reports of the potential development of cancer of the mouth and throat from the use of chewing tobacco.

At about 1958 or 1959 I instituted a program of sending each panel member a Christmas card from FRI. I included a handwritten personal message in each card. Those messages had a theme related to farm life. The theme was never contrived but usually one that grew out of my experience or attitude toward life. Three such messages are given here to illustrate the nature of my Christmas cards to the panel. The first example was the card sent at the 1981 Christmas. It contained an illustration of an abandoned hay rake standing in a vacant field. The card included this personal message:

> I recently visited the small farm in Northern Missouri where I was born. The old house had long been unoc-cupied and is now as abandoned as the hay rake

pictured on this card. I also visited the little country church I attended in my youth. It was still in good condition and far from being abandoned. That church seemed to symbolize the stability of the spiritual edifice that is built within the human soul. Let us not abandon that edifice.

The 1987 card contained an illustration of a winter farm scene with snow on the ground and stars in the heavens. My message on that card was distinctly farm related:

A city boy was invited to spend a weekend with a farm family. His first night there brought an amazing comment as he gazed skyward. He had literally never seen the stars in the heavens before. At the farm there were no city lights to block a view of the heavens. Maybe that is one reason farm families feel a special closeness to God.

Another card, sent at Christmas 1988, contained a lone winter tree silhouetted against a star-filled night sky. It contained this message:

The tree on this card does not stand alone. It reaches out to embrace the stars. There are times when we may think we stand alone wrestling with personal problems. It is not so. There is always a higher power where help can be found. Reach out and embrace that power.

My letters containing occasional reports of answers to special questions and the Christmas cards with my personal message brought numerous personal letters from panel members. The "lone tree" card brought a number of very touching letters. Members would often write to tell us of additions to their families, sickness, injuries, deaths, vacations, and other of their own personal lives.

This personalization of the relationship with panel members was never designed as a pure "business" operation. It was instead an extension of my interest in serving the interests of agriculture and showing an appreciation to those who were cooperating with FRI in performing that service. If you call that "business," then there was a business motive. That, however, was in harmony with my philosophy that the businessman is or should be, in fact, a servant of the people. FRI was therefore helping agribusiness serve commercial farm families more effectively. Our research operation would not be effective if we lacked credibility. We therefore wanted members of our panels to understand our objective and to know us as a person and to believe in our operation.

We did not ask panel members to render service without compensation. We gave each member a specified number of "merit points" for completing and returning a questionnaire on time. In addition, we gave a bonus of 50 percent to those members who returned all of the studies sent to them during our operating year and a bonus of 25 percent to those who missed only one study. Merit points could be redeemed in good quality merchandise as premiums. We supplied members with a catalog or a lengthy list of items that could be obtained. Each item carried the number of merit points needed for redemption. We had arrangements with a well-recognized supply house and had our members send their orders for premiums directly to us. We then sent the orders on to the supply house, and they took the responsibility for shipping the items and billing us for the cost. If any member was dissatisfied with a premium we wanted the member to know that we assumed responsibility for keeping them satisfied. We would have a heavy flow of orders for premiums starting in October and carrying through until December. These were used as Christmas gifts. We would have another heavy flow of orders in April or May preceding school graduation and weddings. One member of our staff devotes from one-fourth to one-half of her time to handling matters related to premiums. Our payment of merit points was not the major reason for receiving the cooperation and loyalty of panel members. In 1989 we included on one questionnaire a list of five specific statements related to panel membership. We asked members to check those they considered important to them. Following are the statements and the percent showing the panel's estimation of the relative importance of each statement:

1. Being a spokesman for fellow farmers—60.9 percent

2. Helping a research organization measure farmers needs—78.8 percent

3. Earning merit points for merchandise premiums—24.1 percent

4. Contributing to agriculture college scholarship funds—42.3 percent

5. It is an honor to be a member of an FRI panel—56.8 percent

Payment of merit points was listed as important by only about one-fourth of panel members, and it was the least important of the five factors. Even though it was rated lowest in importance of any of the factors, there may be a hidden value in that it permits us to provide a token of appreciation and might thus help to call attention to the other factors that are considered of substantially greater importance than are merit points.

In 1987 we instituted a practice of giving scholarships to students studying agriculture in an agricultural college in one or more of the states in which we operate. In 1991 we gave three $500 scholarships to such students. We indicated to our panel members that if they did not wish to redeem their merit points we would contribute money to a scholarship fund in the name of FRI and in honor of farmers cooperating with us in our research work. A combination of the various reasons for membership undoubtedly accounts for the high percentage of returns we obtain on most studies. Those returns range from 80 to 93 percent. In fact, we guarantee an 80-percent return except in very rare cases where an unusually long and difficult questionnaire is involved.

The bookkeeping to record mailings, returns, credits for merit points earned, premiums ordered, and debits for merit points used is substantial. That information together with codes for each demographic factor on our Personal Data Sheet is kept on a 4 x 6-inch record card for the individual member. That system of record keeping was instituted in 1947 and is still the method used. A computer expert would wonder why we could not become modern and place all records on a computer. One answer is that we must include on every questionnaire mailed the panel member's identification number. We always use a number rather than a name as a means of guaranteeing the confidentiality of information provided us. There is a wealth of information on those 4x6 cards covering more than forty years. They are in fact a multiple accumulation of case histories showing changes in the farming operations of individual farmers. Changes such as acres operated, ownership, kinds of crops, acres planted by type of crop, economic class, membership in farm organizations, level of education, livestock operation, changes in numbers and types of livestock, number of years of farming, and, of course, age are all included on each member's card. It is hoped that some researcher, perhaps in rural sociology or agriculture economics—and a super expert in computer programming—will sometime in the future develop a way to use this stored information to show changes in the pattern of work and life on the farm by individual farm families rather than farm families in the aggregate.

Types of FRI Research

One of our early studies (1949) involved measuring the extent to which farm families listened to radio. While at Miami University I had created and used a form to be used by individuals in keeping a diary of their radio listening. That diary form was broken into fifteen-minute segments covering the time period 5 a.m. to midnight for each of the seven days in a week. My client had no information that showed radio listening by farm families. We therefore asked our panel members to keep a radio listening diary with separate diaries kept by each adult member of the family. From those diaries we were able to chart radio listening separately for male and female adults and relate each fifteen-minute segment of each day to specific radio stations. The results of that research project provided valuable information to the client in allocating its advertising budget.

There were three major radio stations that stood out in attracting farm family listening. They were WOWO in Ft. Wayne, Indiana; WLW in Cincinnati, Ohio; and WLS in Chicago. Each of these stations had 50,000-watt power and covered a large area. Local and some regional stations had significant followings, but the three majors mentioned were dominant. Of the three, WLS was outstanding. It had chosen to concentrate much of its programming to meet the interests of farm people.

Because of the farm audience rating of WLS among farm families in the northwest third of Indiana, I thought the station might be interested in those results and willing to pay us something for it. My Indiana client gave me permission to negotiate with WLS for the purchase of that segment of our findings. I had become acquainted with George Biggar, an officer of WLS, when I was with the Institute of Transit Advertising in Chicago. I therefore wrote him to ascertain whether WLS might be interested in our Indiana data. The result of my negotiations with the Chicago station was their purchase of our findings of the WLS coverage of farm families in Indiana for a modest sum.

I had no further contact with WLS until January 1955 and that was with Glenn Snyder, general manager of the station. It was in the form of a letter written as satire designed to call critical attention to the unfortunate placement of a radio commercial for the laxative gum, Feenamint. The commercial was aired during the normal dinner hour. It pulled no punches. It brought the bathroom to the dining room table. I sent the following letter to Mr. Snyder:

January 25, 1955

Mr. Glenn Snyder
General Manager, WLS
1230 Washington Avenue
Chicago, Illinois

Dear Glenn:

An inspiration for a promotion piece to stimulate increased listening to WLS came to me the other evening when I was listening to one of your programs. The piece would follow the general pattern of a radio commercial, but could also be sent out as a direct mail folder or letter to lists of men and women throughout the WLS listening area.

If you also wanted to get a little novelty into your promotion this commercial could be cut on a platter and the record sent to a select mailing list. You might also get a number of firms that pipe music to their employees to play your record once or twice. The theme of the promotion piece would undoubtedly appeal to the management of many firms as a way to increase the production of employees.

Here is the suggested promotion piece:

> Are you sluggish at your work today? If you are you probably did not listen to your favorite radio station during your dinner hour at home last night. May I recommend that tonight you invite WLS into your home at 6:15 and then listen attentively to the information, advice, and counsel from Feenamint. Do this while you are dining. With your 6:15 WLS guest whispering the marvels of a gentle laxative, one that does not work in the stomach but in the lower tract where it eliminates mostly waste, you will get increased satisfaction from your dinner. It will reassure you that if your dinner is not easily digested you can just chew Feenamint after dinner and not worry. Such reassurance in itself will probably help to relax you and make your dinner even more enjoyable. The whisper of your WLS friend, Mr. Feenamint, is undoubtedly a better dinner companion than is Beethoven or Brahms or Bach. Your children will love Mr. Feenamint, too, particularly at dining time. And the next time you have friends in for dinner be sure to tune in WLS for the reassuring and comforting dinner "music" of Mr. Feenamint.

When you use this promotion as a mailing piece you would need some sort of closing phrase before your signature. You could use very truly yours, sincerely yours, refreshingly yours, aesthetically yours, or laxatively yours. Or you might give some thought to the possibility of using "yours for rapid waste elimination."

That is a little negative though, so you might want a more positive closing "yours for cleaner bowels." —That will really put guts into your promotion.

Sincerely,

C. H. Sandage

P.S. I had planned to copyright this to protect myself but finally decided against it. I know you can be trusted to pay me a reasonable sum when you make use of this suggestion for promotion.

Glenn Snyder caught the satire in my letter and called me suggesting that sometime when I might be in Chicago to stop by his office for some conversation. I took advantage of that suggestion and did meet with him. We talked about farm radio listenership and the attention WLS was continually giving to developing programs of interest to farm families. It was natural that WLS would be interested in farmers since the station was owned by *Prairie Farmer*, a magazine directed exclusively to the farm market. At that conference he asked that I make a proposal for a study of the listenership of farm families in the WLS coverage area. That area included a large portion of Illinois and lesser portions of Indiana, Michigan, and Wisconsin.

I developed a proposal to ask a large sample of farmers to answer a short questionnaire. I proposed asking the agricultural county agent in each county of the WLS coverage area to select a sample of farmers and mail them an envelope supplied by me in which would be a letter, a questionnaire, and a pre-stamped, addressed envelope for returning the completed questionnaire to me. A total of 4,275 stamped envelopes were mailed to the county agents in the coverage area. Some of these envelopes may never have been mailed by the county agents but 1,366 completed questionnaires were returned. It was the first comprehensive measurement of actual farm radio listening made for a specific station coverage area. Most listening measurement studies did not have a large enough sample to show the listenership for actual farm families.

WLS seemed to be highly satisfied with that 1955 study and in 1957 commissioned FRI to make another study and include television viewing as well as radio listening. A different approach was used for that study. In this study we wanted even a larger sample than the one used in 1955 and to mail our request and questionnaire directly to farmers rather than through county agents. We selected from a detailed list of operating farmers 17,640 names of persons to whom we mailed a double postcard containing our letter and a short, straightforward questionnaire. Our letter could be detached and the questionnaire, pre-addressed and stamped, returned to us. We received 2,493 usable questionnaires.

The results from all three studies confirmed the dominance of WLS among farm families. The station now thought it was in a position to emphasize that dominance in its solicitation of advertising from agribusiness firms.

One of WLS's pieces of promotion came to the attention of Joseph H. Sierer, a salesman for the radio representative firm of Edward Petry & Co., Inc. The Petry Company served as a representative of WGN in soliciting advertisers to advertise on their station. Because the WLS promotion piece placed WLS significantly ahead of WGN in reaching the farm audience, Petry sent the memo, reproduced here, to all Petry salesmen in all their offices across the United States.

Edward Petry and Co., Inc.
400 N. Michigan Ave.
Chicago Wh 4-0011

TO: All Salesmen—All Offices
FROM: Bill Steese
RE: Sales Letter on WGN

August 6, 1958

Joe Sierer has written the letter below to a farm advertiser on behalf of WGN.

cc: Chicago   Atlanta   Boston   Detroit   Los Angeles
St. Louis   San Francisco

Miss Pamela Tabberer
Liller, Neal, Battle & Lindsey
Walton Building
Atlanta, Georgia

Re: Big Crop
Armour Fertilizer Works
WGN-Chicago

Dear Pam:

Without attempting to pose as a research expert, here are some pertinent questions in connection with the Farm Family Radio Listening in WLS Land ... December 1957, Prepared exclusively for WLS by the Farm Research Institute, Urbana, Illinois.

1. *Who and what is the "Farm Research Institute"?*
   What national, or even regional acceptance do they enjoy? What other farm research have they undertaken? What acceptance has it had, other than by the firm financing it? What lists of research sources does FRI appear in, if any? Being widely unknown, why—as with most generally unknown firms—do they fail to identify themselves further in this study, other than by location and the name of the president? Instead of being handled by professionals, is this possibly a college or university paid-research project?

2. *With one of the stated purposes of this study being to determine the Radio listening pattern of farm*

340

*families at different periods of the day, why should
the county-area covered be restricted to the WLS 0.5
m/v coverage?*

Doesn't the nationally accepted NCS No. 2, clearly
show that WGN, and at least one other Chicago
station, cover a substantially larger area than
WLS? What then about farm listening in those
ADDITIONAL counties in the five mid-western
states where Armour Fertilizer has distribution?
Doesn't a study confining listening habits of 243
Radio stations to the specific signal pattern of ANY
ONE OF THEM obviously develop "bias" in favor of
the restricting station?

3. *What is the source of the farm family list used?*

Why wasn't the source of the list included in the
introduction of the study? By what method was this
list, supposedly including from 85-90% of all farm
families in the area surveyed, reduced to 100 families in each county (except in Iowa)? Why wasn't
the method disclosed? What percent of total farm
families in the area is represented by the 17,640
questionnaires mailed? And, what percent of total
farm families is represented by the 2,493 usable
questionnaires returned?

4. *With replies received from 178 counties, and a total
of 2,493 questionnaires returned, doesn't this figure
on an AVERAGE OF ONLY 14 REPLIES PER
COUNTY?*

With the study showing the lowest county return
supplying only 4 replies, and with 38 counties
having "fewer than 10," and the county producing
the highest return providing only 29-wouldn't most
counties be in the 15-20 replies category? Going
back to the county average of 14, if in WLS-Land 2
farm families in each county admitted they were
Methodists (or Baptists, Rosicrucians, or Holy Roll-
ers) can we then with statistical accuracy claim
that 14.3% of all Mid-western farm families are
members of this particular denomination or sect?
Since the percent of farm families ostensibly pre-

341

ferring WLS vary by time segments from 6.3% to 19.2%, can't we assume then an average of about *only 2* WLS mentions per county? Does the "exceedingly large and well distributed" sample provide substantial "confidence in the validity of results", or does the exceedingly *small* county sample offer the possibility of only compounding errors?

5. *Was the questionnaire a "simple, straightforward request" as FRI indicates?*

Is the statement of purpose on the questionnaire entirely clear to farm-family respondents? What is a "survey of farm Radio listening"? Does it concern itself only with "farm Radio" (programming) listenership, or do the research people more precisely mean "Radio listening on farms"? Isn't it perfectly conceivable that many—*if not all, or most*—respondents would naturally interpret this as it is obviously stated and meaning listening to FARM-Radio, as opposed to more general Radio programming?

6. *If, as the study claims, there was no element of bias, why then do the seven time segments chosen embrace ONLY THOSE TIMES when WLS (as shown in SRDS) programs ALL Their weekday FARM RADIO service?*

Isn't it highly probable that NONE of the other 242 stations listed by respondents feature purely farm service programming in all seven of these time segments? Doesn't this overwhelmingly "load" the survey in favor of WLS? How does it affect stations like WGN which don't sign on until 5:30 AM when one of the time-segments is 5:00-6:00 AM? Isn't this obvious bias?

7. *Don't all nationally accepted Radio research companies now admit people listen to PROGRAMS and PERSONALITIES ...not to a set of station call letters.*

While many listeners have "favorite" stations that can be measured on a call letter basis for broad segments, as NCS does with "daytime" and "nighttime," what other nationally accepted research now tries to measure 1/4 hour, 1/2 hour, or hourly listening by *station call letters* rather than program listenership? Isn't this questionnaire actually based on antiquated research methods, and produces data without validity? Isn't it true that the only kind of meaningful farm family facts for your serious consideration that this type of study could produce would come from a more general, and in line with modern research, more correct question such as, "What Radio station do you listen to most frequently"?

8. *How can MORE THAN ONE station be LISTENED TO "MOST FREQUENTLY" (as the questionnaire asks) in a specific time segment?*

   Why is this obvious error further compounded by asking the respondents to "write in call letters of stations in the space provided for each given time"? Why, by the preparation of the form, do they encourage respondents to list as many as *three* stations listened to MOST FREQUENTLY in each time period?

9. *Even accepting this obvious fallacy, why then does the Farm Research Institute admit that "A substantial number of respondents did list more than one station, but in extracting information from the returned cards to get the figures for Table I, ONLY THE FIRST MENTIONED STATION WAS USED"?*

   Isn't this suspect "loading" to take advantage that WLS used-to-be "the" FARM station and their call letters might still first come to mind? Yet what relationship, if any, has this to actual listening performance? (How many people still "say" they have Frigidaires, when they actually own a wide variety of electric refrigerators of other brands?) What kind of research integrity considers as valid a summary table from multiple station listings, but based only on the FIRST station listed in any group?

10. *Why are the total sets-in-use or homes-using-radio, figures so completely at variance with those from*

nationally accepted FARM studies by Dr. Forrest Wahn and others?

(5:00-6:00 AM	47.9%
6:00-7:00 AM	81.7%
11:30-12:00 NN	67.2%
12:00-12:30 PM	77.5%
12:30-1:00 PM	59.5%
1:00-1:15 PM	43.0%
6:00-7:00 PM	57.6%)

11. *Why does FRI include all stations listed by each family in Tables II and III, but only the first one listed in Table I?*

12. *Who are the respondents to this study?*
Are they men, women or children? And what percentage of each?

13. *Can you give complete credibility to a study financed by a single Radio station and undertaken by a relatively unknown research company?*
Have you ever seen a single-station financed study, such as this, that didn't show the bankrolling station *tremendously ahead of all competition?* In such a situation isn't there always greater possibility of the use of the age-old method of asking a "loaded question" to get a desired answer?

14. *With single-station participation isn't it relatively easy for any station setting out to prove a point to devise a "seemingly" unbiased route to that end?*

15. *In fact can't you prove almost anything you want with one survey or another?*

16. With that in mind *isn't it wiser to rely on the decided advantages we've already shown from NATION-ALLY RECOGNIZED surveys like NCS No. 2 and the April-May, 1958 NSI that WGN will give Big Crop over WLS?*
Nationally accepted research has shown WGN with far more coverage and audience advantages for BIG CROP than WLS. Your own agency media and account levels, as well as the client, had previously agreed on WGN's *qualitative* and *quantitative* FARM

344

audience advantages. All these point to the fact that WLS was the farm station. WGN now is the farm station in the Midwest!

17. *With the manager of the Armour Fertilizer Works in Chicago Heights admitting he wasn't overly impressed with the results from your past use of WLS, isn't this the time to test WGN's farm pulling power in the Midwest? Isn't this the only final "survey" that counts?*

All the best,

Joseph H. Sierer
EDWARD PETRY & CO., INC.

That memorandum raised serious questions concerning the validity of FRI's research. Glenn Snyder of WLS sent me a copy of the Petry memorandum and asked my advice on what might be done about it. Instead of giving specific advice, I sent him a detailed letter, a copy of which follows, in which I provided evidence to establish the validity of FRI's WLS study.

September 3, 1958

Mr. Glenn Snyder, Manager
Radio Station WLS
1230 Washington Boulevard
Chicago 7, Illinois

Dear Mr. Snyder:

The letter of Mr. Joseph Sierer is indeed an interesting one. He raises a number of questions about the December 1957 WLS study. Every true researcher welcomes constructive criticism and evaluation of any research study from other researchers. Some of Mr. Seirer's questions are pertinent and penetrating, while others seem to be strained and inappropriate.

Perhaps it is important to reemphasize the primary objective of the WLS study. It is practically impossible to obtain from regular radio research agencies radio listenership data in sufficient detail to provide a meas-

345

ure of various segments or components of the listening audience. This is particularly true when it comes to measuring the strictly farm audience. Breaking population figures at the under 2,500 category will not give a true picture of farm listening.

It is obviously unfair and often dangerous for an advertiser to buy radio time on the basis of research data that do not delineate the specific audience that the advertiser must reach. An advertiser that wishes to reach a purely farm audience should have information that would provide a measure of purely farm listening. If such an advertiser must select a limited number of stations out of the large number available in his efforts to reach a farm market, very substantial help could be obtained from a measure of the relative position of such stations among farmers in the areas to be covered.

The study under discussion was not undertaken to provide absolute figures of farm radio listening, but rather relative figures to permit a classification of individual stations on the basis of relative use by farm people.

I believe that most researchers who might evaluate the short questionnaire under discussion in the study would agree that it does not discriminate against any radio station. NO station is named and no wording used that would suggest any specific station. Respondents were completely free to write in any station in answer to the question. Answers would not provide a measure of the absolute size of the radio audience either in total or to specific stations. The study was not designed to obtain that kind of information. Data should, however, provide a measure of the relative position of different stations in the total listenership picture.

Perhaps one of the best ways to check the validity of the WLS study would be to compare it with other studies which were conducted on a different basis. This I have done since receiving your letter.

During the week of November 17-23, 1957, a University of Illinois study was made of radio listening in Champaign County, Illinois. This was a carefully con-

346

ceived and executed study that would meet the research standards of the most fastidious researcher. A sample of farm men and women and urban men and women was selected on a random basis. Each individual in the sample was provided a 7-day diary broken into fifteen minute segments of time from 5:00 a.m. until midnight. Each respondent was to record on the diary form the call letters of the radio stations listened to during any 15-minute segment of time.

The size of the sample ranged from 124 to 141 for each of the four sample segments. The effective size is much greater when it is recognized that each respondent reported 532 quarter hours of time.

Some data from that study have been extracted for purposes of comparison with the WLS study. The total number of quarter hours of radio listening to WLS and WGN, as reported by respondents in Champaign County, was taken as a base for comparing the relative position of those two stations among respondents. The results of that comparison are shown below.

Percentage of the Total Quarter Hours of Radio Listening to WLS and WGN Given to Each of the Two Stations (Champaign County, Ill. for Week of November 17-23, 1957)

Kind of Listener	Size of Sample	Station WLS	WGN
Urban Men	124	41.2%	58.8%
Urban Women	141	51.3	58.7
Urban M&W Combined	265	47.6	52.4
Farm Men	125	79.2	20.8
Farm Women	131	67.6	32.4
Farm M&W Combined	256	72.1	27.9
WLS Study			
Total (All States)	2493	79.4	20.6
Illinois Only	1191	78.0	22.0

347

The results of this analysis are most revealing. They high-light the reason that a study like the WLS study was necessary. They show that WGN had relatively more urban listenership than did WLS in Champaign County; figures for urban men and women combined were 52.4% for WGN and 47.6% for WLS, but look at the figures for farm listening. There the combined listening of farm men and women showed WGN with only 27.9% as compared with 72.1% for WLS. The relative strength of WLS among farm men was even more pronounced.

For purposes of easy comparison, percentage figures calculated on the same basis are shown from the WLS study under question. Of the 2,493 persons who responded to the WLS study, 1,043 mentioned WLS and 270 mentioned WGN. Using the sum of these two figures as a base, it shows WLS with 79.4% and WGN 20.6%. These figures are almost identical with the figures for farm men radio listening as shown from the Champaign County study, a remarkable substantiation of the WLS study.

If this is not enough, there is still additional evidence. Another diary study was made among farm men in all of Illinois during the second week of December 1957. This study was made by the Farm Research Institute for another client, and detailed findings are, therefore, not available to others. I may say, however, that this study was also a diary study covering a full week and covered every county in Illinois. A total of 825 commercial farmers in Illinois responded. This represented more than 90% of the total number who received a diary form to be completed. The sample was the panel of commercial farmers in Illinois operated by the Farm Research Institute. Panel members were recruited on a random basis, and the representativeness of the panel has been subjected to many tests, with positive results in each case. Percentages showing the relative position of WLS and WGN among farm men as shown by that diary study were almost identical to the percentages obtained in the December, 1957 WLS study and the November, 1957 University of Illinois study.

Both the Champaign County study, which was a University of Illinois study, and the total state study among commercial farm men, which was a Farm Research Institute study, were under my supervision. Thus, Mr. Sierer might question the validity of those studies because of my position in them. This perhaps calls for some comments concerning my research background, even though I reluctantly enter into this aspect of Mr. Sierer's criticism. This is perhaps called for because the Farm Research Institute is a single proprietorship and is largely synonymous with C. H. Sandage.

The pertinent elements in my background can be found in *Who's Who in America*. I received my Ph.D. degree from the University of Iowa in 1931. I have had fairly extensive publication in the form of books, monographs, and articles in the fields of advertising and research. From 1935 to 1937 I was Chief of the Division of Communications of the U.S. Bureau of the Census. As such, I was in charge of the first census of radio broadcasting ever taken. I served for two years as Visiting Professor of Business Research on the faculty of the Harvard University Graduate School of Business Administration. I also served on a full-time basis for two years as Director of Research of a significant organization in the commercial field.

One of my books is titled, *Radio Advertising for Retailers*. A substantial portion of that book was the result of extensive research into retailer use of radio advertising. It has been quoted extensively and used by many in the radio advertising field. I pioneered the use of the radio listening diary as a method for measuring the composition in detail of the radio audience to specific stations in a given area. I have been credited, and I believe accurately, for having been the first person to develop and use the diary for measuring individual rather than family listening. I have had in the past numerous discussions with the A.C. Nielsen organization in respect to the use of the listening diary. It is interesting to observe that Nielsen now uses the method extensively. Unfortunately, his samples are not sufficiently large to permit a delineation of important segments of the total listening audience.

My primary occupation is that of university professor. The Farm Research Institute is, therefore, a small organization that has not concerned itself with self-promotion for purposes of substantial growth and expansion. The Institute has been in operation for eleven years. It has no connection with the University and is operated purely as a part-time research venture on my part. Its methods of operation have been copied by at least two nationally organized research agencies. One of those agencies has used the consulting services of Institute personnel in developing its plan of operation.

It may be of some value to give you a partial list of clients that have been served by the Farm Research Institute. The list includes Reynolds Metals, Purina Mills, Nutrena Mills, Keystone Steel and Wire, U.S. Department of Agriculture, Capper's Farmer, American Foundation for Animal Health, Swift and Company, and the Illinois Agricultural Association. Each of these clients came to the Institute unsolicited.

I have not attempted to take up point by point the issues raised by Mr. Sierer. I frankly believe most of them are not pertinent or valid. May I illustrate by a specific comment on his item 4 where he raises some question concerning the sampling on a county by county basis. Most data in the WLS report were shown on a total area or total state basis. The fact that the sample was scattered over the entire area rather than chosen from counties close to Chicago should be recognized as a favorable factor for objectivity. The total sample of 2,493 is a tremendous one. A critic of sampling procedure might more properly raise the question of respondent bias; thus the 2,493 respondents represented only 14.1% of the total mailing. While the total mailing list was selected on a random basis, one could question whether the 14% who responded were representative of the 86% who did not respond. If the results of the WLS study did not correspond so dramatically with other studies made independently of the WLS study and made on a basis where statistical validity could not be subject to question, then this question of respondent bias might be highly important. In view, however, of the supporting evidence of these other studies, we must rule out the presence of respondent bias in the WLS study.

May I say that the Champaign County study referred to is public property and available to any and all who wish to avail themselves of it. Unfortunately, we (the University) have not been able to finance the publication of the results of that study. Detailed findings, however, are available from IBM runs, and any person or persons should feel free to make an appointment to go over the data and extract any portions they wish for personal use.

I would like very much to sit down with Mr. Sierer and discuss any aspects of that study he wished to discuss. The same is also true in respect to the WLS study.

Sincerely,
C. H. Sandage
President

Glenn Snyder used my letter as a part of a brochure in which this whole issue raised by the Petry people would be answered and in doing so would increase the acceptance of WLS as the dominant farm station. He included the following introduction to the brochure:

Recently, the national sales representative of Station WGN raised a series of questions regarding the validity and reliability of a farm listening survey made for WLS and the qualifications of the gentleman under whose direction the survey was conducted....Dr. C. H. Sandage of the University of Illinois.

At the outset, we wish to make clear that WLS has no desire nor intent to engage in any controversy with Station WGN. We have a very high regard for that station and have long enjoyed a most cordial relationship with its management and personnel. We intend to maintain that relationship. But the question raised by its national representatives so reflect on the integrity of the survey

351

and the man responsible for it that we feel it is necessary to reply.

After his introduction, he included a complete reproduction of the biographical information on me carried in *Who's Who in America* and *American Men of Science*.

Our work in measuring the character and quality of the pure farm audience listening to radio and viewing television was extensive. Actually, our studies for WLS were secondary and supplementary to detailed measurement of the farm radio and television audiences for our Indiana and Illinois co-op clients. We developed periodic measurements for those two clients regularly throughout the more than forty years we have served them. However, our early work with WLS and the Petry controversy focused both regional and national attention on FRI as a company that specialized in studying the farm market. It established our credibility and brought us additional business. Because the operation of FRI was secondary to my full-time teaching, I developed no program to solicit business. I was content to serve my two major clients and other clients who came to us voluntarily.

The Keystone Steel and Wire Company came to us unsolicited and asked us to help them answer one of their problems in the selection of advertising media. Keystone had, for a number of years, sponsored the "National Barn Dance" program broadcast regionally on WLS. They came to us at a time when television was expanding rapidly but there was no information available to Keystone to indicate the extent to which the "National Barn Dance" on the radio might be losing audience to television. We agreed to try to answer that question for them. We did so by measuring the pure farm audience to both radio and television with emphasis on the Saturday nighttime period. Our studies clearly showed that farm families were increasing their ownership of television sets and substantially shifting their evening attention in broadcasting from radio to television. As a result of these findings, Keystone revised its media schedule to concentrate their evening use of broadcasting to television and limit their use of radio to early morning or noontime periods.

Indiana and Illinois co-ops used the results of our broadcast studies especially as a help in selecting local radio stations and specific programs to carry their advertising. It was only because of our large samples of farm families, in which every county in the respective states was included, that realistic data on local station coverage of the farm market could be made.

Measuring Print Media Coverage

Our two major clients were interested in farm family use and attention given to all media of communication. We, therefore, made periodic studies of print as well as broadcast media. All of our studies were specifically commissioned and the results became the property of the individual client. The work we did for our Indiana and Illinois people was therefore not available, at least through us, to anyone else. We were, however, free to do research for any other client interested in media penetration of the farm market. After our extensive research for WLS, the owner of that station (*Prairie Farmer*) asked us to measure the readership of farm families in Illinois and Indiana, the two states served by their publications. At that time we had approximately 1,000 commercial farmers as panel members in each state. We mailed each panel member a questionnaire in which we asked them to write in the name of the farm papers and farm magazines received regularly. Other detailed questions were included in our questionnaire. From the some 2,000 questionnaires mailed, we received for tabulation 949 from Indiana and 817 from Illinois. Those figures are mentioned to emphasize the ability of FRI to provide clients with a sufficiently large sample to permit detailed analysis by area and various demographic factors. Our report provided *Prairie Farmer* with extensive information which was used by both their advertising department and editorial staff.

We did several studies for *Capper's Weekly*. The first was in the early 1950s and the last in 1957. Our first study revealed areas of weakness. Management made changes designed to correct declining readership and circulation. Our later studies were designed to measure the reaction of readers to changes and chart attitude changes. Unfortunately for *Capper's Weekly*, their decline was slowed but not stopped.

We also did work for *Farm Quarterly*. Regretfully, we were brought in when the publication was in financial difficulty and our findings and recommendations came too late to keep them from folding.

We also did readership studies for *Big Farmer* and *Successful Farming*. We made two studies for the latter. One was a straightforward readership study while the other developed comparisons with a state farm publication, *Prairie Farmer*, and its major national competitor, *Farm Journal*. We used a semantic differential measurement instrument to provide a basis for comparing attitudes of farmers toward those three publications. The measurement instrument contained a seven-point scale for each of six pairs of polar adjectives and brief descriptive phrases. They were: friendly/unfriendly; good for me/bad for me; believable/unbelievable; knows my problems/doesn't know them; dependable/undependable; valuable/not valuable. *Successful Farming* ranked third on all scales but only slightly behind its national competitor. The study uncovered specific areas of weakness and permitted the publication to improve these areas.

A group of state farm publications covering eight Midwestern states had developed a group advertising and sales operation under the label Mid-West Farm Unit. That unit asked us to develop a detailed readership study covering all eight states. We worked with a committee of five separate state papers that covered all eight states in developing a questionnaire and approach to collecting data. I wanted to use our panels in Indiana and Illinois and personal interviews in the other six states, but some members of the client committee rejected that idea. We therefore used personal interviewers in all eight states to call on farm families at the home site. Our sample consisted of 200 completed interviews in each area.

As a personal experiment, I wanted to test out the difference of data collection via personal interviewers versus our fixed panel. I therefore, as a test, mailed to our Indiana panel the same questionnaire that was being used by the personal interviewers. The results showed there were some differences, but none were significant.

The key question used in the Mid-West Farm Unit study was designed to measure the "thoroughness" of reading. Most readership studies emphasized the amount rather than the thoroughness of reading. In other words, the common question was "Did you read all or some or none." It was my belief that a person could hastily read or skim all or most articles but could not say that the articles had been thoroughly read. I believed that the "thoroughness of reading" factor would be better than the "circulation" factor in evaluating a publication as an advertising medium. It was suggested in our report that one could calculate the cost per thousand of thorough readers in contrast to the cost per thousand of recipients of the publication. Because our study included all publications received by the respondents, cost per thousand thorough readers could be compared for each publication. That measurement became quite effective.

A truly great compliment for FRI came to our attention when *Progressive Farmer* asked us to do some readership studies for their publication. The *Progressive Farmer* publisher provided us with information supplied to them by the Mid-West Farm Unit. The essence of that report follows:

> Farm Research Institute was selected because of their reputation, experience, and expertise in the farm magazine study field.
>
> The Farm Research Institute is an independent research organization that specializes in farm-oriented market research. FRI has been studying and analyzing the farm market for almost 30 years. The Institute is headed by Dr. C. H. Sandage....
>
> In 1972 Midwest Unit Farm Publications engaged Farm Research Institute to undertake the "Farm Media Study of Eight Midwest States." Before making the contract with FRI (Dr. Sandage), the Midwest Unit made a comprehensive survey on the subject of farm media among advertising agencies and advertisers. A total of 221 executives of advertisers and agencies throughout the United States who had a direct interest in the farm market responded. The survey included not only questions on attitudes toward media, but perhaps most important of all, a question to determine which research organization would have the most acceptance with this

group if it were to make a penetrating study of farm publications.

A check list type question was used. Twelve prominent research organizations were listed. Farm Research Institute at Urbana, Illinois, which is the organization of Dr. Charles Sandage, was checked by more respondents than any other organization.

Determining Question:

"Which of the following research firms would have the greatest acceptance among farm advertisers and farm oriented agencies if it were to make a preference-type study of farm publications?"

Results:

Farm Research Institute (Sandage)	41.9%
Simmons	34.6
Chilton Research Services	25.7
Market Facts	26.5
Marplan	14.0
Elrick and Lavidge	11.8
Erdos and Morgan	9.6
Winona Interviewing Service	8.8
Bisbing Business Service	7.4
Eastman Research	3.7
Central Surveys	2.2
Other	15.4

We had no research panels in any of the sixteen Southern states served by *Progressive Farmer*. We therefore asked a list house to randomly select 12,000 names of farm and ranch operators in those sixteen states. Each name on the list was sent a mailing which consisted of a questionnaire, a covering letter, and a postage-free return envelope. We attached a quarter to each letter with the thought that this would increase responses. We obtained a response rate of 49 percent.

A year after this study was completed, *Progressive Farmer* asked us to do another study. We used the same general approach in this as in the first one, with one exception. We selected a mailing list of only 10,000 instead of 12,000. We included a one-dollar bill instead of a quarter as an incentive. This was done partly to test the relative value of the larger versus the smaller incentive. In this second study we obtained a response rate of 61 percent. Thus it could be inferred that a one-dollar incentive would produce a 24-percent greater return than that obtained by the twenty-five cent incentive.

FRI did other research studies in the general area of communication. One was done for the U.S. Department of Agriculture. It consisted of researching the extent to which farm families were familiar with or had heard about various publications of the USDA. We also determined the extent to which various publications were read and the attitude of the reader toward the publications. The respondents were given an opportunity to comment in their own language on their reaction to various publications.

Another communication type study dealt with farm family use of and attitude toward the state-supported bookmobile program.

Purchase Inventories

Some very important research done by FRI consisted of three types of studies. One had members of our research panels keep monthly or quarterly diaries of their purchases of farm inputs. A second had members report on a rather long list of products what they had purchased in the past six months and to check those items they thought they would probably buy in the next six months. The third type was to measure attitudes, likes, dislikes, and other elements or factors that might influence buying behavior.

In all three of these approaches emphasis was placed on learning and trying to understand the needs and wants of farmers and to report such findings to agribusiness firms and educational institutions as a help to them in serving the agricultural market.

Diary information permitted one to measure share-of-market obtained by individual suppliers and for individual brands. Cross-classification of data also permitted one to determine which segments of the agricultural market were being best served. Longitudinal data permitted a supplier to test the effectiveness of various advertising and merchandising programs.

The measurement of past purchases and forecast of future purchase probability provided an opportunity to measure the degree to which individuals could accurately forecast the probability of future purchases. Our experience with that type of research indicated that about 40 percent of those who said they would probably make purchases in the next six months did not do so. On the other hand, a somewhat similar percentage of those indicating no probable purchase in the next six months did in fact make a purchase. We found that the error in forecasting became a fairly consistent one and thus provided a fairly accurate forecast. If the same degree of error exists from period to period then such erroneous data can and does in fact provide an accurate basis for forecasting.

Measurements of attitudes, likes, dislikes, etc., provided valuable information in the selection of appeals to be used in promotion and the particular qualities of a product or service to be emphasized.

The particular kind of research discussed above was discontinued after a number of years of use. It was reintroduced in a modified form in the late 1980s. The modification consisted in eliminating the forecasting part of the "inventory" of purchases. It was thus used primarily to measure share-of-market by suppliers, by brand, and with share-of-market measured for different market segments such as region, size of farm operation, type of farming, economic class, and so forth.

Reverse Flow of Information

Considerable attention has been given in this chapter to researching various aspects of the mass media of communication. The reader should not infer that the space devoted to the mass media here is a measure of the ratio of such research to the total research of FRI. Indeed, most of the research effort of FRI has been devoted to providing a reverse flow of information. Thus, in addition to information from agri-business, government agencies, and educational institutions flowing *to* farmers via broadcasting and magazines, FRI has been providing a flow of information from farmers to agri-business firms, government agencies, and educational institutions. Our panels of commercial farm families in effect serve to provide "editorial content" through FRI in the form of research reports distributed to those serving the farm market. That editorial content has been multifaceted. It has included the measurement and reporting of buying behavior. It has given attention to the likes and dislikes, attitudes and beliefs, satisfactions and dissatisfactions, operating problems and search for solutions by farm families. FRI has also experimented with the development of an economic confidence factor to measure changes in the farmer's conception of economic conditions. The distribution of this reverse flow of information as provided by FRI has been to specific rather than mass audiences. The "subscribers" to the information provided by farmers are the individual clients. In this computer age one might visualize this as providing a network of 2,000 or more farm operators (reporting stations) supplying data to FRI. The client can then use its modem to plug into the database accumulated from that network.

Chapter 17

Off the Beaten Path

There has been a facet of my life which is perhaps difficult to classify. It involves the use of communication to stimulate, needle, criticize, and jar one's thinking. The communication has generally been in the form of letters, verse, or short essays. Some have been straightforward but many have been in the form of satire. I have been encouraged to include some examples of such communication.

Marry Your Work

I will start with some verses labeled "Marry Your Work." This was created in my middle age. It was designed as a reply to those who sometimes chided me for "working so hard." I had never really thought about how hard I was working. I was brought up in a family who probably never heard of the term "work ethic" but who nevertheless adhered to or practiced that ethic. It was a way of life and necessary if we were to survive. We were taught to enjoy life and that work was actually a part of that joy. It was out of that background that "Marry Your Work" was created.

MARRY YOUR WORK

Does work involve struggle,
And struggle bring pain,
To those who love life,
But are 'fraid of the rain?

Is work just a job
To bring bread and milk
To those who want beauty
Or the world's finest silk?

Is the job just a jail
Where slaves become clay
Through a crushing of spirits
By the toil of the day?

Does the worker take care
In the job that is sought,
To see that his service
Is most dearly bought?

Is work a mere product
To be sold at a store,
Or bargained for silver
On the plane of a whore?

If all these are true—
Then man is not free;
He's either a slave
Or a Simon Legree.

But man would not fret
From work's heavy toll,
If labor were pleasant
And brought joy to the soul.

Well, labor is pleasant
If looked on aright;
It can make the days short
And the evenings most bright.

Just marry your work—
Be polygamous, too,
If more than one job
You can faithfully do.

Take care in your choice
And pick a good "wife,"
One that brings comfort
Or surcease from strife.

Don't marry for silver,
For then you may fail
To find in your work
Your own holy grail.

So marry for love
Of the job to be done;
And work will bring joy
That is truly great fun.

Philosophical and Religious Perspective

I suppose in any autobiography, reflections on life, or personal history the question of religion must be discussed. I have always considered myself as being a religious person and have held membership in a particular church since the age of twelve. Even so, I have never been an active church member, but that has not diminished my concern for or interest in the philosophical and spiritual aspects of religion. Perhaps some insight into my attitude on the subject can be gleaned from the letter I wrote to a preacher in Oxford, Ohio, when I was a professor at Miami University. I attended the church service at which the preacher delivered a sermon titled "Is God Emeritus?" In that sermon he considered that God was some being or power outside the individual and resided "somewhere in the heavens." The preacher made no reference to the idea that God might reside in the soul of an individual if permitted to enter and that in such case He should not be retired and given emeritus status. That failure violated my basic belief and hence stimulated the following essay.

IS GOD EMERITUS?

(A statement written in 1942)

An eminent churchman recently presented to his congregation a sermon entitled "Is God Emeritus?"—a title borrowed from an article by Shailer Matthews.

The preacher presented, in what appeared a very logical manner, a case for belief in a personal God, but a God that is outside the individual. He emphasized the ability of such an outside God to give poor mortals hope, ideals, and a power outside self to which one could appeal for assistance in maintaining hope and ideals. Criticism was heaped upon those people who depend upon self, individually and collectively, as the primary method of attaining the "better life."

It seemed to me that my preacher friend missed the vital element in this God business. To me an *inside* God is much more vital than an *outside* one. The former is personal, intimate, close, always present and willing to whisper advice, encouragement, and direction to our worthwhile efforts. It places emphasis on the importance of *you* and *me* in the social scheme of things—that *we* can feed the multitudes and house the poor if we do not retire the active God to an emeritus status.

This inside God concept is neither new nor out of harmony with the literature of Christianity although most devout Christians probably prefer the outside God. But does not the handbook of Christianity emphasize that God "created us in his image?" And is it not difficult to tell the actual from the image? Which, therefore, is you and which is God? Could they not both be housed in the same frame? There is, therefore, no important conflict between the inside God idea and Biblical literature.

Let us then analyze the importance of this inside God concept as a factor in the attainment of Christian ideals. What are these ideals or God-like qualities which most people seem to believe desirable? A partial list would include happiness, love, charity, social benefit, honesty, integrity, service. I submit that the "God in you" rather than the "God in the heavens" will be infinitely more effective in the promotion of these qualities.

If you allow your "other self" to whisper words of encouragement, prompt you to develop a well-balanced routine of work and play, point out examples of your past successes and emphasize the fact that future successes are possible, encourage you to seek avenues of work which will be of vital interest, and focus attention on the good qualities possessed by your neighbors and fellow workers, you will find yourself in possession of greater power, love, and happiness than can be found from major dependence upon an outside God. Furthermore, much more in the way of social advancement will be achieved. Those dependent upon the "God in the heavens" are apt to assume the let-George-do-it attitude. Such people will often implore their outside God to have mercy on themselves or on the world, to take care of the poor, to guide nations and individuals in the proper paths, etc.

Would it not be much more effective to implore the God in you to take hold of *your* other self and thus give you some power over your own destiny and the destiny of society? Would not this cause you to recognize your own responsibility as well as ability to do something worthwhile and constructive? By such a process you can transform yourself from a grouch to an interesting person. You can develop a keen interest in the welfare of humanity—slum clearance, adult education, improved business methods, fair dealings, true service to humanity. You can reduce sickness—psychologists tell us that not more than one-half of our "illness" is the result of organic disorders. Thus, at least one-half of our sickness is the result of emotional or mental unbalance. The God in *you* can treat these problems most effectively. Why supplicate an outside God to banish fear, anger, despondency, worry, boredom, when you have within yourself such power? There are sufficient actual Dr. Jeykel and Mr. Hyde case histories on file to establish the power of this claim.

It was not an outside God that motivated Franklin, Edison, Adams, Keller, Nightingale, Curie, Lister, Lincoln, Darwin, and others like them. In fact, it might almost be said that, when one places dependence on an outside God and ignores the God within, the real, the vital God has been retired to the rank of God emeritus.

It is when the inside God has been put on the shelf that we cheat, try to exploit our neighbor, seek special privilege, lose sight of human welfare, seek excessive profits, sell adulterated merchandise, use false advertising, fake our tax reports, fail to give an honest day's work for an honest day's pay, plunge a nation into periodic depression and eventually revolution. All these things we have in too great an abundance. Yes, God is emeritus—has been retired from active service in all too many instances, and that is deplorable.

This essay was written fifty years ago. In rereading it now, I can see that some might place me in the "New Age" cult. Nothing could be farther from the truth. In no way do I now, nor have I ever, equated man with God. Man and God are two separate and distinct entities. God is ethereal, not seen by the human eye, not limited in space. Those qualitites permit God to be anywhere and everywhere, not as man but as God. It permits God to reside in man but not to be man. In no way can man be God. God can be a faithful counselor to those who will open their hearts and let Him in.

The Drug War

The importance of the individual and the power of the mind was expressed in another poem labeled "An Ode to LSD," written in the early years of the drug culture. It was never published and had little or no circulation. LSD was perhaps the most talked about drug at that time. It was replaced in apparent popularity with drugs such as cocaine and crack. It had a rebirth when in

1991 it was reported as the "drug of choice" among the young experimenters with drugs. The "Ode" follows:

AN ODE TO LSD
(February 1968)

I wanted to take a trip
To some far, faraway place
It seemed my strongest wish
To resign from the human race.

But how could I get away?
Could I call for a magic spell
That would lift me above the clouds
And out of my dismal hell?

I was told of LSD
And of other acid pills
That would send me on a trip
With unearthly thrills and chills.

They said with these I could escape
From all that is real in life
And while I was on the trip
Could forget the world of strife.

I was not told, however
That an acid trip could kill
And that those who take the journey
Might forever lose their will.

I closed my eyes and thought and thought
I stretched, and I stretched my mind
I called upon my inner powers
To help me my world to find.

My will, my mind, my inner soul
Combined to let me see my star
And yet they let me come back home
When I had traveled far and far.

So don't be fooled by LSD
Don't let it kill your mind and soul
Instead depend upon your will
To help you travel toward your goal.

As the drug culture became more widespread, the federal government became concerned and in the late 1980s established a program designed to curb the spread of drug use. A so-called "drug czar" was appointed to head the "War on Drugs." Major emphasis was placed on controlling the supply of drugs, thus presumably making them unavailable for use. The strategy of that "war" was to destroy the raw material from which drugs are created and/or its supply. I could not conceive that such a strategy could succeed. There would be entrepreneurs who would find ways of providing drugs and drug addicts ways to buy them. I wrote the following essay.

Is the War on Drugs Doomed to Fail?
(September 1989)

The drug war had been going on for some time before President Bush's formal declaration. That declaration has committed our government to seriously enter the fray to destroy the enemy—drugs and those who produce and peddle them.

Can the war be won in a relatively short time, or will it continue for a number of years, or will it ever be won? What will the strategy be?

The current strategy seems to focus on the production and distribution of supply with minimum or no attention given to the demand for drugs. That strategy is doomed to fail. As long as there are addicts, emerging addicts, and significant social users with money, ways will be found by entrepreneurs to provide supplies regardless of the risk.

Addiction is not limited to chemical dependence. Psychological and social addiction can be equally strong. The so-called drug culture is more sociological than physiological.

The drug war may never be won unless frontal attacks are made on the demand side of the equation. Can such an approach ever be successful? Some support for the possibility of success might be found in a review of what has happened in the case of tobacco.

It was just 25 years ago that the Surgeon General issued his first report on the physiological dangers resulting from the continued use of tobacco, especially cigarettes. During the 25 years since that report, the use of cigarettes by people in the United States has been cut in half. This reduction has been greater in some segments and less in other segments of the population.

This decline has been brought about almost completely by education and peer pressure. No attempt has been made to destroy the production of tobacco and tobacco products or curtail their distribution. Instead, the government tobacco "cartel" continued to subsidize farmers who grow tobacco and collect its ransom from distributors and users. The reduction has been brought about almost completely as the result of educational efforts on the part of agencies such as the American Cancer Society, the American Heart Association, the American Lung Association, the Advertising Council and the cumulative influence of peer pressure.

Let me illustrate with an individual case study. This writer started using tobacco in the early 1930's. He became an avid and probably an addicted pipe smoker. His pipe became a constant companion. He smoked it before and after meals, in private and public transportation facilities, in various public gatherings such as conventions, in restaurants, at cocktail parties, in his university office, at faculty meetings and in his graduate seminars. Several of his graduate students and young colleagues viewed him as a role model and became pipe smokers themselves. Four years ago he quit smoking. This was not because of doctor's orders but essentially because of the incessant bombarding of facts issued by various agencies and by peer pressure. No longer was it socially acceptable to smoke at parties, in many public places and in many other situations where people congregated. It took 20 years for the educational bombardment and social pressure to cause this pipe smoker to

371

break the habit. Changes in the cultural climate were especially powerful.

The American experiment with Prohibition is an example of losing the war when strategy was applied primarily to the supply side of the issue. Attempts to eliminate or control supply may well have exacerbated the problem. The "speak easy" and the social acceptance of violating the law became a common part of the culture.

The success with education in reducing tobacco consumption, and the failure of attempts at supply control in the case of alcohol, should give pause to our generals plotting strategy in the drug war. Maybe private and quasi-governmental agencies could take the initiative to fight the drug war by attacking the demand side of the issue. A crack in the sociological armor encasing the consumption of alcohol is already noticeable. Statistics indicate some decrease in the use of hard liquor. Perrier water is becoming a common item at cocktail parties. The emerging health and physical fitness culture is casting new light on the effects of alcohol consumption on health. The crack in the armor can be widened when the persuasive power of leadership by example is exerted by those who serve as role models for others to follow. When this occurs various media of communication, especially television, will recognize the trend and by mirroring that trend accentuate its contagious effect.

It is not suggested here that no attention be given to curtailing the supply of drugs or to interdict and punish the drug dealer. The primary thesis is that efforts devoted to controlling supply are doomed to fail, but a long-range effort to alter demand would result in some real progress. The billions of dollars now being devoted to fighting producers and distributors of drugs is largely wasted. Transferring money to support efforts at modifying consumer behavior would probably be much more productive. Money could be used to stimulate entrepreneurs to create new approaches to education and develop leadership among students in our grade and high schools to work toward a drug free school environment.

In writing the essay, I was not naive enough to think emphasis on demand could result in a quick solution to a major problem. It seemed obvious that any major reduction in the demand for drugs would take years to accomplish. The success in reducing the demand for tobacco should give hope in the case of drugs. Attention to the element of social addiction when added to various kinds of communication might hasten a decline in drug use. Having drug-free role models in secondary schools and colleges could affect the actions of young people.

Social and Cultural Conservatism

In 1978 the University of Illinois appointed a new chancellor, Dr. William P. Gerberding, to head the Champaign-Urbana campus. He had served as executive vice chancellor at UCLA before coming to Illinois. Soon after he arrived, he spoke at a Conference on Feminine Scholarship on the U of I campus. In that speech he was reported in the local *News Gazette* as having said, "I detect a social and cultural conservatism that surprised me" on the UI campus. "I sometimes have the queasy feeling that I have moved out of the mainstream and into the backwater."

In comparing students at the U of I with those at UCLA, he observed that "The students I have spoken to as a rule tended to be more obviously career oriented and in general more conventional toward authority." Just about the only exception, among the student leaders...was a couple of students on the *Daily Illini* student newspaper who were "more like students I'm used to—more acerbic, and critical," he said.

I was moved to write him and challenge some of his statements as reported in the *News Gazette*. My letter, as it appeared in the newspaper, is reproduced here.

373

March 3, 1978

Dr. William P. Gerberding
101 West Meadows
Urbana, Illinois 61801

Dear Dr. Gerberding:

This is probably a strange way for a neighbor to introduce himself. I live two doors west, but on the north side of the street from you.

This introduction is strange in that it is prompted by Tuesday's *News Gazette* report of your speech to the Conference on Feminine Scholarship, held on the U of I campus. I am not only your neighbor but also a retired University of Illinois professor. I have in the past also held visiting professorships at Harvard, University of Pennsylvania, and the University of California (Berkeley). I was on the Berkeley Campus as a member of an academic committee meeting there the day after the People's Park uprising. I was on our local campus during student riots in the past decade. My observation of student thought and action is, therefore, not entirely parochial.

It is in the light of my experience and observation that I was disturbed by the tenor of your speech, at least as it was reported in the *News Gazette*. The tone of that report would suggest that you denigrate conservatism and relegate it to the stagnant backwater left from the rushing of the mainstream of social and political thought. Popular usage of terms would use liberalism as being the opposite of conservatism, and perhaps in your frame of reference would say that liberalism represents the mainstream.

May I observe that it is conceivable (even possible) that conservatism is carving a new channel in the river of life, and soon will be, if not already, the mainstream of intellectual thought.

Words carry different meanings to different people, and it may be confusing to observe that the 1978 conservative is a true liberal, vitally concerned with the welfare of society. Such a person can become a real activist in fighting those "liberal" policies which have brought bankruptcy to New York City.

As one foreign observer of U.S. policy has recently said, "The United States has pursued policies of taxing work, production and thrift, and subsidizes leisure, inactivity, unemployment, and consumption."

Has not the liberal in terms of your frame of reference looked to government as the solver of all social and economic problems? Has not the experience of the last few decades demonstrated that that is an erroneous concept?

Would it not be an intellectually stimulating and socially valuable undertaking to challenge students to fight for a redressing of grievances produced by the "liberalism" of the past several decades? Should we not try to change the system that "subsidizes leisure and inactivity," and which makes it possible for one to collect more money for unemployment insurance than from working?

Should we fight for a Constitutional amendment that would force government to operate on a balanced budget? Should we fight for a curtailment of the growing power of big government? Should we concern ourselves with the excessive power of organized labor? Should we fight to re-establish individual dignity and *responsibility*, as against the concept that the government owes us a living? Should we fight to re-establish the responsibility of parents for their youngsters' actions, particularly in respect to youngsters' disregard for public and individual property? (Note the vandalism in schools, as well as private property.)

It may be that I have misinterpreted your philosophy. My only source was the *News Gazette* report. I agree with you that students should have a critical mind, but not necessarily acerbic. The most effective critical mind is one that is not really negative, but attempts to develop solutions to problems after weighing all of the "pros" and "cons" of the situation.

It may be that the great University of Illinois, located in the midst of fertile corn and bean fields, is in an admirable situation to exercise outstanding leadership in developing the faculty to provide viable solutions to many of our social, political, and economic problems. There may be merit in being somewhat detached from the heat of racial riots, bankrupt cities, powerful and corrupt labor unions, and the excessive growth of big government. Such detachment may facilitate more objective and reasoned solutions.

I am confident that the University community and the entire state of Illinois are looking forward to your strong leadership in developing and implementing goals designed to put America on the road to real progress.

Sincerely,

C. H. Sandage

Dr. Gerberding replied with a warm and gracious letter in which he thanked me for challenging his statements as reported in that newspaper story.

Citizens for an Alcohol-Free Congress

In the early days of the presidency of George Bush, he nominated John Tower to be secretary of defense. When hearings were held by the appropriate Senate committee to determine whether that committee would recommend to the full Senate that he be confirmed or not confirmed, strong opposition developed. One of the major charges made as a basis for questioning his qualifications to hold that important office was his presumed affinity for booze. It occurred to me that emphasis on booze, particularly by a group many of whose members undoubtedly had comparable affinity, was used to cover other reasons for recommending against confirmation. I thought that zeroing in on the one factor—booze—was hypocritical for members of a distinguished Senate committee.

I thought it might be interesting to use satire as a way of perhaps calling attention to such camouflage. I did this by writing an "open letter to citizens." That letter is reproduced on page 378.

The reader will note that a special letterhead was prepared to recognize a presumed specially organized citizens' interest group with a distinguished board of trustees. The names of the trustees used in the letterhead were real persons with factual professional titles. Also note the slogan in the letterhead, "Sauce for the Congressional Goose is Taboo for the Cabinet Gander."

That letter was mailed to each member of the Senate committee and to a few newspapers. It brought some comment in the press and replies from some committee members. I am glad to state here that Senator Sam Nunn, chairman of that committee, replied with a most thoughtful letter.

Protest Against Promoting Home Equity Loans

In the early 1980s there was a strong development by financial institutions to encourage homeowners to borrow money and use the unpledged equity in their home as security. Promotion pieces and advertising messages tended to emphasize that the hidden assets in the equity in a home were often unrealized by the owner. Why not, the ads would say, take advantage of that asset by borrowing against it and using the newfound cash to "live it up," take a vacation, buy that new automobile, and so forth.

Not all ads were that blatant and some would emphasize using this means to help pay for a youngster's education, consolidate credit card debt into a lower cost instrument, remodel their home, and so on. It occurred

LIBERTY

Citizens for an Alcohol Free Congress
2003-B Philo Road, Urbana, IL 61801

Sauce for the Congressional Goose
Is Taboo for the Cabinet Gander

An Open Letter to Citizens:

In the waning days of February 1989 the Senate Armed Services Committee voted 11 to 9 to recommend that their colleagues not approve the nomination of John Tower as Secretary of Defense. It was symbolic that the decision was taken during the only month in which there is a National holiday honoring a U.S. President and Commander-in-Chief of all armed services.

The Group of Eleven can thus be commended for providing the news media with great quotes on the numbing effects of alcohol on the clarity of thought and the danger to the nation if regular users of alcohol were given positions of leadership in our government. It took great courage to voice concern on a matter of such personal nature. Indeed, members must have had strong personal experience to support their courage.

The struggle of the Eleven to persuade other members of the Senate to follow their example merits citizen support. Perhaps there should be a vehicle, a citizens' organization to which individuals could become members that would make it easy to show their support.

A dedicated group of concerned citizens has taken this challenge seriously. The names of some members of the group appear as officers and trustees on our letterhead. You are one of a small group we are asking to respond to the concept of a special citizens organization. We suggest the name <u>Citizens for an Alcohol Free Congress</u> (CFAFC). Please let us know if you think it is a good or bad idea.

Would you suggest that we invite selected members of Congress to join us as charter members and perhaps honorary trustees? Invitations could go to those who could supply leadership based on broad personal knowledge and experience. Perhaps some members of the Group of Eleven would qualify.

Please send us your ideas. Use the back of this letter or your own paper to send your comments. Would <u>you</u> like to become a member?

Sincerely yours,

C. H. Sandage

C. H. Sandage
President

to me that there were two basic negatives that were obviously missing from advertisements but which should be brought to the attention of both borrowers and lending institutions. The primary negative for the borrower was the consumption of assets today and the increase in consumer debt. The extra negative or danger for the individual borrower was that pledging the equity built up in their home as security for a loan would generally be in the form of a second mortgage. Much of that equity was the result of monetary inflation. Should the future bring about deflation or economic changes that would result in the borrower's loss of job and income, the borrower could lose not only the equity that existed at the time of the new loan but also the entire home.

In 1987 I took the opportunity to write a friend who was president of a local bank that had been advertising avidly for people to borrow against the equity in their homes. I created a one-time letterhead that I thought epitomized the results of what might happen to many who were persuaded to take out a home equity loan and fritter the proceeds away. The letter included a picture of two bums on a park bench with a caption in which one bum recognized the other as his former investment adviser. The pertinent comments in my letter are reproduced here.

> ...Having given you my honest evaluation of the excellent record of you and your bank, I am permitting myself to voice what might appear to be a negative comment. You may have sensed a note of negativism in my "specially prepared new letterhead." The creation of the "letterhead" was triggered by listening to radio advertising, reading newspaper advertisements, and reading your direct mail piece plugging the merits of home equity loans. I cannot eradicate from my brain visions

of numerous families in the early 1990's who had their homes taken over by banks that had been so generous with their home equity loans in 1987.

I think my next "special letterhead" will place emphasis on a family who had postponed purchases of vacations, Mercedes-Benz's, boats and fur coats and had used their bank to help them save until they could pay cash for those special "want" things and services. It will picture a happy, well dressed family in a 1990 setting giving thanks to their bank for its past solid financial counseling.

Will encouraging people to go into debt via credit cards and home equity loans in order to have things *now*, even though it means mortgaging one's future, be laying the foundation for a good old-fashioned depression in the future?

Speaking now, in 1992, the reference in my 1987 letter to potential bad times coming in the early 1990s was prophetic.

How to Handle Solicitors

There are kinds of causes that bring people to one's door to solicit signatures on petitions or contributions in the form of money to support a cause. Those activities have tended to bother me. Many of those who call are paid solicitors. They cannot give any information on how much of one's contribution would go for paying the solicitor, paying central office administrative costs, or how much is actually used to promote the cause in question.I eventually developed a fairly routine procedure in responding to such house calls. I might ask the caller whether he or she is a student. If yes, I ask what year they are in, what they are majoring in, and what they want to do after graduation. I ask the extent to which they are dedicated to the furtherance of the cause for which they are working. Generally, such an approach discourages the individual and he or she is happy to go to the next house.

Occasionally, there is a caller in whose cause I can believe or a desire is kindled to help the individual caller, not by signing anything but by giving an outright cash donation. This latter is rare.

One caller represented an organization whose purpose was to save the whales. I could gain nothing from the caller concerning the extent to which whales were in danger or what were the crucial reasons why one should support an organization dedicated to further that objective. I changed my usual questioning approach and told the caller that I had my own cause: to save the sheep. I pointed out that I could not stand to hear the bleating of a lamb being slaughtered for its meat. I wondered how anyone could really enjoy eating a lamb chop. I would much prefer to eat whale steak than something carved out of an innocent lamb. I pleaded with the caller to support my cause. The caller did not stay long.

After that episode, I began to think that maybe I had something there. Why not not only save the whale, but domesticate it and make it a source of food for humanity? If this were done, it could take much of the pressure off of slaughtering sheep. I therefore developed a promotion piece as a satire on this Save the Whale operation.

I developed a special CHS Company letterhead and prepared a one-page description of the objective of my company and invited the recipient of this "Dear Investor" letter to buy stock in my new company. The purpose of the new company was to develop whale farms. I recognized it would be probably impossible, certainly exceedingly expensive, to "fence" in a portion of an ocean where whales might be cultivated for human consumption.

It then occurred to me that there was a naturally fenced body of water, namely Lake Michigan, which could be used as the locus for a real whale farm. Now it was recognized that the whale is a salt water mammal. We, therefore, would plan over time to acclimate whales to a fresh water environment. There are other things that we would undertake over time to enhance those characteristics that were most favorable for marketable whale meat.

I even pointed out in my prospectus that the governments of the states bordering Lake Michigan—Wisconsin, Illinois, Indiana, and Michigan—were arranging for legislative approval of such a venture and the issue of licenses to further the operation.

A young professor at a noted graduate school of business where the case method was the basic teaching approach became interested in developing a whale farm as an instructional case to highlight the importance of entrepreneurship. That should eventually add to the instructional literature in the field.

New Use for an Old Raw Material

That professor had noted and become enamored of another entrepreneurial venture that I had undertaken some years earlier. That had to do with the creation of a new ready-to-eat cereal. The raw material for the product was plentiful and quite low-cost. It, however, had outstanding qualities. Some of these were high fiber content, no cholesterol, low calorie, and so on. The product would have a variety of natural flavors, such flavors being inherent in the basic raw material. All of this would be toasted and presented to the public in a very attractive package. The package would be designed to not only appeal to customers but also to managers of supermarkets to provide good shelf space for it. The raw material for the product was sawdust. Thus, because of the variety of plants from which the sawdust could be obtained, we could offer such flavors as maple, walnut, cherry, peach, apple, plum and others depending on the demand by consumers. The reader may well find this product on the grocery store shelves. It has not yet been named, but a name copied after "Grape Nuts" might be appropriate. You could have Cherry Nuts, Peach Nuts, Apple Nuts, etc.

Stop Sign Episode

Sometime in the late 1980s and early 1990s I got involved with the Urbana City Council in a matter associated with a stop sign on Colorado Street, a primary traffic street although only about four blocks long. It had a four-way stop at the crossing of another primary traffic route but no other stops until someone persuaded the city council to authorize the addition of a stop on Colorado at the point where George Huff Drive entered the street. George Huff is a short residential street that stops at Colorado. It therefore forms a "T" rather than a crossroad.

Many of the regular users of Colorado Street were angered by what they considered to be a nuisance stop. One resident obtained more than 100 signatures on a petition to the city counsel to remove the sign. A significant number of citizens wrote letters of protest.

I did not protest the sign but instead wrote a letter to the mayor of Urbana in which I indicated some confusion as to the purpose of a stop sign at that particular location. I asked for the rationale that the city used to justify such a sign. No response resulted from my inquiry.

Several weeks later, I sent the city via the mayor an invoice for $4.29 to cover the extra expense I incurred in the form of gasoline and wear on the brakes and tires as a result of the stop-and-go requirement. That did bring forth a reply from the mayor but no rationale except that it was a city council and not a city administration matter.

Several months later a traffic officer stopped me after I had run through that particular stop sign. He asked me if I knew why he had stopped me. My reply was "yes." I asked him why it had taken him so long to flag me down since I, along with a lot of other people, had been regularly ignoring that stop sign. I told him that I knew this was an act of civil disobedience and started to explain my reason for doing so. The officer said he better call his sergeant and let him handle the case.

The sergeant arrived in only two or three minutes. When I started to explain my reasons for my action, he said he agreed that the sign was a nuisance, that the police department had strongly recommended against placing the sign there, but that the department was overruled by the city council. He felt sorry for me but indicated that I would probably have to pay the fine.

I went home and wrote a letter to the city council explaining the reason for my civil disobedience. I also sent a copy of that letter to the local daily newspaper, and it appeared in the letters to the editor section. This brought telephone calls and congratulatory letters and eventually action by the city council to eliminate the sign. A copy of that letter as it appeared in the *News Gazette* is reproduced here, along with the item that appeared announcing the removal of the stop sign.

Unnecessary stop sign
warrants disobedience

To the Editor:

I recently was ticketed for failing to observe a stop sign on Colorado Avenue where George Huff Drive joins that street. I admit that I only slowed and paused when driving through that sign. This act of civil disobedience could be viewed as a protest against what is generally considered a nuisance and an unnecessary stop sign.

Evidence seems to indicate that only a few residents of the area sought such a sign and brought strong pressure on city officials to enact legislation. The action ignored the strong recommendation of traffic experts that the sign was not needed. That recommendation came after extensive monitoring of traffic.

The sign brought substantial protest from many area citizens. Letters and telephone calls were directed to aldermen and administrators. Officials were asked to provide evidence, and information supporting the sign was never forthcoming. Additional protest was presented in the form of a petition signed by more than 100 motorists using Colorado.

The current attention given by city officials to the Colorado/George Huff stop sign comes after traffic officials ostensibly permitted persons to ignore the sign for three or more years. Their traffic monitoring had demonstrated that the sign was not justified as a safety measure, hence manpower could better serve the city by allocating time to other areas and problems. Could it be that the current activity is designed primarily to bring additional revenue?

It has not been easy for me to resort to civil disobedience. I suspect, though, it was also not easy for a black person to disobey the law that prohibited riding in the front of a bus or sitting at a white person's table. It is in that light that I confess my disobedience. If my protest would bring about the elimination of a recognized nuisance, I would consider my $50 well spent.

C.H. Sandage

Urbana

Excerpt from the *News Gazette*
(Tuesday, April 3, 1990)

■ Approved removal of stop signs on Colorado Avenue at the intersection with George Huff Drive.

Alderman Bonnie Tarr, Democrat Ward 7, said residents in her ward felt the stop sign is more of a hazard than a help because drivers who aren't aware of the sign drive through it, she said.

Joked Alderman Michael Pollock, D-5, after the vote: "I want to call attention to all you who call us Stop Sign City, USA, that we're removing a stop sign."

An interesting postscript to this episode is worth reporting. A friend invited me to lunch one day and when I arrived others had been included and were present. After lunch my friend said he had a presentation to make to me. He read a letter addressed to me from the mayor of Urbana and then presented me with an actual stop sign symbolizing the one that I had been able to get removed from Colorado Street. The mayor's letter is sufficiently interesting to reproduce here.

I review this here primarily as an example of the importance of citizen concern and the power of communication in bringing about change.

June 26, 1990

Mr. C. H. Sandage
106 Meadow Dr.
Urbana, IL 61801

Dear Mr. Sandage:

On behalf of the people of Urbana (especially the thousands who travel Colorado Avenue), it is my pleasure to write and express my most sincere gratitude and undying admiration for the community service you have performed for us all.

It has been my pleasure to serve the people of Urbana as a member of the Council since 1973 and as Mayor since 1977. I have met hundreds of mayors, many state legislators, congressmen, governors, vice presidents, presidents, and more bureaucrats than you can count. Never in all of my years have I seen an exhibition of power such as you have demonstrated.

Whoever said "The pen is mightier than. the sword" surely had C. H. Sandage in mind. A couple of letters, a phone call or two and, "puff," no more stop sign. Never mind that I had asked the Council not to put the sign in, never mind that the City Engineer said it wasn't needed, never mind that the State of Illinois said it did not meet warrants, but a letter from C. H. Sandage and the problem is solved.

I am reluctant to push my luck, but could you next work on property tax relief, solid waste, commercial and industrial development or maybe funding for education.

My very best to you and yours.

Sincerely,

Jeffrey T. Markland
Mayor

The Debate on Fluoridation

The debate on the wisdom of adding fluorides to drinking water as a way of protecting teeth against decay has been going on for many years. A group of citizens in Urbana kept the debate alive with frequent letters to the editor denouncing the addition of "poisonous" fluorides to the local water system.

In August 1988 a review of the pros and cons of fluoridating drinking water appeared in the local newspaper. It was after reading that article that I wrote a somewhat satiric letter to the paper and that letter was eventually printed as reproduced here.

Letters to the editor, *News Gazette*
(September 6, 1988)

Eureka! Pipe smoking prevents tooth decay

To the Editor:

The "Debate over Fluoridation" article in the *News Gazette* of Aug. 28 was both revealing and confusing. However, it did cause me to review the history of my own tooth cavities.

That rumination revealed that I developed several tooth cavities in my earlier years, but had none after 1930 (I was born in 1902).

I could not remember when my drinking water was seasoned with fluoride, but I think it was after 1930. But I did remember that I started to smoke a pipe in 1929 and that my dentists have commented on two things: (1) tobacco stains on my teeth, and (2) the absence of cavities.

Eureka! Smoke a pipe and free yourself from developing holes in your teeth. I am now suggesting dentists urge patients to take up pipe smoking to prevent tooth decay and forget about possible side effects.

C. H. SANDAGE

Urbana

Misplacement of Commercials Draws Attention

Another bit of satire included in a letter to the editor resulted from a radio commercial I had heard while listening to my car radio. I was jarred by the type of product being advertised immediately after a serious commentary by a noted newsman. The newsman closed his commentary with the statement, "And now this message." My letter as printed in the *News Gazette* (November 3, 1985) follows.

Hemorrhoid radio ad timely for listeners

To the Editor:

I enjoyed the thoughts on doctoring in the Oct. 20 *News Gazette*. Reading it reminded me of my reaction to a hemorrhoid radio commercial that followed a Dan Rather program. My thought caused me to write the following to Gary Cummings, manager of WBBM radio station.

I often enjoy listening to Dan Rather's five-minute program which comes on at 4:25 p.m. on your good station. Today, immediately after his program, your hemorrhoid commercial came on. It seemed to me that you could increase the impact of that commercial if it were prefaced with the statement, "If Dan Rather gives you a pain in the ass, listen to the following message."

C. H. SANDAGE
106 The Meadows, Urbana

I was pleased to note that some weeks after my letter, a different product was advertised following the newsman's commentary.

Statehood for the District of Columbia

In the late 1980s there was substantial debate concerning the merits and demerits of statehood for the District of Columbia. Attention was often given to the idea that D.C. residents were essentially disenfranchised in respect to national matters. It seemed to me that many of those who were advocating statehood were more interested in the effect statehood would have on the balance of political power in national matters than in escaping as "wards" of the national government. I prepared the following open letter to members of Congress outlining some suggestions as to how the question might be resolved.

August 29, 1990

An Open Letter to Congress:

The question of statehood for the District of Columbia is a current topic for debate. Those who favor statehood point out that the population of the District is greater than the population of some of the fifty established states. They also emphasize that most of the residents are not represented by voting members in either the House of Representatives or the Senate of the United States. Even though they can vote in national presidential elections and, in general, are accorded most of the privileges and responsibilities of United States citizenship, including federally imposed taxes, comments can thus be made that District residents are subjected to taxation without representation.

Those opposed to statehood offer various reasons for their opposition. They point out that because of the dominant position of the Federal Government in the District, statehood would tend to make the state a captive of the federal government. It might also reduce the emphasis on the federal government as an umbrella over all states. Opponents of statehood point out that the federal government should concentrate on national matters and leave state and local matters to the respective non-federal legal entities. It would, therefore, be unfortunate to have the federal government closely associated with one particular state.

Let me suggest an approach that could meet most of the problems related to the issue of statehood for D.C. The federal government should be a part of no single state. It should operate more like an enclave in which emphasis is placed on dealing primarily with national affairs. This could be enhanced by not giving statehood to the District and, at the same time, giving District residents representation in the U.S. Congress if the following steps were taken:

a) Eliminate completely the District of Columbia.
b) Have that geographic area merged with the state of Maryland.
c) Recognize all of the U.S. Government buildings and offices as being comparable to embassies of Nations.
d) Change the name of the city of Washington to Columbia, Maryland.
e) Make the official address of the federal government buildings and offices (embassies) Washington, USA.

Under this arrangement no eligible voter would be without representation in the United States Congress. No one could be classified as being disenfranchised. All federal elected officials and many, if not most, members of the staffs of federal government officials and agencies maintain their official and voting residence in one or another of the fifty states. Thus, everyone living in what is now the District of Columbia, whether attached to the federal government or the infra-structure supporting federal operation, would have complete voting rights at the state level. Permanent residents of Columbia, MD would vote in Maryland and most federal personnel would vote in their respective individual states. Also, it would place emphasis on the federal government as an umbrella over all states rather than as an isolated district.

C. H. Sandage
Urbana, Illinois

The letter received some response, both favorable and unfavorable. If nothing else, it stimulated my interest in following the continuing debate on the issue.

Change Martin Luther King Day to Ethnic Day

The 1992 Democratic presidential campaign revolved around the notion of "change," with the inaugral of the newly elected president, Bill Clinton, following only two days after Martin Luther King Day. Because much of the campaign rhetoric focused on representing cultural and ethnic diversity in the selection of cabinet members and other appointive officers, it occurred to me that it would be not only appropriate but a warmly welcomed change to recognize all ethnic groups with a special "day" rather than single out only one for such honor. I therefore wrote the following letter and sent it to a number of newspapers, members of Congress, television personalities, syndicated columnists, and others.

January 20, 1993

To the Editor:

The Martin Luther King Day was celebrated on January 18. That day gave us all an opportunity to think of the value of ethnic diversity. Dr. King is representative of only one ethnic group. We have a multiplicity of such groups in the USA. Would it not, therefore, be appropriate and valuable to recognize all such groups? This could be done by expanding the MLK Day to include all ethnic groups. With that change the day would logically be called Ethnic Day.

Such a day would highlight the melting pot goal in this nation that has welcomed diverse cultural and ethnic groups. It could call attention to factors that serve as adhesive to bind the groups together. These might include a common language, a political system that makes all persons equal in the voting booth, a social system that rewards individual initiative, an economic system that converts hope into reality, and the uplifting power of freedom.

C. H. Sandage
Emeritus Professor
University of Illinois

Chapter 18

Epilogue

In 1985 I established a personal charitable corporation titled the Sandage Charitable Trust. This became a part of my plans and procedures for the distribution of the assets that might be in my estate. Of course, my first objective was to make sure that my wife, Elizabeth, would be financially independent and that she could continue to maintain the life-style to which she had become accustomed. After the allocation of funds for Elizabeth and family members, there should be funds that could be allocated for other purposes.

While such funds would not be great, they would probably be substantially greater than would normally be expected of one who had spent most of his productive life in academic work. My accumulation of assets came not only from my salary as a professor but also from book royalties, business consulting, my Farm Research Institute, and fortunate investments. It would probably be sufficiently large that unless part of it was distributed to eleemosynary institutions the inheritance tax would consume much of it. The establishment of a personal charitable trust provides a vehicle for both the avoidance of an inheritance tax and the allocation of resources in support of charitable work described or specified in the charter of the trust. Of course, assets could have been distributed directly to some operating organization, but it was my thinking that greater value would result if my wife, Elizabeth, and a board of trustees of my choice were given the opportunity and responsibility for monitoring the distribution of income from the corpus during Elizabeth's lifetime than might otherwise be done. Elizabeth shares my philosophy and together with the board of trustees will serve as good monitors. It would be understood that the SCT would be dissolved and the corpus distributed to an operating institution when Elizabeth is no longer willing or able to function as an overseer.

It would be logical to ask why not distribute the total estate to family even if the amount to be distributed were diminished by the inheritance tax. The answer requires some review of my philosophy of life and the part an individual should play in that life. I believe that an individual is only a part of a larger entity that we call society. In addition, the individual just may be a part of a plan directed by a Higher Power. If the latter is true, then the individual is really a steward of the talents he may have inherited or had given to him. As a steward he must be held responsible for applying these talents appropriately.

I accept the concept of stewardship. I believe the first financial responsibility is to take care of family needs. Children and grandchildren can often be injured if monetary gifts are sufficiently large to sublimate their own feeling of personal achievement. If there is no incentive to cultivate one's talents and achieve, there will be little contribution to self or society. We have seen the wasted lives of those who have lost their initiative because of the largesse given in the name of love and compassion by biological or governmental parents.

I am proud of my son, my two grandsons, and Elizabeth's son and daughter in their achievements and particularly in their independence and satisfaction derived from their own personal achievements. I congratulate and award them but hopefully not stifle them by removing or desensitizing their initiative.

The charitable area in which I am most interested is that of education. The educational institution in which I am most interested is Graceland College. That institution gave me great help in cultivating what talents I might have, stimulating me to achieve. The philosophy of life acquired from my parents and Graceland has, I believe, provided me with a positive outlook and an acceptance of basic human values.

In my academic work I majored in economics with minors in business and history. Most of my teaching has been in the field of applied economics and business. As noted earlier, my philosophy of business stretches far beyond the narrow concept of making monetary profit. In fact, profit should be viewed as a measure of the extent to which the needs and wants of consumers have been adequately served. Thus business is the product of ethical and moral behavior combined with a set of moral and ethical values. It is my view that Graceland College has done and is doing a good job of making that combination and developing it in its classrooms and campus environment. It is for that reason that I have provided some financial support to Graceland for many years. It is also why the income from the corpus in the Sandage Charitable Trust is to be earmarked primarily for support of various aspects of business and economic education at Graceland.

In 1988 Graceland, through my stimulation and minor financial support, established the Center for the Study of Free Enterprise and Entrepreneurship. That is an example of what is now being done and can expect to be done in the future as a result of SCT and other financial support.

The mission of the Sandage Charitable Trust is rather completely set forth here. Its life is temporary. I expect that its contribution to the development of future leaders and workers in the field of business will be substantial and contagious by the work of Graceland College, the institution that will, in essence, perpetuate the concepts provided by the Sandage Charitable Trust.

Appendix A

A Positive Approach to Advertising

Reprinted from Journalism Quarterly *39, no. 4*
(Autumn 1962)

A Positive Approach to Advertising

By C. H. Sandage*

Advertising people, like most humans, are sensitive to criticism. Because of the nature of advertising it perhaps receives more than its share of criticism. Too often the advertising man becomes defensive instead of striving to understand the true nature of advertising and concentrating on its positive values.

The criticism of advertising is of two kinds: 1) that which is directed against the methods of individual practitioners, and 2) that which holds that the total advertising process is neither socially nor economically justified.

In many respects criticism should be welcomed. Nothing could be worse for advertising than to have the public ignore it. Criticism should thus stimulate us to continually reassess the social and economic contributions of advertising and to be eternally vigilant in reducing malpractice.

It is probable, however, that greatest progress will be achieved in meeting criticism, not by defensively an-

---

*This article is based upon a talk given by Dr. Sandage before the Association of National Advertisers in New York.

swering each critic, but rather by concentrating on a positive approach. Let us distinguish clearly between the institution of advertising and advertising as a tool.

When Professor Potter, the Yale historian, refers to advertising as "the institution of abundance," he is not talking about individual advertisements and commercials, or specific workers in the vineyard. Instead, he is talking about broad social or economic functions that society wants performed and which have been assigned to a given institution to perform. Thus, society has assigned to the institution of religion the broad function of serving the spiritual needs of man. To the institution of law has been assigned the basic functions of administering justice and preserving a constitutional form of government. And to advertising, according to Potter, has been assigned the function of helping society achieve abundance.

The manner in which advertising operates to help achieve abundance is not always understood or at least not always tied back to the basic goal of abundance. But basically society holds advertising responsible to *inform* and *persuade* members of society in respect to products, services and ideas. An additional responsibility that is becoming more and more significant is that of education in consumerism—the development of judgment on the part of consumers in their purchase practices. This is extremely important in a society that places emphasis on the freedom of consumers to choose what they will buy. A failure to understand or to accept these facets of advertising in their total social context probably gives rise to much of the criticism of advertising.

Actually, much of the criticism is not basically against advertising as much as it is against abundance, persuasion and the concept of consumer freedom of choice. Many in our society who have achieved relatively high abundance seem to have a guilt complex growing out of our Puritan heritage. Instead of recognizing this for what it is, they attempt to unload their guilt feelings by holding advertising responsible for their "transgressions."

Perhaps one fact of our positive approach to meeting the criticism against advertising would be not to talk so much about advertising as such, but to examine the philosophy of abundance as a social goal and, if it appears to be good, then to present its merits forcefully.

There is much in our modern culture to support the concept of abundance. The search for means to provide abundance has been a concern of economists and philosophers for centuries. It has motivated the actions of governments both here and abroad. Our own Employment Act of 1946 stated that "It is the continuing policy and responsibility of the Federal Government to use all practicable means . . . to promote maximum employment, production, and purchasing power." We hear much these days of unemployment as politicians and economists debate issues and seek remedies. Certainly few would deny that full employment is a national goal—only the means of achieving it is at issue.

Of course, there is little justification for employment and production for their own sake. These are inextricably related to consumption. Full employment, at least in America, can be maintained only if consumption, here or elsewhere, is at a high level. Consumption may be at the individual or societal level or both, but there must be an abundance of consumption.

In a free society the nature of consumption is determined primarily by consumers themselves. They decide, through their actions in the marketplace, how many people will be employed to supply them with tobacco, clothing, homes, automobiles, boats, golf balls, cosmetics, air conditioners, books and paintings to hang on their walls. They decide, too, how much of their purchasing power will be spent to support preachers, private schools, research foundations, art galleries and symphony orchestras. In a little different fashion but still basic, they determine through their votes at the polls how much they will buy in the form of defense hardware, public school buildings, teachers' services, public parks, highways and help for the less fortunate.

It is this freedom of the consumer to choose that bothers so many of the critics of advertising. They seem to hold to the philosophy that consumers are not really capable of making wise decisions and that they would be better off if some supposedly more intelligent person or group made all consumption decisions. Of course, this is not really new. History shows that this debate has been going on for centuries. Our free enterprise system which emphasizes individual rights is based on the philosophy that we shall not have a dictatorial elite telling us what to do—but there are still some who would substitute a commissar for the free consumer. Advertising is criticized on the ground that it can manipulate consumers to follow the will of the advertiser. The weight of evidence denies this ability. Instead, evidence supports the position that advertising, to be successful, must understand or anticipate basic human needs and wants and interpret available goods and services in terms of their want-satisfying abilities. This is the very opposite of manipulation. To the extent that consumers are not capable of making purchase decisions that will maximize their own satisfactions, the solution lies not in taking the right of decision from them, but rather in raising their level of education in consumerism. This, frankly, is a function of and an opportunity for advertising.

A part of the process in consumer education and in implementing freedom of choice is to supply consumers with adequate and accurate information about all of the alternatives available to them. The extent to which performance falls short of the ideal is a matter of concern to all, but it does not diminish the social need in having these functions performed.

It is probable that most laymen and many advertising practitioners do not understand the basic social and economic goals and functions of advertising. This results in the layman making value judgments on the basis of his reaction to individual advertisements and individual practitioners. It is like the parent who criticizes all education because he does not like a given school or becomes irritated by a particular teacher. If people understand the functions and believe in the goals of an institution, they will accept certain annoyances and irritations which are superficial flaws in an otherwise worthwhile system. It is only when annoyances and irritations become too severe that dangers arise and a reaction sets in. But the very nature of advertising will never permit the complete elimination of some irritation—no more than we can expect all salesmen to become popular to all clients or all politicians to have unanimous support of their constituents.

It is unfortunate that laymen in general have no real appreciation of the broad goals and functions of advertising. It is even more unfortunate that many practitioners fail in this respect. This is damaging to the individual practitioner and to the profession. It places too many in the category of an artisan rather than a professional. They are bricklayers rather than architects. As such, they are bound to be married to their tools rather than to see their tools as means to an end. They, thus, have neither a basic philosophy to guide their action nor a solid foundation on which to build their practice. Under such circumstances, they cannot effectively support advertising to their social critics or become fired with a feeling that they are making a vital contribution to social well-being. This is more apt to lead them to concentrate solely on a personal goal of making money. Let me hasten to add that it is essential to make money, but those who set this as their goal generally make less money than those who concentrate on providing a product or service that serves some specific segment of society.

Let me document this plea for a basic social philosophy to guide the advertising practitioner with a quotation from the Rev. E. J. Walker. Mr. Walker was an ad man who left advertising to enter the ministry. In explaining his action he pointed out that he used about the same techniques as a preacher as he did as an ad man. "The only real difference," he said, "is that I no longer work with tongue in cheek. I am completely sold on my product." He further said, "I had become so embroiled in techniques of selling that I had never developed an overall philosophy of advertising. Techniques had become an end in themselves." Practitioners generally recognize the importance of being sold on the products they advertise, but too many are unaware of the importance of being sold on the institution of advertising itself.

And the Rev. Robert E. Peterson, writing in the *Saturday Review* on May 12, and commenting on what he considers the sin of advertising, said, "The public service ads are often moving, poetic, and truthful. But let a sponsor wave a checkbook in front of Madison Avenue and idealism is drowned by a passion to move a product instead of moving people."

In contrast to these gentlemen, there are advertising men who use techniques not only to move people to products that will satisfy their needs and wants, but also to sell people on ideas that have broad social significance of a non-product character. The history of the Advertising Council provides vivid testimony to this.

There is hope that the institutional functions as well as the tools of advertising might be applied to the area of world peace. Paraphrasing Lincoln, we might observe that no world can long exist half rich and half poor. Since advertising is the institution of abundance, might not advertising play an important part in educating and stimulating people in underdeveloped areas to seek abundance through their own efforts once their basic needs have been met? Is this not a far better approach than that which is implicitly involved in the proposals of some who would have us sink to their levels rather than having the underdeveloped nations rise to ours? Advertising, of course, cannot do the complete job, but is it not conceivable that it can present the goal of abundance in a manner that would stimulate such people to improve their skills and increase their labor to reach the goal?

There are equally dynamic and positive values provided by advertising in other non-material areas. It modernizes freedom of speech by supplying the necessary facilities for distributing individually held ideas to the masses. It makes it possible for individuals, groups and corporations to become their own editors and publishers and, in most cases, frees them from the blue pencil of the newsman and the audience limitations of the soap box in the town square.

Perhaps enough has been said about some of the positive values of advertising. Emphasis has purposely been placed on broad social and economic values such as contributor to material abundance, minister to consumer needs and wants, vital stimulator and persuader as an antidote to lethargy, implementer of freedom of speech, champion of consumer freedom of choice and believer in the inherent dignity of man. Of course, other agencies in society contribute to the furtherance of these values, too, but advertising men are important members of the team that promulgates them.

Let us now turn for a moment to a consideration of how these positive values can best be implemented and presented to the public.

Perhaps it will be agreed that the most important single element in the promulgation of these values is the quality of the men and women who work in the field of advertising. This front has sometimes been neglected, and it must be strengthened. Too much emphasis has been placed on hiring and training craftsmen and not enough on educating for understanding. It is probable that too many employers have sought only bright young men and women, probably college graduates, but with no attention given to their understanding of advertising and its social and economic values. They then proceed to train these people as craftsmen only and leave them to their own devices to attain a professional foundation for their work. Such craftsmen may be able to converse brilliantly on production problems or media allocations, but how can such people be expected to contribute positively to the public image of advertising in sophisticated discussions of the socio-economic effects of advertising?

Much has been written in the advertising press about the professional aspects of advertising. The prevailing attitude appears to be that advertising is first and foremost a business and that it should forget about trying to become a profession. To this I must say that advertising will continue to have a weak public image until the field of practice is built on a more professional base and craftsmanship is recognized as means to an end not as an end in itself.

The surgeon could be viewed as a skilled craftsman, but, if he were only that, his public image would be quite different from what it is. As a foundation for his crafts-manship, his medical education has provided a strong philosophical base.

In law and accounting, fields perhaps more compa-rable to advertising, methods of training practitioners at one time were comparable to methods still common in advertising. It was enough to read Blackstone or McKinsey or to serve as an apprentice in some office. This has long since passed. Now major dependence is placed on well-developed programs of professional edu-cation in leading colleges and universities.

Conditions are rapidly changing in advertising itself. There has been a strong movement toward the develop-ment of professional advertising education since World War II. This movement has been generated by univer-sities rather than by practitioners. Its center is in the Midwest but it is spreading all over the nation. In general, such professional advertising education has been built on a strong liberal arts base. Then attention has been given to the social and economic values of advertising, combined with sufficient training in advertising skills to make the graduate a worthy prospect for his first employer. A few universities also have developed a graduate program in advertising education in cooperation with other areas such as psychology, communications, economics, marketing and sociology, which permits the training of scholars who wish to teach advertising at the college level. It is in support of this type of graduate program that the James Webb Young Fund for Education in Advertising was established.

The development of strong programs in advertising education at both the undergraduate and graduate levels in our universities may well provide the most potent single force in changing the public image of advertising. Such education is now providing the philosophical foundation for effective practice. It is moving toward research programs that will hopefully answer some of the basic economic issues and test hypotheses at the operational level.

There is growing recognition among leaders in the field of advertising practice of the values of professional advertising education. There is, however, great need for such leaders to join forces with educators to maximize the values of professional education to the profession and to society.

Some specific suggestions are presented here to stimulate thought and, hopefully, action in respect to the implementation of professional advertising education.

Suggestions deal with two important groups. The first consists of the people already in advertising practice. The second group includes the young men and women of college age who in a few short years will be assuming positions of advertising leadership and influence in our society.

As far as the first group is concerned—those already working in the area of advertising—some of the following specific steps might be taken:

1. Provide wide distribution of advertising literature that is already available which explains the economic and social role of advertising. This would help to emphasize the positive aspects of advertising and provide a better balance of literature to the public that has a deep interest in advertising. Such positive literature could have as wide a distribution as *The Waste Makers* if advertising people would help promote it.

2. Sponsor seminars for employees on the functions of advertising—to be conducted by advertising educators and acknowledged statesmen in the field. (One ad agency is already planning such seminars.)

3. Disseminate information on advertising educational programs to staff members so they will be more knowledgeable to intelligently discuss advertising education when young men and women solicit their advice.

4. Encourage key people in the field of practice to teach advertising subjects at night school or take leaves of absence to join the faculties of our universities for a full year's instructional experience.

5. Establish recruitment programs which give adequate recognition to college graduates majoring—or at least evidencing some strong interest—in the field of advertising.

The benefits from such a program are bound to be substantial. In essence, this will mobilize manpower resources already available in the advertising industry to enhance their own understanding of advertising's role in society and to present that role more effectively to the public.

The second set of proposals deals with educational efforts at the college level. Professional advertising education is quite new. It was non-existent at the time that many of the present leaders in advertising practice were getting their education. We are still in a transitional era between dependence on general and self-education and professional education for advertising practitioners. The trend, however, is obvious. It is a trend that perhaps holds more promise for the solid growth of advertising toward professional status than any other single development. To hasten this development the following are presented:

1. Establish a committee composed of representatives of all facets of advertising to make or direct a truly comprehensive study of advertising education—perhaps to supplement the current study being done by Dr. Vergil Reed. Some of the areas to be covered in such an endeavor might include an appraisal of the following:
   a. Basic objectives of a sound advertising educational program;
   b. Needs of the advertising profession that can be met most effectively through planned education;
   c. Current character and quality of advertising education;
   d. Matching needs against current programs to earmark areas requiring strengthening;
   e. Quality of students now being attracted to advertising educational programs and, if nec-

essary, exploring the means for attracting the kinds and numbers of students needed;

    f. Contributions that might be made by practitioners as part-time teachers and teachers as part-time consultants.

Without awaiting the results of such a study the following steps could be taken by people in the field of practice:

1. Provide scholarship funds for worthwhile students at the undergraduate level. Other industries are doing this on a wide scale—why not advertising?

2. Encourage and render financial support of graduate programs in advertising. We need more and we need better qualified advertising teachers. This is one of the major objectives of the James Webb Young Fund, which deserves support as well as others like it.

3. Subsidize basic research to be directed by university departments of advertising.

4. Endow chairs of advertising in selected universities.

5. Establish even closer liaison with advertising educators and give moral support and understanding to their efforts to uncloud the truth.

The positive values of advertising are substantial. These values need to be emphasized both to those who now work or who plan to work in the vineyard and to the general public. Advertising may not be a profession, but if those who work in it do not have a professional philosophy concerning its social and economic functions, we cannot expect the public to have a favorable image of either the institution or its practitioners.

Appendix B
Published Works of
C. H. Sandage

BOOKS

Advertising Theory and Practice (12 Editions, 1936-1989). Editions 1-4 (1936-1955); Editions 5-9, with Vernon Fryburger (1958-1975); Editions 10-12, with Fryburger and Kim Rotzoll (1979-1989). Publishers: Editions 1-11: Richard D. Irwin, Inc., Homewood, Illinois; Edition 12: Longman, Inc., White Plains, New York.

Radio Advertising for Retailers. Cambridge, Massachusetts: Harvard University Press, 1948.

Editor, *The Promise of Advertising.* Homewood, Illinois: Richard D. Irwin, Inc., 1961.

C.H. Sandage and Vernon Fryburger, eds. *The Role of Advertising.* Homewood, Illinois: Richard D. Irwin, Inc., 1960.

C.H. Sandage and Arnold M. Barban, eds. *Readings in Advertising and Promotion Strategy.* Homewood, Illinois: Richard D. Irwin, Inc., 1968.

Advertising in Contemporary Society, with Kim Rotzoll and James E. Haefner. Columbus, Ohio: Copyright Grid, Inc., 1976.

CONTRIBUTING AUTHOR

"Advertising the Product." In *Marketing by Manufacturers,* edited by Charles F. Phillips, 299-329. Chicago: Richard D. Irwin, Inc., 1946.

"The Sales Program: (Advertising, Brand Policy, Personal Selling, Distribution)." In *Marketing by Manufacturers,* Revised Edition, 267-334. Chicago: R.D. Irwin, Inc., 1951.

"The Role of Advertising in Modern Society." In *Changing Perspectives in Marketing,* edited by Hugh G. Wales, 185-196. Urbana, Illinois: University of Illinois Press, 1951.

"Report of the Network Study Staff to the Network Study Committee." In *Network Broadcasting,* Two Volumes, Network Study Staff, Washington, D.C.: Federal Communications Commission, 1957.

"The Role of Advertising in Modern Society." In *Marketing in Transition*, edited by Alfred L. Seelye, 270-277. New York: Harper & Brothers, 1958.

"Using Advertising to Implement the Concept of Freedom of Speech." In *The Role of Advertising—A Book of Readings*, edited by Sandage & Fryburger, 221-223. Homewood, Illinois: R.D. Irwin, Inc., 1960.

"Basic Functions of Advertising." In *The Promise of Advertising*, 146-159. Homewood, Illinois: R.D. Irwin, Inc., 1961.

"The Newspaper as an Advertising Medium: Problems and Opportunities." In *Diagnosis & Prognosis in Journalism*, edited by John E. Drewry, 159-165. University of Georgia Bulletin, 1962.

"Too Little for Advertising's Future." In *Advertising—Today/Yesterday/Tomorrow*, 397-400. McGraw-Hill Book Co., Inc., 1963.

"Some Observations about Advertising Education." In *Frontiers of Advertising Theory and Research*, edited by H.W. Sargent, 155-164. Palo Alto, California: Pacific Books, 1972.

"Introduction." In *The paws of refreshment—the story of Hamm's beer advertising*, by Moira F. Harris. Minneapolis, Minnesota: Pogo Press, 1990.

"Some Challenges for Advertising." In *Occasional Paper in Advertising* 1, no. 2 (May 1966). Special Editor.

"Some International Challenges to Advertising." In *Occasional Papers in Advertising* 1, no. 2 (September 1967). Journal Committee Chair.

MONOGRAPHS

The Motor Vehicle in Iowa. Iowa Studies in Business—Study No.1, Iowa City, Iowa: State University of Iowa, 1928.

Motor Vehicle Taxation for Highway Purposes. Iowa Studies in Business—Study No. 11, Iowa City, Iowa: State University of Iowa, 1932.

Department Stores and Radio Advertising. New York: Mutual Broadcasting System, Inc., 1948.

Qualitative Analysis of Radio Listening in Two Central Illinois Counties. Bureau of Economic and Business Research, Bulletin Series No. 68, Urbana, Illinois: University of Illinois, 1949.

Building Audiences for Educational Radio Programs—An Experiment in Audience Promotion. Institute of Communications Research, Urbana, Illinois: University of Illinois, 1951.

JOURNAL ARTICLES

"Some Phases of Motor Vehicle Transportation in Iowa." In *Journal of Business* 7, no.4 (April 1927): 8-9, 19.

"The Question of Motor Vehicle Subsidy." In *The Bulletin of the National Tax Association* XV, no.1 (October 1929): 14-18.

"A Program for Ohio Highway Finance." In *Miami Business Review* II, no.6 (March 1930).

"What it Costs to Go to College." In *Miami Business Review* VII, no.2 (November 1934).

"Student Expenditures for Clothing." In *Miami Business Review* VII, no.3 (December 1934).

"Consumer Market Data for the Miami Valley." In *Miami Business Review* XI, no.6 (March 1940).

"Price Control and Inflation." In *Miami Business Review* XIV, no.1 (November 1942).

"Reconversion and Postwar Financial Problems." In *Miami Business Review* XV, no.4 (April 1944).

"Radio Listening." In *Miami Business Review* XVII, no.3 (March 1946).

"The Universities and Education in Business." In *Journal of the American Association of Collegiate Registrars* 18, no.2 (January 1943): 175-185.

"Measuring the Quality of the Radio Audience." In *Opinion and Comment* (University of Illinois Bulletin) IX, no.3 (August 1947): 1-8.

"Educators View Advertising." In *The Advertiser's Digest* 15, no.4 (April 1950): 1-3.

"Institutional Ads for Retailers." In *Sales Talk* 8, no.9 (September 1951): 14-15.

"The Role of Advertising in Modern Society." In *Journalism Quarterly* 28, no.1 (Winter 1951): 31-38.

"Ludgin Comments on Advertising Education Challenged by University Spokesman." In *Advertising Age* (November 1951).

"Institutional Ads for Retailers." In *Sales Story* 5, no.3 (March 1952): 2-3.

"A Philosophy of Advertising Education." In *Journalism Quarterly* 32, no.2 (Spring 1955): 209-211.

"Advertising as a Percent of Sales: (Report of data from 2,300 manufacturers giving their expenditures for advertising as a percent of 1954 sales)," with S.R. Bernstein. In *Advertising Publications* (1956).

"Do Research Panels Wear Out?" In *The Journal of Marketing* (April 1956): 397-401.

"What Do Your People Think of You?" In *American Cooperation* (1959).

"The Inequalities of Television Franchises." In *Journal of Marketing* (July 1959): 22-25.

"What Farmers Think About Advertising." In *Journalism Quarterly* 36, no.4 (Fall 1959): 455-459.

"Importance of Advertising to Cooperatives." In *Patrons Guide* XIV, no.3 (Spring 1962): 16-17.

"A Positive Approach to Advertising." In *Journalism Quarterly* 39, no.4 (Autumn 1962): 451-456.

"Too Little for Advertising's Future." In *Printer's Ink* (June 1963).

"Nichols Cup to James Webb Young." In *Linage—Alpha Delta Sigma* XVII, no.3 (Spring 1965): 9.

"Education and the Advertising Industry." In *Occasional Papers in Advertising—Interdisciplinary Approaches to Advertising Education* 1, no.1 (January 1966): 93-102.

"Illinois Farmers' Use of Media During Arab-Israeli Conflict," with Arnold M. Barban. In *Journalism Quarterly* 45, no.2 (Summer 1968): 336-337.

Book Review: "Advertising in America: The Consumer View." In *The Journal of Business* 42, no.2 (April 1969): 250.

"What Farmers Think About Consumer Protection," with Arnold M. Barban. In *Journalism Quarterly* 47, no.1 (Spring 1970): 147-151.

"A Study of Reisman's Inner-Other Directedness Among Farmers," with Arnold M. Barban, Waltraud M. Kassarjian, and Harold H. Kassarjian. In *Rural Sociology* 35, no.2 (June 1970): 232-243.

"The Right to Know." In *Grassroots Editor* (May-June 1971).

"Some Institutional Aspects of Advertising." In *Journal of Advertising* 1, no.1 (1972): 6-9.

"The Press and Advertising." In *Advertising in Contemporary Society* (1976): 127-136.

"How Farmers View Advertising," with Arnold M. Barban and James E. Haefner. In *Journalism Quarterly* 53, no.2 (Summer 1976): 303-307.

"Student Attitudes Toward Advertising: Institution vs. Instrument," with John D. Leckenby. In *Journal of Advertising* 9, no.2 (1980): 29-32.

CONFERENCE PROCEEDINGS, ETC.

"The Viewpoint of a Marketing Specialist." Second National Conference, Institute for Consumer Education—Bulletin No.2 (July 1940): 64-69. Stephens College, Columbia, Missouri.

"Recent Trends in the Psychology of Advertising." First Advertising and Sales Promotion Conference (April-May 1942), Ohio State University: 56-61.

"What Educators Think About Advertising." AFA Convention (1949), Houston, Texas.

"Marketing Aspects and Techniques." Packaging and Materials Handling Short Course (October 1952), Chicago, Illinois: 28-33.

"Using Advertising to Implement the Concept of Freedom of Speech." Convention of Association for Education in Journalism (August 1958).

"Advertising: What farmers think of it." In *The Country Guide* (a brochure), Winnipeg, Canada.

"Basic Functions of Advertising." The Fifth District Conference of The Advertising Federation of America (May 1961), Cincinnati, Ohio.

"Basic Functions of Advertising." In *Advertising Functions, Critics, Ethics, Morals, Responsibility: Five Addresses From the Fifth District Conference of the Advertising Federation of America*, 5-17. Cincinnati, Ohio: Scripps-Howard Newspapers.

"Consumers Not Commissars must make the choice...." Retitled speech to The Fifth District Conference of The Advertising Federation of America, *Advertising Age* (May 15, 1961), Reprint, Bradham Advertising, Inc., Charleston, South Carolina.

DATE DUE

GAYLORD

PRINTED IN U.S.A.